D1804163

Explaining Process and Change

Economics, Cognition, and Society provides a forum for theoretical and empirical investigations of social phenomena. It promotes works that focus on the interactions among cognitive processes, individual behavior, and social outcomes. It is especially open to interdisciplinary books that are genuinely integrative.

Ulrich Witt, Editor. *Explaining Process and Change: Approaches to Evolutionary Economics*

Explaining Process and Change
Approaches to Evolutionary Economics

Edited by
Ulrich Witt

Ann Arbor
THE UNIVERSITY OF MICHIGAN PRESS

Copyright © by the University of Michigan 1992
All rights reserved
Published in the United States of America by
The University of Michigan Press
Manufactured in the United States of America

1995   1994   1993   1992   4 3 2 1

*A CIP catalogue record for this book is available from
the British Library.*

Library of Congress Cataloging-in-Publication Data

Explaining process and change : approaches to evolutionary economics /
edited by Ulrich Witt.
    p.   cm.—(Economics, cognition, and society)
  Papers from a symposium held at the University of Freiburg in
Germany, 1988, and additional papers covering important areas of
research.
   Includes bibliographical references and indexes.
   ISBN 0-472-10291-5 (cloth : alk. paper)
   1. Economics—Congresses.   2. Evolution—Congresses.   3. Economic
development—Congresses.   4. Technological innovations—Economic
aspects—Congresses.   I. Witt, Ulrich.   II. Title: Evolutionary
economics.   III. Series.
HB21.E96   1991
338.9—dc20   91-34077
                                                                                  CIP

Preface

Evolutionary economics is a label that many people associate with Schumpeterian dynamics, that is, the way industrial capitalism develops under the pressure of technological innovations. However, this is not all that can be connected with the term *evolutionary* in economics. In the summer of 1988 a symposium was held at the University of Freiburg in Germany—for the last two decades the home university of F. A. Hayek and, thus, a place of symbolic meaning—to explore the breadth of research that comes under the label of evolutionary economics. Some of the chapters in this volume emerged from this symposium, and some other papers covering important areas of research have been added. The result is a collection of papers on special topics that, taken together, may help to identify the contours of a broad and promising approach to economics.

It is a pleasure to thank all those who have contributed in one or other way to make this volume possible. I thank the Volkswagen Foundation for financial support of the symposium. Thanks to all colleagues who offered a paper and to all who sacrificed their time reviewing papers considered for publication in this volume. I have profited much from their advice. Besides the authors who cross-refereed their papers I have to thank Hans Albert, Stephan Boehm, Wilhelm Brandes, Erik van Damme, Malcolm Dunn, Frank C. Englmann, Eirik Furubotn, James D. Hess, Terence W. Hutchison, Erich Kaufer, Sigrid Müller, Fritz Rahmeyer, Ekkehart Schlicht, Rolf Schmachtenberg, Dieter Schmidtchen, Hermann Schnabl, Gerald Silverberg, Gunter Stephan, Manfred Tietzel, Heiner Ursprung, and Murray Wolfson. Finally, I want to thank two anonymous referees for their helpful comments on all papers and, in particular, Timur Kuran who acted as a most engaged series editor and provided detailed suggestions about how to improve the volume.

Contents

Part 1. Introduction

1. Evolution as the Theme of a New Heterodoxy
   in Economics   3
   Ulrich Witt

Part 2. Toward a Formal Theory of Process and Change in the Economy

2. Explaining Reciprocal Behavior in Simple Strategic
   Games: An Evolutionary Approach   23
   Werner Güth and Menahem E. Yaari
3. Evolution of a Field of Socioeconomic Forces   35
   Peter Weise
4. Imitating Evolution: Collective, Two-Level Learning
   Processes   49
   Hans-Paul Schwefel

Part 3. Socioeconomic Evolution and Economic Growth

5. The Factors of Production of Evolutionary Economics   67
   Joseph A. Weissmahr
6. A New Theory of "Modern Economic Growth"   81
   Günter Hesse
7. Innovation, Cultural Evolution, and Economic Growth   105
   Viktor Vanberg

Part 4. Conceptual Problems and Policy Implications

8. Information, Transactions, and Catallaxy: Reflections on
   Some Key Concepts of Evolutionary Market Theory   125
   Manfred E. Streit and Gerhard Wegner
9. The Implementation of Industrial Policy in an
   Evolutionary Perspective   151
   Alexander Gerybadze

Contributors 175
Name Index 177
Subject Index 181

Part 1
Introduction

CHAPTER 1

Evolution as the Theme of a New Heterodoxy in Economics

Ulrich Witt

Evolution has become a fashionable word in economics. For example, several recent books include it in their titles (Boulding 1981; Nelson and Winter 1982; Clark and Juma 1987; Foster 1987; Hanusch 1988; Gordon and Adams 1989). The positions from which these authors write range from the Schumpeterian tradition to the institutionalists and even to the post-Keynesians. The difficulties involved in trying to identify the common elements in these "evolutionary approaches" would seem to be matched only by the diversity of their theoretical backgrounds. Indeed, with the exception of cases based on an analogy with biological evolutionary theory, similar diversity also appears in attempts made over the past few years to identify the essential features of an evolutionary approach in economics (e.g., Hirshleifer 1982; Gowdy 1985; Day 1987; De Bresson 1987; Winter 1987; Allen 1988).

Therefore, it may be appropriate for an introductory chapter to briefly explain what contributions to evolutionary economics, including those in the present volume, seem to have in common. The next section is devoted to such a classificatory attempt. The third section then discusses how common features might be merged into a broader evolutionary paradigm in economics and how the latter might possibly compare with the theory of natural selection in biology that is often held to be paradigmatic for explaining evolutionary phenomena. It will be argued that, for a proper notion of socioeconomic evolution, an appreciation of the crucial role of novelty, its emergence, and its dissemination is indispensable. The fourth section continues by highlighting some implications of such an assessment. As the range of questions addressed

---

Some of the ideas in this paper have been fostered by the stimulating intellectual atmosphere of the Santa Fe Institute, Santa Fe, New Mexico. I owe thanks to B. Arthur, P. David, R. Herrnstein, J. Holland, S. Kauffman, and D. Lane for exhilarating discussions during my stay at the institute in the autumn of 1989. Financial support by the Fritz Thyssen Foundation is gratefully acknowledged. Most helpful comments on an earlier draft of the paper have been made by J. Irving-Lessman, T. Kuran, J. A. Weissmahr, and two anonymous referees.

in the chapters in this volume is significantly wider than that commonly found in current discussions of evolutionary economics, the fifth section briefly outlines how each of the contributions relates to a broader view of socioeconomic evolution. In the last section, some tentative conclusions are drawn.

Process and Change as Key Features

Looked at more closely, the first characteristic of all the existing contributions is that they tend to interpret the term *evolutionary* in much the same way. They use it to convey the idea that, in the design of economic theory, emphasis should be placed on process and change as the key elements in the economic realm. This message was present in the earliest, though for a long time isolated, contribution by Schumpeter (1934). Most of the authors combine this emphasis with often explicit arguments directed against orthodox neoclassical economic thought. In fact, hardly any contribution to evolutionary economics has been published in recent years that has not, at least in its introduction, criticized neoclassical economics in one way or another. There is no doubt that neoclassical economics was originally developed within the analytical framework of statics and comparative statics. Yet, more recently, considerable efforts have been made to develop notions about dynamic aspects, and neoclassical theory can, therefore, no longer be charged with having a completely blind spot with regard to the problems of process and change. To give but a sample, there are neoclassical theories of individual decision cum learning processes (De Groot 1970), of market processes (Fisher 1983), of economic development and growth (Lucas 1988), and even of innovation (Binswanger and Ruttan 1978), and of long-term institutional change (North 1981).

Thus, while emphasis on process and change is a constituent element in evolutionary economics, as such it cannot be said to be the distinguishing feature. Rather, it is the manner in which these themes are approached that differs from, and is not compatible with, the neoclassical paradigm. In the latter, change is always interpreted as reactive. Individual agents or economic aggregates are viewed as responding to events that affect the basis of decision making. Economic actors are portrayed as attempting to adapt optimally to new conditions imposed on them. They are not credited in any way with creating the new conditions themselves. The reason for this narrow interpretation is the very core of the neoclassical paradigm, the synthesis of optimization and the equilibrium concept. Used together, the two ingredients rule out any explanation of individual behavior other than that of adapting to changing circumstances. This can easily be demonstrated.

As is well known, the synthesis was based on an analogy with classical mechanics (Wolfson 1987; Mirowski 1988, chap. 1; Ingrao and Israel 1990). In mechanics, disequilibrium is identified with free energy that is instantaneously dissipated in the process of restoring equilibrium. The economic analogue to free energy is a kind of psychic energy, drive, or motivation to act on the part of the individual agent. It is associated with a difference between the realized and the feasible utility index, that is, with a potential deviation of an individual's current choices from those he or she prefers most among the feasible choices. The analogy suggests that this drive or motivation is dissipated once the individual has achieved the constrained maximum.

If, in the realm of market transactions, the constraints, as determined by prices and initial endowments or income, are such that the individual optima of all agents involved are mutually compatible, a market equilibrium exists. By assumption, in market equilibrium, no agent is driven or motivated to change anything. Further changes, which of course do take place, must generally be considered to be caused by factors other than the individuals' behavior within the model, that is, as exogenous. These changes are either not explained at all, or their explanation is left to other disciplines. The consequence is that important aspects of the changes occurring in modern economies are excluded from the scope of neoclassical theory. Among other things, no explanation can be offered for entrepreneurial activities, for technological process, for changing preferences, or for newly emerging administrative and political ideas and skills.

The second feature that contributions to theoretical heterodoxy emerging under the label of evolutionary economics seem to share is opposition to the self-imposed constraints implied by the neoclassical interpretation of change. While it is certainly true that many causes of change are outside the domain of economics, there are important examples, such as those just mentioned, that clearly result from the behavior of the economic agents. It is these changes that must be treated as endogenous in an evolutionary approach (i.e., as something to be subjected to explanatory efforts). Quite naturally, contributions to this new heterodoxy usually start by attacking and abandoning or modifying the ingredients of the neoclassical synthesis: the optimization hypothesis, the equilibrium concept, or both. In so doing they align themselves with earlier heterodox traditions that, by taking the new evolutionary perspective, can be merged into a broader vision.

New Analogies or a New Synthesis?

One source of critical reasoning to which it may be worthwhile to return, and which, in fact, is sometimes referred to in the new heterodoxy, is the behavioral theory of the firm. This theory questions the notion of a decision maker who, unconstrained in his or her information-processing capacity and imperturbable in his or her desires, has no difficulty in identifying optima (Simon 1955; March and Simon 1958; Cyert and March 1963; March 1978; more recently extended by Heiner 1988). If problems in determining what is optimal are notorious in decision-making processes, the neoclassical motivation-to-adapt hypothesis derived from the analogy to the free-potential notion in mechanics no longer works. This was the reason the satisficing hypothesis was suggested.

Another source of critical ideas that the new heterodoxy increasingly appreciates is the tradition of Austrian and subjectivist economics. Here, emphasis is put on the inherently subjective and "kaleidic" nature of future prospects created in the decision maker's imagination (Hayek 1952; Shackle 1958 and 1972; Lachmann 1976; Menger 1981, chap. 1; Wiseman 1983; Buchanan and Vanberg 1990). If the imagination of choices and constraints is volatile and subject to the individual invention of novelty, not only is the rather naive, static utility theory of neoclassical economics inadequate, but the very notion of simultaneous convergence of individual adaptations to an equilibrium state is also questionable.

An attempt to integrate ideas from such diverse strands as these into a broader evolutionary paradigm in economics seems to require a more elaborate and detailed notion of socioeconomic evolution and evolutionary theory. Yet, at present, the conceptual and methodological foundations for an evolutionary approach in economics and the social sciences are little developed. Several attempts have been made to borrow a foundation from biology, where Darwin's theory of natural selection is, for many, the prototype of an evolutionary theory (see Hirshleifer 1977). In the 1950s there had been a controversy on whether something analogous to the argument of natural selection—survival of the fittest—could be used to justify the optimization hypothesis in the context of market behavior (Alchian 1950; Penrose 1952; Winter 1964). The debate may have helped to prepare the ground for the new analogy. It was, at least, significant for the approach developed by Nelson and Winter (1982) who, on the basis of a loose analogy to the theory of natural selection, merged Schumpeterian ideas with the behavioral theory of the firm. There are also many other contributions in various fields of economics and the social sciences built on more-or-less sophisticated analogy constructions (e.g, Boulding 1981; Aldrich and Mueller 1982; Boyd and Richerson 1985; Schmid and Wuketits 1987; Hannan and Freeman 1989).

However, the new analogy is not without pitfalls, as the validity and the boundaries of possible homologies between the social sciences and biology are unclear. Direct application of concepts from biology within the domain of economics may, in some cases, be appropriate. This can be argued where there is reason to believe that biological constraints have an impact on economic behavior, for instance, where peoples' economic behavior is subject to inherited (i.e., genetically programmed) regularities. A case in point is the discussion about arguments taken from sociobiology.[1] An attempt to establish evolutionary economics simply by opening up and exploiting an analogy between biology and economics, in contrast, is in danger of inducing biased and arbitrary interpretations of economic phenomena. Their potential inappropriateness may make such interpretations nearly as misleading as those resulting from the old analogy between mechanics and neoclassical economics.

Typically, there is a tendency to perfunctorily apply and overinterpret the triple notion of variation, selection, and replication in the attempt to describe and explain socioeconomic change. Variation, selection, and replication are key notions in Darwin's theory of the origin and evolution of species, that is, where information processed and changed in the course of evolution is biochemically encoded information, and where the mode of generating and processing such information is that of self-replicating macromolecules (Eigen 1988). It is by no means evident, however, why information generated and processed by human intelligence within the framework of human culture should be subject to similar, or even the same, regularities as those observed for genetic information. On the contrary, there are many obvious differences in the generation, transmission, and storage of the two kinds of information.

Human memory, imagination, and creativity working in parallel in a huge number of individual brains generate a variety of, and a growth rate in, cultural information unmatched by genetic processes. Unlike the latter, new cultural information is searched for and created deliberately in response to problems perceived or imagined by the human mind. Moreover, social learning and interindividual communication, individual recognition and imitation of successful solutions developed elsewhere, all speed up the propagation of new information in the cultural sphere. Accordingly, novelty—imagined, implemented, imitated—can be expected to play a much more significant role in explaining socioeconomic evolution than in explaining biological evolution. Although the corresponding conjectures can certainly also be expressed in terms of the triple notion of variation, selection, and replication, this scheme is unlikely to contribute much to the understanding of the specific properties of socioeconomic evolution.

A proper notion of socioeconomic evolution thus presupposes adequate theories of man-made change, of its particular sources and driving forces, and an understanding of the pivotal role of novelty. In this sort of evolutionary approach, ideas from both the subjectivist camp and the behavioral theory of the firm might be merged in a natural synthesis. The Austrian and subjectivist

---

1. Cf. Witt 1991. Interestingly, however, there seems to have been a two-way transfer in the case of the development of evolutionary game theory; for the latter, see Maynard Smith 1982; Selten 1983; Van Damme 1987, chap. 9.

positions can be interpreted as a plea for an economic theory in which the creation and dissemination of novelty plays the part it deserves (Witt 1989). What is missing, after all, in the subjectivists' contributions to accounting for evolutionary phenomena is a thorough understanding of the nature of novelty and the process by which it emerges. Although the dynamics are presumably complex, analytical progress beyond the mere statement of Shackleian "kaleidics" seems to be feasible in future research. Apart from the creativity problem, the process by which novelty emerges also involves a motivational problem. If novelty emerges in the human mind, what motivates the individual to imagine, implement, or even search for novelty? Since the not-yet-known cannot be subjected to any kind of maximization, the optimization hypothesis is clearly inadequate here. As discussed elsewhere, the motivation to search for something unknown can, however, be explained on the basis of the satisficing approach developed in the behavioral theory of the firm (Witt 1992, chap. 3).

Nonlinear Dynamics and Schumpeterian Themes

The possibility of novelty emerging and intervening in current economic processes poses intricate methodological and conceptual problems (see Witt 1992, chap. 1). One of these, which is relevant here, is a rethinking of the mathematical tools available for describing and analyzing the properties of economic processes. In line with its mechanical analogy, the neoclassical interpretation of change focuses on converging processes.[2] The basic dynamic pattern pictured in this interpretation is, roughly outlined, the following: an "exogenous shock" distorts the equilibrium in which an individual, or a collection of interacting individuals, had reached their mutually compatible constrained maxima. Thus displaced from a state of rest, the individual or collection of individuals readjust in such a way that, as time elapses, the deviation from equilibrium, either the former equilibrium or a new one, decreases and eventually vanishes. The process of adaptation converges to a new state of rest.

For obvious reasons, this notion is not adequate for capturing the dynamic patterns of evolutionary processes. Although some partial features may be characterized by a converging process, it is impossible to fully explain evolution by focusing on only that one facet of its dynamics. It is not clear, however, how a mathematical characterization of the whole evolutionary process might be achieved. Among the suggestions that have been made is the

---

2. The analogy to so-called conservative mechanical systems, i.e., systems moving along a close equilibrium orbit, which is sometimes suggested for business cycle models (see Gabisch and Lorenz 1989, chap. 4), will be ignored here.

conjecture that socioeconomic evolution is a globally unstable process that passes through phases of relative stasis alternating with phases of rapid growth and expansion (Day 1984; Day and Walter 1989). The background of the corresponding model is a complicated switching between ever more productive cum population-intensive technoinstitutional regimes, each one of which, once having culminated, tends to stagnate and break down.

An idea that might alternatively be suggested is that of a stochastic process in a high dimensional state-space in which a vast number of multiple equilibria exists. The equilibria visited sequentially may differ strongly with regard to their phenomenological attributes. Historical circumstances cumulate randomly in such a way that a temporarily or locally stable equilibrium, which has been attained, is sufficiently destabilized or a deviation beyond the attracting domain of that equilibrium (a "critical mass") is produced. As a consequence, the evolutionary process is attracted to another one of the multiple equilibria. The direction of the transition in a multidimensional phase-space is determined by random effects. It is here that the recently growing interest in modeling transitions between different economic regimes, that is to say, attractors in a phase-space, on the basis of nonlinear dynamics has a role to play in evolutionary economics. In the sciences, nonlinear phase transitions like these are sometimes referred to as self-organization phenomena and are related to evolutionary processes (Prigogine 1976; Haken 1978, chap. 7; also Silverberg 1988; Lesourne 1989).

Two approaches that differ in the properties of the stochastic processes they imply have been developed, one by Weidlich and Haag (1983) and Haag, Weidlich, and Mensch (1987) and the other by Arthur, Ermoliev, and Kaniovsky (1986 and 1987) and Arthur (1988). Up to now, these contributions have essentially been employed in investigating bimodal models, that is, models in which a potential transition between two opposing equilibrium states or attractors is considered. This is, of course, once more only a partial aspect of evolutionary processes. If, as in the second of the suggested approaches, the process ends up being "locked in" almost surely to one of the opposing equilibria, this notion could even be interpreted as just a more complicated convergence problem in a neoclassical spirit.[3] An interpretation that is appropriate for modeling evolutionary processes would have to assume transitions between very large numbers of alternative attractors scattered over a multidimensional phase-space, a problem that, in its complexity, does not yet seem analytically tractable.

Regardless of which mathematical concept seems the most promising, none of them have yet found or, perhaps, even considered an answer to the question of how the emergence of novelty may be adequately represented in a

---

3. See the applications surveyed by David (1989), several of which tend in that direction.

formal treatment of the evolutionary process. All of the models refer to a known set of attractors and to a given, finitely dimensional phase-space in order to characterize the features of the hypothesized processes. Thus, they implicitly assume that all implications of (future) evolution can be characterized in terms of already known properties: "there is nothing new under the sun." Unfortunately, however, positive suggestions of how to proceed otherwise seem to be unavailable. In general, few efforts have been made to inquire into the epistemological and methodological consequences of "real novelty" (Popper and Eccles 1977, chap. 1) that emerges during evolution. This situation is markedly different from the epistemologically less problematic diffusion research that can be based on the assumption that all properties of diffusing novelty have already been revealed, at least to the scientific observer. A formal theory of novelty has not yet appeared, and it may well be that the mathematical concepts adequate for describing and analyzing evolutionary processes will be strongly dependent on such a theory.

In contrast to the diffusion of novelty, the crucial role of its emergence for socioeconomic evolution is not universally recognized in evolutionary economics, especially in the Schumpeterian tradition. Schumpeter never developed a theory of novelty, and he showed no interest in one. In Schumpeter 1934, the emergence of novelty was referred to the domain of "inventions," something Schumpeter deemed trivially and abundantly available and irrelevant for economic analysis. As is well known, his concern was with "innovations," that is, the carrying through of new combinations of resources, the large-scale implementation of already existing inventions, by outstanding entrepreneurial talents. Interestingly, implied in the notion of the Schumpeterian entrepreneur there was, at least as far as economics is concerned, an unorthodox elitist theory of motivation and a rudimentary theory of creative imagination.

In his later work, Schumpeter (1942)—perhaps under the influence of the intellectual climate at Harvard University (see Stolper 1979)—abandoned even these rudiments. He submitted, instead, that entrepreneurial capacity and imagination had become a matter of routine so that there was no particular motivational problem involved any more. However, the distinction between invention and innovation is arbitrary, as becomes obvious when one tries empirically to separate them in the study of the development of new techniques or products. Nevertheless, the distinction has been accepted, in the Schumpeterian tradition, as an argument for excluding and belittling the problem of novelty. In fact, the distinction was necessary for Schumpeter's move to a more conventional interpretation of the entrepreneurial role, which, in turn, was helpful in transforming the Schumpeterian themes into the present industrial innovation and R&D versions of neoclassical economics (see, e.g., Kamien and Schwartz 1982; Baldwin and Scott 1987).

In the neoclassical interpretation, "innovation" is a somewhat misleading metaphor for a special class of investment problems. All properties of the innovation are supposed to be known already, at least in probabilistic terms. Accordingly, the decision about whether or not to innovate (i.e., invest in a new venture) is treated in terms of constrained maximization and equilibrium concepts. Given the ambiguous assessment of his own seminal contribution (e.g., in Schumpeter 1935), and the susceptibility of Schumpeter 1942 to neoclassical reinterpretations, it is perhaps not surprising that Schumpeter and the writers in his tradition have not met with general approval in evolutionary economics. True, with its many useful empirical and historical investigations into actual industrial innovations (Freeman 1982; Nelson 1984; Scherer 1984; Dosi 1988) and its extensions into the theory of business cycles and long waves (Mensch 1979; Kleinknecht 1987), the Schumpeterian tradition is by far the most prolific at present. But there are often doubts about whether, and to what extent, the respective contributions actually share the common ground of the heterodox approach to socioeconomic evolution characterized here. Moreover, in its somewhat narrow, technology- and industry-oriented research program, the heuristic potential of the Schumpeterian tradition for developing evolutionary economics further may be rather limited.

About the Chapters in this Volume

Because it has been so prolific, the Schumpeterian, technology- and industry-oriented tradition is sometimes identified with evolutionary economics. For the reasons I have given, this is unfortunate. There are other promising traditions, and the new heterodoxy portrayed here as possibly merging in an evolutionary paradigm is, therefore, much broader in scope and method. Indeed, if the evolutionary approach is to be understood as offering an alternative to the neoclassical synthesis of optimization and equilibrium, its scope should be expected to be of similar universality. Theoretical and conceptual problems will have to be addressed and solved on many levels and in many applications in economics.

Unfortunately, however, a coherent, evolutionary paradigm comparable in generality and acceptance to the neoclassical paradigm is still far from existing. Even a common language and common interpretative pattern are not yet fully developed in the contributions to the new heterodoxy. Thus, much as it had been my intention to select a sample of the work that would give an idea of the broad spectrum of problems and methods in the most recent research into evolutionary economics, the result is a collection of contributions from different areas that still await being related to each other in future research. In my subsequent remarks, I will try to give the reader an impression of the chapters' messages together with some view of the relationships between the contributions and broader evolutionary vision. However, many of the connections still need exploration for a fully developed picture of evolutionary economics to emerge.

The chapter by Güth and Yaari begins a section that highlights selected aspects of formal theorizing about evolutionary phenomena in economics. The particular question of how reciprocal behavior evolves, which Güth and Yaari address, belongs to the wider class of problems posed by explaining altruism and cooperative behavior in Prisoner's Dilemma games (see Sugden 1986 for an elementary introduction). A key issue in this literature is to clarify how the dilemma may be overcome—as various empirical instances seem to indicate—despite the fact that individual rationality dictates the adoption of noncooperative or selfish strategies. Retaliation by those who have been treated noncooperatively although they themselves cooperated (i.e., ex-post reciprocation of unfair behavior) might deter noncooperative behavior. Such a deterrent effect will develop if reciprocation, that is retaliatory reaction, is expected to occur regularly. However, even this is difficult to explain on the basis of individual rationality. The damage caused by unfair treatment has to be borne anyway, and ex-post reciprocation of unfair treatment causes costs on top of this. Güth and Yaari show how, maintaining the rationality assumption, the emergence of reciprocal behavior may be explained by the evolution of appropriate individual preferences in a reproduction process. Reciprocal behavior may be an evolutionarily stable strategy in the sense of evolutionary game theory. Such an interpretation implicitly presupposes, of course, that the theory of biological evolution is directly applicable to Güth and Yaari's problem.

The chapter by Weise presents an example of economic dynamics that may be governed by a nonlinear, stochastic process. The focal point is, as in the chapter by Güth and Yaari, the theory of preference. This time, however, it is not the impact of genetic endowment ("nature"), but the impact of the social environment ("nurture") that is considered—two influences that may well coexist according to present understanding (see Witt 1991). Weise wants to get away from the purely formal and static notion of preferences prevailing in microeconomics. He suggests using Lewin's field theory from social psychology as a foundation—thus the title of his chapter. However, Lewin's theory does not offer any dynamic notions. Weise provides these in a model that describes the interactive changes that may occur in individual preferences, if an individual's preferences depend on the preferences of other individuals. That is, he models a frequency dependency effect involved in preference formation. In a dynamic interpretation, this effect usually implies nonlinear phase transitions, as was recognized in the context of consumer demand theory by Granovetter and Soong (1986). As far as the dynamics are concerned, Weise's model, unlike that of Granovetter and Soong, is a thorough application of the approach developed by Weidlich and Haag (1983). Thus, it belongs to the class of bimodal transition models. It implies a rather complicated, potentially cyclical, process of preference changes with fluctuations between stages of high and low conformity pressure.

The point of departure in the chapter by Schwefel is once again ideas taken from the biological theory of evolution. However, in contrast to the direct application of such notions in Güth and Yaari's model, Schwefel is seeking generality. He looks for supraindividual forms of intelligence that may be applicable or already at work elsewhere. Schwefel identifies them in basic properties of genetic variation and selective replication and tries to translate them into abstract learning rules. These rules may be interpreted as general devices to adapt myopically in an unknown, "rugged" landscape (Kauffman 1989). Converted into computer algorithms, their properties and relative advantages can, on an abstract level, be investigated and compared. Schwefel's two-level learning rules thus offer a powerful simulation tool and a theoretical background for rethinking rationality concepts within an evolutionary perspective. (Similar efforts are currently under way in the discussion of genetic algorithms and classifier systems in computer science and economics, see Arthur 1989a; Holland 1989). Schwefel is right in being very cautious, at the present stage, in drawing parallels to economics. Yet his insights into "collective intelligence" accumulated in abstract learning or adaptation rules may well provoke deeper thought about the role of the individual in evolutionary adaptations of multipart systems such as the economy and society. The framework outlined in his chapter can thus, for instance, help to provide a more thorough understanding of cultural evolution and the "pretense of knowledge" (Hayek 1988).

The three chapters in part 3 consider an issue that should be an important touchstone in discussing the fruitfulness of an evolutionary approach to economics: the explanation of economic growth in the long run. Though the chapters emphasize different aspects, they converge in the assessment of where growth theory needs revision and extensions if it is to fit an evolutionary approach. The chapter by Weissmahr contains a plea for abandoning the traditional theory of factors of production as handed down through generations of economists since the classics. In Weissmahr's view, these factors of production—land, labor, and capital—do not allow the forces that actually drive long-term growth to be understood. Weissmahr claims, and he thoroughly reconstructs relevant parts of the history of economic thought to support his argument, that the classical factors of production are an abstraction. In this regard, economists have been led astray partly by an overly descriptive account of the historical forms of production of the time and partly by the desire to make the theory fit normative arguments of moral philosophy. In order to recognize the truly driving forces of the growing human capacity to produce and consume, Weissmahr asks what makes land, labor, and capital "productive." Quite in line with an earlier conjecture by Boulding (1981), he wants human creativity and solar energy-flow to be properly appreciated in answering that question. Accordingly, he argues for knowledge, energy, and time as factors of production in an evolutionary approach.

The chapter by Hesse begins from a very similar basic assessment. Hesse is interested in explaining why industrialization has occurred, and why it has started in the northern parts of the world. Using development economics as his base, he briefly reviews the standard explanation—which is, of course, based on the classical theory of the factors of production—and shows that it is difficult to bring into line with the actual historical events. Industrialization, as a special case of long-term economic development, cannot be understood, he submits, unless the role of human creativity in changing production techniques is acknowledged and understood. Energy utilization is a crucial aspect here. However, Hesse prefers to interpret energy supply as a basic constraint of human production activity, one among several basic constraints. Another such constraint, albeit a dynamic one, is the development of population density. In an agricultural society, increasing population density requires respective intensification of land use for calorie production. There are many ways to do this, as the author shows, and geographically they differ significantly. Indeed, because of its specific climate conditions, northwestern Europe was the region with one of the greatest disadvantages in this respect. As population density nevertheless rose drastically, human creativity was challenged to find ways of calorie production other than a simple intensification of land use.[4]

The chapter by Vanberg focuses on economic growth from a different point of view: an attempt is made to contribute to an evolutionary interpretation from the perspective of constitutional choice theory (see Buchanan 1990). If human creativity is the driving force behind economic growth—as argued in the preceding two chapters—then innovations can be expected to play a crucial role in historically observed growth processes. This is the assumption from which Vanberg begins. He wants to inquire into the incentives and constraints that constitutional environments, interpreted as a set of prevailing rules, imply with regard to innovative behavior. More precisely, he explores the question of what kind of rules induce experimental processes that enhance organizational and institutional innovations, on the one hand, and technological innovations, on the other, or, to put it in different terms, what distinguishes the first kind of experimental process from the second. In the light of

---

4. On this basis, Hesse has worked out a new theory of industrialization, which he has described in various publications over the last decade. The outline in this volume is the first publication of this new theory in English.

the abstract relationships between information-processing rules and collective intelligence considered in Schwefel's chapter, a similar relationship may exist, it may be conjectured, between the evolution of constitutional rules that a population of individuals have adopted and their capacity to generate and experiment with innovations, where there may be differences between organizational or institutional innovations and technological innovations. Vanberg builds on ideas suggested by Nelson and Winter (1982) and, most importantly however, on Hayek's theory of cultural evolution (recently summarized in Hayek 1988). Vanberg offers a unified framework of cultural, organizational, and technological experimentation processes that provides an important extension of an evolutionary theory of economic growth as it has taken shape in the chapters of part 3.

Part 4 of the volume is devoted to conceptual problems and some policy implications. The chapter by Streit and Wegner is devoted to the question of what role transaction costs can play in an evolutionary economic theory. As is well known, transaction costs are a central concept of the new, neoclassical, institutional economics (Demsetz 1968; Furubotn and Richter 1984; sometimes also called "transaction-cost economics," see Williamson 1986). In contrast to the neoclassical interpretation, Streit and Wegner relate their approach to the Austrian and subjectivist tradition. They emphasize, in the spirit of Hayek (1945 and 1978), the knowledge problem involved in market transactions and, hence, reflected in transaction costs. Knowledge of this kind needs to be produced and kept up to date—a necessary prerequisite for market coordination that, however, is costly to provide. If the knowledge is contained in easily identifiable and reliable institutional conditions, transaction costs are sunk. This, of course, is not generally the case. If institutional change is a persistent phenomenon—as it seems evident in an evolutionary perspective—current transaction costs still have to be incurred. Obviously, these costs cannot be known before institution-specific knowledge has been achieved, and, hence, they cannot be subject to optimization. A straightforward question, then, is why people do incur these ex-ante unknown costs? Streit and Wegner's answer is that they are accepted as the price for the chance of discovering profitable resource reallocation possibilities. The authors' interpretation not only contrasts with the neoclassical treatment of transaction costs and market coordination, but also with the theory of arbitrage suggested by Kirzner (1973 and 1979) in his influential Austro-American theory of the market process.

The chapter by Gerybadze, connecting with a major research interest of the Schumpeterian tradition, evaluates performance and the effectiveness of innovation-enhancing industrial policy programs that are and have been particularly fashionable in Western Europe and Japan. From a theoretical point of view, these programs have been suspected, in the spirit of Hayek (1988), of being examples of "constructivist rationalism." However, as Gerybadze points out, there may be a theoretical argument that favors a particular kind of industrial policy intervention. The argument is contingent on the diagnosis of a critical mass problem, that is, a case of nonlinear dynamics figuring prominently within evolutionary economics. Expressed in game-theoretic terms, the underlying problem is that of a coordination game (Lewis 1969; Sugden 1986, chap. 3). A choice has to be made between two alternative conventions, and the pay-offs increase with increasing relative adoption of either one of the conventions—a frequency dependency effect. Innovations are related to this in that they often require the acceptance of new standards that are like conventions (David 1987). Even though an innovation (new standard) could be beneficial if accepted by everyone, there may be no chance of it being adopted because the development is "locked in" (Arthur 1989b) to an old, common standard by the frequency dependency effect. Gerybadze suggests that, in such a situation, a coordination kind of industrial policy intervention may be helpful, possibly even necessary, in inducing a collective transition to the new standard, and he explains in more detail how such a policy could be designed.

Conclusions

An attempt has been made to work out common assessments and assumptions in a newly emerging heterodoxy in economics that can be related to an evolutionary approach. Some sources and predecessors of the various branches of this heterodoxy have been identified. A common position in this literature turned out to be its emphasis on features of process and change in the economy. As a consequence, the concepts of optimization and of converging dynamics and stationary states (in particular market equilibria) characteristic for neoclassical economics, are met with skepticism or even open opposition. The chapters in this volume reflect this position. They are selected from a broad range of topics to indicate the demand for generality attributed here to the evolutionary approach. Notwithstanding the fact that the relationships between the various problems discussed still await thorough exploration, each of the contributions to this volume indicates, in its particular field, how an evolutionary approach is gradually taking shape, and how it may contribute to explaining economic process and change.

REFERENCES

Alchian, A. A. 1950. "Uncertainty, Evolution, and Economic Theory." *Journal of Political Economy* 58:211–51.
Aldrich, H., and Mueller, S. 1982. "The Evolution of Organizational Form: Technol-

ogy, Coordination and Control." In *Research in Organizational Behavior,* ed. B. M. Staw and L. L. Cummings, 4:33–88. Greenwich, Conn.: JAI Press.

Allen, P. 1988. "Evolution, Innovation, and Economics." In *Technical Change and Economic Theory,* ed. G. Dosi, C. Freeman, R. Nelson, G. Silverberg, and L. Soete, 95–119. London: Pinter.

Arthur, W. B. 1988. "Self-Reinforcing Mechanisms in Economics." In *The Economy as an Evolving Complex System,* ed. P. W. Anderson, K. J. Arrow, and D. Pines, 9–31. Redwood City: Addison-Wesley.

Arthur, W. B. 1989a. "On Classifier Systems and Models of Learning in Economics." Santa Fe Institute. Mimeo.

Arthur, W. B. 1989b. "Competing Technologies, Increasing Returns, and Lock-in by Historical Events." *Economic Journal* 99:116–31.

Arthur, W. B., Ermoliev, Y. M., and Kaniovsky, Y. M. 1986. "Strong Laws for a Class of Path-Dependent Urn Processes." In *Stochastic Optimization: Proceedings of the International Conference,* ed. V. Arkin, A. Shiryayev, and R. Wets, 287–300. Berlin: Springer.

Arthur, W. B., Ermoliev, Y. M., and Kaniovsky, Y. M. 1987. "Path-dependent Processes and the Emergence of Macrostructure." *European Journal of Operational Research* 30:294–303.

Baldwin, W. L., and Scott, J. T. 1987. *Market Structure and Technological Change.* New York: Harwood.

Binswanger, H. P., and Ruttan, V. W. 1978. *Induced Innovation: Technology, Institutions, and Development.* Baltimore: Johns Hopkins University Press.

Boulding, K. E. 1981. *Evolutionary Economics.* Beverly Hills: Sage.

Boyd, R., and Richerson, P. J. 1985. *Culture and the Evolutionary Process.* Chicago: University of Chicago Press.

Buchanan, J. M. 1990. "The Domain of Constitutional Economics." *Constitutional Political Economy* 1:1–18.

Buchanan, J. M., and Vanberg, V. J. 1990. "The Market as a Creative Process." Center for Study of Public Choice, George Mason University. Mimeo.

Clark, N., and Juma, C. 1987. *Long-Run Economics: An Evolutionary Approach to Economic Growth.* London: Pinter.

Cyert, R. M., and March, J. G. 1963. *A Behavioral Theory of the Firm.* Englewood Cliffs, N.J.: Prentice-Hall.

David, P. A. 1987. "Some New Standards for the Economics of Standardization in the Information Age." In *Economic Policy and Technology Performance,* ed. P. Dasgupta and P. L. Stoneman, 206–39. Cambridge: Cambridge University Press.

David, P. A. 1989. "A Paradigm for Historical Economics: Path Dependence and Predictability in Dynamic Systems with Local Network Externalities." Center for Economic Policy Research, Stanford University. Mimeo.

Day, R. H. 1984. "Disequilibrium Economic Dynamics—A Post-Schumpeterian Contribution." *Journal of Economic Behavior and Organization* 5:57–76.

Day, R. H. 1987. "The General Theory of Disequilibrium Economics and of Economic Evolution." In *Economic Evolution and Structural Adjustment,* ed. D. Batten, J. Casti, and B. Johansson, 46–63. Berlin: Springer.

Day, R. H., and Walter, J. L. 1989. "Economic Growth in the Very Long Run: On the

Multiple-Phase Interaction of Population, Technology, and Social Infrastructure." In *Economic Complexity,* ed. W. A. Barnett, J. Geweke, and K. Shell, 253–89. Cambridge: Cambridge University Press.

De Bresson, C. 1987. "The Evolutionary Paradigm and the Economics of Technological Change." *Journal of Economic Issues* 21:751–62.

De Groot, M. H. 1970. *Optimal Statistical Decision.* New York: McGraw-Hill.

Demsetz, H. 1968. "The Cost of Transacting." *Quarterly Journal of Economics* 82:33–53.

Dosi, G. 1988. "Sources, Procedures, and Microeconomic Effects of Innovation." *Journal of Economic Literature* 26:1120–71.

Eigen, M. 1988. "Macromolecular Evolution: Dynamical Ordering in Sequence Space." In *Emerging Syntheses in Science,* ed. D. Pines, 21–42. Redwood City: Addison-Wesley.

Fisher, F. M. 1983. *Disequilibrium Foundations of Equilibrium Economics.* Cambridge: Cambridge University Press.

Foster, J. 1987. *Evolutionary Macroeconomics.* London: Allen and Unwin.

Freeman, C. 1982. *The Economics of Industrial Innovation.* 2d ed. London: Pinter.

Furubotn, E., and Richter, R. 1984. "The New Institutional Economics." *Journal of Institutional and Theoretical Economics* 140:1–6.

Gabisch, G., and Lorenz, H. W. 1989. *Business Cycle Theory—A Survey of Methods and Concepts.* Berlin: Springer.

Gordon, W., and Adams, J. 1989. *Economics as a Social Science: An Evolutionary Approach,* Riverdale, Md.: Riverdale Co.

Gowdy, J. M. 1985. "Evolutionary Theory and Economic Theory: Some Methodological Issues." *Review of Social Economy* 43:316–24.

Granovetter, M., and Soong, R. 1986. "Threshold Models of Interpersonal Effects in Consumer Demand." *Journal of Economic Behavior and Organization* 7:83–99.

Haag, G., Weidlich, W., and Mensch, G. 1987. "The Schumpeter Clock." In *Economic Evolution and Structural Adjustment,* ed. D. Batten, J. Casti, and B. Johansson, 187–226. Berlin: Springer.

Haken, H. 1978. *Synergetics.* Berlin: Springer.

Hannan, M. T., and Freeman, J. 1989. *Organizational Ecology.* Cambridge, Mass.: Harvard University Press.

Hanusch, H., ed. 1988. *Evolutionary Economics—Applications of Schumpeter's Ideas.* Cambridge: Cambridge University Press.

Hayek, F. A. 1945. "The Use of Knowledge in Society." *American Economic Review* 35:519–30.

Hayek, F. A. 1952. *The Sensory Order.* London: Routledge and Kegan Paul.

Hayek, F. A. 1978. "Competition as a Discovery Procedure." In *New Studies in Philosophy, Politics, Economics, and the History of Ideas,* 179–90. Chicago: University of Chicago Press.

Hayek, F. A. 1988. *The Fatal Conceit.* London: Routledge.

Heiner, R. A. 1988. "Imperfect Decisions in Organizations." *Journal of Economic Behavior and Organization* 9:25–44.

Hirshleifer, J. 1977. "Economics from a Biological Point of View." *Journal of Law and Economics* 20:1–52.

Hirshleifer, J. 1982. "Evolutionary Models in Economics and Law." *Research in Law and Economics* 4:1–60.
Holland, J. H. 1989. "Using Classifier Systems to Study Adaptive Nonlinear Networks." In *Lectures in the Science of Complexity,* ed. D. Stein, 463–99. Redwood City: Addison-Wesley.
Ingrao, B., and Israel, G. 1990. *The Invisible Hand: Economic Equilibrium in the History of Science.* Cambridge, Mass.: MIT Press.
Kamien, M. I., and Schwartz, N. L. 1982. *Market Structure and Innovation.* Cambridge: Cambridge University Press.
Kauffman, S. A. 1989. "Adaptation on Rugged Fitness Landscapes." In *Lectures in the Science of Complexity,* ed. D. Stein, 527–618. Redwood City: Addison-Wesley.
Kirzner, I. M. 1973. *Competition and Entrepreneurship.* Chicago: University of Chicago Press.
Kirzner, I. M. 1979. *Perception, Opportunity, and Profit.* Chicago: University of Chicago Press.
Kleinknecht, A. 1987. *Innovation Patterns in Crisis and Prosperity.* London: Macmillan.
Lachmann, L. M. 1976. "From Mises to Shackle: An Essay on Austrian Economics and the Kaleidic Society." *Journal of Economic Literature* 14:54–62.
Lesourne, J. 1989. "Self-Organization as a Process in the Evolution of Economic Systems." Paper presented at the International Symposium on Evolutionary Dynamics and Nonlinear Economics, Austin, Tex.
Lewis, D. 1969. *Conventions: A Philosophical Study.* Cambridge, Mass.: Harvard University Press.
Lucas, R. E., Jr. 1988. "On the Mechanics of Economic Development." *Journal of Monetary Economics* 22:3–42.
March, J. G. 1978. "Bounded Rationality, Ambiguity, and the Engineering of Choice." *Bell Journal of Economics* 9:587–608.
March, J. G., and Simon, H. A. 1958. *Organizations.* New York: Wiley.
Maynard Smith, J. 1982. *Evolution and the Theory of Games.* Cambridge: Cambridge University Press.
Menger, C. 1981. *Principles of Economics.* New York: New York University Press.
Mensch, G. 1979. *Stalemate in Technology.* Cambridge, Mass.: Ballinger.
Mirowski, P. 1988. *Against Mechanism—Protecting Economics from Science.* Totowa, N.J.: Rowman and Littlefield.
Nelson, R. R. 1984. *High Technology Policies: A Five-Nation Comparison.* Washington, D.C.: American Enterprise Institute.
Nelson, R. R., and Winter, S. G. 1982. *An Evolutionary Theory of Economic Change.* Cambridge, Mass.: Harvard University Press.
North, D. C. 1981. *Structure and Change in Economic History.* New York: Norton.
Penrose, E. 1952. "Biological Analogies in the Theory of the Firm." *American Economic Review* 42:804–19.
Popper, K. R., and Eccles, J. C. 1977. *The Self and Its Brain.* Berlin: Springer.
Prigogine, I. 1976. "Order Through Fluctuation: Self-Organization and Social System." In *Evolution and Consciousness: Human Systems in Transition,* ed. E. Jantsch and C. H. Waddington, 93–133. Reading, Mass.: Addison-Wesley.

Scherer, F. M. 1984. *Innovation and Growth: Schumpeterian Perspectives.* Cambridge, Mass.: MIT Press.
Schmid, M., and Wuketits, F. M., eds. 1987. *Evolutionary Theory in Social Science.* Dordrecht: Reidel.
Schumpeter, J. A. 1934. *The Theory of Economic Development.* Cambridge, Mass: Harvard University Press.
Schumpeter, J. A. 1935. "The Analysis of Economic Change." *Review of Economics and Statistics* 17:2–10.
Schumpeter, J. A. 1942. *Capitalism, Socialism, and Democracy.* New York: Harper.
Selten, R. 1983. "Evolutionary Stability in Extensive Two-person Games." *Mathematical Social Sciences* 5:269–363.
Shackle, G. L. S. 1958. *Times in Economics.* Amsterdam: North-Holland.
Shackle, G. L. S. 1972. *Epistemics and Economics.* Cambridge: Cambridge University Press.
Silverberg, G. 1988. "Modeling Economic Dynamics and Technical Change: Mathematical Approaches to Self-organization and Evolution." In *Technical Change and Economic Theory,* ed. G. Dosi, C. Freeman, R. Nelson, G. Silverberg, and L. Soete, 531–59. London: Pinter.
Simon, H. A. 1955. "A Behavioral Model of Rational Choice." *Quarterly Journal of Economics* 69:99–118.
Stolper, W. F. 1979. "Joseph Alois Schumpeter—A Personal Memoir." *Challenge* 21:64–69.
Sugden, R. 1986. *The Economics of Rights, Cooperation, and Welfare.* New York: Basil Blackwell.
Van Damme, E. 1987. *Stability and Perfection of Nash Equilibria.* Berlin: Springer.
Weidlich, W., and Haag, G. 1983. *Concepts and Models of a Quantitative Sociology.* Berlin: Springer.
Williamson, O. E. 1986. "The Economics of Governance: Framework and Implications." In *Economics as a Process,* ed. R. N. Langlois, 171–202. Cambridge: Cambridge University Press.
Winter, S. G. 1964. "Economic 'Natural Selection' and the Theory of the Firm." *Yale Economic Essays* 4:225–72.
Winter, S. G. 1987. "Natural Selection and Evolution." In *The New Palgrave Dictionary of Economics,* ed. J. Eatwell, M. Milgate, and P. Newman, 3:614–17. New York: Stockton Press.
Wiseman, J., ed. 1983. *Beyond Positive Economics?* London: Macmillan.
Witt, U. 1989. "Subjectivism in Economics—A Suggested Reorientation." In *Understanding Economic Behavior,* ed. K. G. Grunert and F. Ölander, 409–31. Dordrecht: Kluwer.
Witt, U. 1991. "Economics, Sociobiology, and Behavioral Psychology on Preferences." *Journal of Economic Psychology* 12, no. 4.
Witt, U. 1992. *Individualistic Foundations of Evolutionary Economics.* Cambridge: Cambridge University Press, forthcoming.
Wolfson, M. 1987. "Science and History: Economics and Thermodynamics." Paper presented at the annual meeting of the History of Economics Society, Boston.

Part 2
Toward a Formal Theory of Process and Change in the Economy

CHAPTER 2

Explaining Reciprocal Behavior in Simple Strategic Games: An Evolutionary Approach

Werner Güth and Menahem E. Yaari

Reciprocal behavior is a tendency on the part of individuals who perceive the behavior of others as being beneficial or harmful to themselves to respond in kind. To simplify matters, our analysis concentrates on situations where it is harm that is being reciprocated. Here, individual A is said to harm another individual B if it is common knowledge that the negative consequences of A's act are serious for B and that A is causing them.

The basic problem of reciprocal behavior is to explain why people engage in costly retribution when the damage to themselves is unpreventable. Our main approach to this problem is the concept of evolutionary stability: we shall try to show that mutants endowed with an incentive to reciprocate have a higher reproductive success. More specifically, it is assumed that, while individual behavior is guided both by the desire to reproduce and the incentive to reciprocate, reproductive success is purely a function of the resources earned via strategic interaction.

Our model is a simple, two-person game where initially both players must choose independently between a fair and an unfair proposal. The game ends immediately if both players pick the same proposal, and this common proposal is then implemented. Payoffs to both players are higher in the case of mutual fairness. In the case of diverging proposals, the player who has chosen fairly can prevent his or her greedy partner from enjoying the fruits of his or her greed, that is, he or she can reciprocate even though the reproductive resources of the fair proposal are no longer available to him or her.

The game to be discussed is simple, but a similar analysis can be performed for more complex game models with more than two players and more than two sequential decision stages. A more important shortcoming of our analysis is that we assume individual rationality for given preferences, al-

---

The authors gratefully acknowledge helpful comments by Reinhard Selten, Eric van Damme, Franz Weissing, Ulrich Witt, and an anonymous referee as well as the financial support of the German Science Foundation DFG and the Israel Foundations Trustees.

though one might also want to derive individual rationality as an evolutionarily stable strategy (ESS; see, e.g., Maynard Smith and Price 1973; Maynard Smith 1982; Selten 1983; Van Damme 1987). One could, for instance, assume two time dimensions so that evolution of behavior for given preferences can develop much faster than the evolution of preferences themselves. Here we do not engage in this more ambitious endeavor but only indicate its likely results.

Another restrictive assumption is complete information, in the sense of both players being aware of each other's preferences, including the desire to reciprocate. A similar analysis is possible for a game model where players are not sure whether their opponents will want to reciprocate. This can be done simply by allowing the opponent to be one of several possible types, with different tendencies for reciprocal behavior. In a further study we shall explore a model that includes the situations of complete and mutually incomplete information as well as the situations of asymmetric incomplete information as special cases.

Our approach can be regarded as a new way of viewing individual preferences. Instead of assuming that individual preferences are exogenously given, we think of an evolutionary process where preferences are determined as evolutionarily stable strategies. An objection to this approach might be that human evolution is much too slow to explain the rather rapid changes in human preferences often observed. We would accept this criticism if our approach were used to explain changes in preferences for consumer products. But for preferences relating to basic human attitudes, such as the desire for reciprocity, this argument does not apply. The desire for reciprocity is not a recent fancy but a typical trait of humans in general, going back to early primates. This point has been discussed by Trivers (1971). (Indeed, reciprocity has been observed also in monkeys, our old ancestors. See, e.g., Maynard Smith 1978.)

In the next section we shall describe our simple game model. This game is analysed in the third section for any pattern of preference for reciprocal behavior. With the help of these results we show, in the fourth section, that the desire for reciprocity can be an evolutionarily stable strategy. We conclude the chapter by summarizing and briefly indicating our further plans for the study of reciprocal behavior.

The Game Model

Two interacting individuals, called player 1 and player 2, are engaged in the game shown in figure 1 in extensive form.

The game starts with the first move of player 1. The moves of player 1 are indicated by capital letters, the ones of player 2 by lowercase letters. The

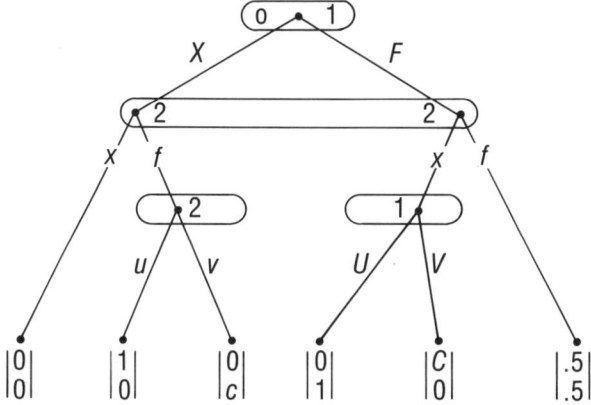

Fig. 1. The game in extensive form with players 1 and 2

letters X and x stand for exploiting the other player, whereas F and f represent the fair treatment move. The label at each decision node indicates the player whose turn it is to move. Note that the two decision nodes following 1's initial move belong to the same information set for player 2, that is, player 2 has to decide between x and f without knowing 1's previous decision. Thus, both players have to decide independently between their exploitative and their fair treatment move.

We imagine that both individuals have to decide how to split a resource whose consumption is positively related to reproductive success. Without loss of generality, the size of this resource can be normalized at 1. In the case of (X,x), where both sides choose to exploit each other, we envisage a very inefficient conflict settlement, for example, risky fights with serious injuries, so that neither party can gain any reproductive success. In the case of (F,f), where both sides choose to treat each other fairly, the result is an equal distribution of the available resource. The payoff vectors (0,0) for (X,x) and (0.5,0.5) for (F,f) should be interpreted either as the amount of resource available for consumption by the two agents or as the reproductive success resulting from consuming it. Since any ordinal transformation of individual payoffs will not affect our results and since reproductive success is assumed to be strictly increasing in resource intake, either interpretation can be used to derive our results.

In the case where the two agents choose opposite moves, that is, (X,f) and (F,x), the player who has made the fair proposal is allowed to decide whether to yield (U, respectively u) or whether to reciprocate (V, respectively v), that is, to prevent the other from enjoying what he or she greedily has taken away. If he yields, then all the resource and all the reproductive success goes to the other (selfish) player. This explains the payoff vectors (1,0) for the play (X,f,u) and (0,1) for the play (F,x,U). If this player chooses to reciprocate, then neither player can enjoy the resource, that is, both players have no resource intake and therefore the same reproductive success, as in the case of (X,x). Ordinarily, this would mean that the payoff vectors for the plays (X,f,v) and (F,x,V) are both (0,0). It is at this point that our analysis departs from customary tradition: We assume that, as far as reproductive success is concerned, vector (0,0) is, indeed, the outcome for both (X,f,v) and (F,x,V). However, as far as agents' preferences are concerned, we assume the outcomes to be $(0,c)$ and $(C,0)$, respectively, and we think of parameters c and C as being determined in an evolutionary process.

The case of $C > 0$ and $c > 0$ is one where both players get satisfaction from reciprocating, in the case of $C < 0$ and $c < 0$ the costs of reciprocation outweigh its pleasures. What we shall attempt to do is show that the situation with $C > 0$ and $c > 0$ is more likely to evolve if the preference patterns expressed by parameters C and c are determined through genetic mutation and evolution.

As long as the game in figure 1 is analyzed solely in terms of pure strategies, there is no loss of generality in assuming that parameters c and C can take on just two value, one positive and the other negative. Consequently, let us assume:

$$C \in \{C_+, C_-\} \quad \text{and} \quad c \in \{c_+, c_-\}, \tag{1}$$

with

$$C_+ > 0 > C_- \quad \text{and} \quad c_+ > 0 > c_-. \tag{2}$$

Note that in the evolutionary game, where parameters c and C themselves are chosen, mixed strategies *are* possible, and they are achieved through distributions of types in the population.

The four possible specifications (C,c) of genetically determined payoff parameters give rise to four different games (in fig. 1) that can be identified by their parameter configurations.

$$(C,c) = \begin{cases} (C_+, c_+) \\ (C_+, c_-) \\ (C_-, c_+) \\ (C_-, c_-) \end{cases} \tag{3}$$

This implicitly assumes that a player knows whether his or her opponent is a reciprocating or a yielding type, that is, that the game is one of complete information. If a player has only probabilistic beliefs concerning the type of his or her opponent, the analysis of the game would have to involve all types of players that are expected with positive probability. What we essentially exclude is the possibility that a yielding type might choose (strategically) to mimic a reciprocating type. A further study will explore a model where such a behavior is possible.

In the next section we will solve the four games shown in figure 1 corresponding to the four possible parameter configurations (C,c) in equation 3. With the help of these results, we then can determine the evolutionarily stable configuration (C,c) of genetically determined preferences guiding reciprocal behavior.

Solution of Games

Let s_i and $\hat{s}_i$ be two possible strategies of player i. We say that s_i dominates $\hat{s}_i$ if, for all possible strategy combinations of player i's opponents, s_i is never a worse reply than $\hat{s}_i$ and if s_i is a better reply than $\hat{s}_i$ to at least one such strategy combination. The strategies that survive repeated elimination of dominated strategies are simply called undominated strategies. For the solution of the four games (C,c), described by figure 1 and equation 3, we will require the choice of undominated strategies by all players. For the case at hand, repeated elimination of dominated strategies yields a unique strategy for both players in all four games (C,c). Therefore, we can determine the solutions of all four games by relying merely on this rather weak rationality condition.

It should be noted that rationality in the sense that players choose undominated strategies can be derived as evolutionarily stable behavior. Imagine a situation where a player i has only two strategies, s_i and $\hat{s}_i$, and where s_i dominates $\hat{s}_i$ with payoffs being positively related to reproductive success. If behavior is genetically determined, all possible strategy combinations of i's coplayers might show up as a result of mutation. Thus, permanent invasion of the population by mutants will completely drive out all $\hat{s}_i$ gene types, since they yield a lower reproductive success than s_i in every completely mixed population where no possible gene constellation is excluded. Unfortunately, this argument cannot be simply extended so that it also applies to repeated elimination of dominated strategies. Another approach would be to model genetically determined learning behavior and to explore whether this will lead to the use of undominated strategies. This indicates that there might be ways to derive rationality in the sense of undominated strategies instead of simply assuming it by an evolutionary analysis whose time unit is infinitesimal in comparison with the time unit that is applicable for changes in the genetically determined incentives for reciprocal behavior.

The Game $(C,c) = (C_+,c_+)$

In case of $C = C_+$ and $c = c_+$, the strategies prescribing moves U and u, respectively, are obviously dominated, that is, both players will reciprocate whenever they have the choice to do so. Thus, after eliminating all strategies prescribing moves U and u, both players have just two possible strategies left, namely XV and FV for player 1 and xv and fv for player 2. The payoff structure for this restricted game is shown in table 1.

In table 1, it can easily be seen that FV is always better than XV regardless which of the two possible strategies player 2 is going to use. Similarly, fv dominates xv in the restricted game. Thus, repeated elimination of dominated strategies yields the unique solution $s = (s_1,s_2) = (FV,fv)$, that is, both players choose fair play, since their opponent is firmly committed to reciprocate. To summarize:

Observation 1. In the case of $(C,c) = (C_+,c_+)$, the solution of the game is the strategy vector (FV,fv).

The Game $(C,c) = (C_-,c_-)$

For $C = C_-$ and $c = c_-$ the strategies prescribing moves V and v, respectively, are dominated. Eliminating these dominated strategies yields the restricted game shown in table 2.

If the opponent is selfish (chooses X or x, as appropriate), then the player's own choice does not matter. But if the opponent is fair (chooses F or f, as appropriate), then the choice of selfish behavior is clearly better. Thus, repeated elimination of dominated strategies yields the solution (XU,xu). Since no one is going to reciprocate, both players make selfish proposals and thereby lose all the available resources.

Observation 2. In the case of $(C,c) = (C_-,c_-)$, the solution of the game is the strategy vector (XU,xu).

TABLE 1. Bimatrix Game Resulting after Elimination of the Dominated Moves U and u for $(C,c) = (C_+,c_+)$

	Player 2	
Player 1	xv	fv
XV	(0,0)	$(0,c_+)$
FV	$(C_+,0)$	(0.5,0.5)

TABLE 2. Bimatrix Game Resulting after Elimination of the Dominated Moves V and v for (C,c) = (C_,c_)

Player 1	Player 2	
	xu	fu
XU	(0,0)	(1,0)
FU	(0,1)	(0.5,0.5)

The Games (C,c) = (C_+,c_-) and (C,c) = (C_-,c_+)

Due to the symmetry of the game, it suffices to consider one of the two possible situations with different incentives for both players to reciprocate. In the case of $(C,c) = (C_+,c_-)$, all strategies s_1 prescribing move U and all strategies s_2 prescribing v are dominated. The restricted game after eliminating all these strategies is shown in table 3.

Obviously, fu dominates xu. Eliminating xu now makes FV a dominated strategy of player 1. Thus, the solution for $(C,c) = (C_+,c_-)$ is (XV,fu), that is, the player who is willing to reciprocate can exploit the other player. For $(C,c) = (C_-,c_+)$, the analogous result is (FU,xv).

Observation 3. The solution of the game is the strategy vector (XV,fu) for $(C,c) = (C_+c_-)$ and (FU,xv) for $(C,c) = (C_-,c_+)$.

Evolutionary Analysis of Incentives for Reciprocal Behavior

With the help of the preceding results, we will now determine the evolutionarily stable parameter configuration (C,c). Let $G = [S_1,S_2; H = (H_1,H_2)]$ be a symmetric game in normal form, that is,

TABLE 3. Bimatrix Game Resulting after Elimination of the Dominated Moves U and v for (C,c) = (C_+,c_-)

Player 1	Player 2	
	xu	fu
XV	(0,0)	(1,0)
FV	(C_+,0)	(0.5,0.5)

$$S_1 = S_2$$

$$H_1(s_1,s_2) = H_2(s_2,s_1)$$

for all

$$(s_1,s_2) \in S_1 \times S_2,$$

where S_1 and S_2 are the sets of pure strategies s_1 and s_2, respectively, and where $H_i(s_1,s_2)$ measures i's reproductive success for the strategy vector (s_1,s_2), $i = 1, 2$. All pure strategies s_i in S_i and mixed strategies $q_i(\cdot)$ with

$$q_i(s_i) \geq 0,\ s_i \in S_i, \quad \text{and} \quad \sum_{s_i \in S_i} q_i(s_i) = 1$$

are considered as possible mutants. We identify the pure strategy s_i with the mixed strategy $q_i(\cdot)$ satisfying $q_i(s_i) = 1$ and denote the set of mixed strategies $q_i(\cdot)$ by Q_i. The payoff functions $H_i(\cdot)$ can be extended from $S_1 \times S_2$ to $Q_1 \times Q_2$ in the canonical way:

$$H_i(q_1,q_2) = \sum_{(s_1,s_2) \in S_1 \times S_2} q_1(s_1) q_2(s_2) H_i(s_1,s_2). \tag{4}$$

A strategy $q_i(\cdot) \in Q_i$ is evolutionarily stable (see Maynard Smith and Price 1973; Maynard Smith 1982; Selten 1983; Van Damme 1987) if the following two conditions hold:

$$H_i(q_i,q_i) \geq H_i(\hat{q}_i,q_i) \quad \text{for all} \quad \hat{q}_i \in Q_i, \tag{5}$$

and

$$H_i(q_i,\hat{q}_i) > H_i(\hat{q}_i,\hat{q}_i) \quad \text{for all} \quad \hat{q}_i \in Q_i$$

with $\quad H_i(\hat{q}_i,q_i) = H_i(q_i,q_i).$ \hfill (6)

Condition 5 says that the evolutionarily stable strategy $q_i(\cdot)$ must be optimal given that the population consists of $q_i(\cdot)$ strategies only. If there is no unique best reply against a population consisting of $q_i(\cdot)$ types only, then, according to condition 6, the evolutionarily stable strategy $q_i(\cdot)$ must be better than any other optimal reply $\hat{q}_i(\cdot)$ against $\hat{q}_i(\cdot)$ in a population consisting of $\hat{q}_i(\cdot)$ types only.

The concept of evolutionary stability as defined here tries to capture, in a static way, the essential aspects of an equilibrium state of a dynamic evolutionary process. Condition 5 implies that, in a population containing the same evolutionarily stable strategy only, there exists no mutant which is better adjusted to this environment. If there would be an equally optimal reply to such an environment, then condition 6 rules out that this mutant can spread out in the population since, in any mixed population with the evolutionarily stable strategy and this mutant, the evolutionarily stable strategy earns a higher reproductive success.

For the evolutionary analysis, we consider both possible parameter values of C and c, respectively, as well as all probability mixtures of both values as possible mutants, that is,

$$S_1 = \{C_+, C_-\} \quad \text{and} \quad S_2 = \{c_+, c_-\}.$$

The reproductive success for all four strategy combinations (C,c) is determined by the solution payoffs for the (C,c) games where one, of course, has to keep in mind that the payoff parameters C and c are completely unrelated to reproductive success. According to observations 1, 2, and 3, the reproductive success for the four possible strategy combinations (C,c) is shown in table 4.

For each of the four possible constellations (C,c) of gene types, the first (second) matrix component measures the reproductive success of player 1(2). With the help of table 4, one can easily see that there exists a unique, evolutionary stable strategy, namely

$$C = C_+ \quad \text{and} \quad c = c_+, \tag{7}$$

since this gene type is always the only optimal best reply regardless of how the population is divided between the two possible gene types.

Proposition. For the game of figure 1 and the space of mutants as described by table 4 there exists a unique evolutionarily stable strategy

TABLE 4. Bimatrix with the Reproductive Success for Both Players and All Four Possible Constellations (C,c) of Gene Types

Player 1	Player 2	
	c_+	c_-
C_+	(0.5, 0.5)	(1, 0)
C_-	(0, 1)	(0, 0)

$C = C_+$ and $c = c_+$, respectively, according to which both players are genetically programmed to exercise reciprocal behavior.

The proposition implies that, after possible adjustments due to short-lived new mutants, the population will settle down to a state where all individuals possess a desire to reciprocate. It thus provides a possible explanation for why humans and their early ancestors developed such a desire to respond harmfully to harm and kindly to kindness. The main reason for our result is that people who allow others to exploit them will finally be exploited and that one will not be exploited if one is genetically determined to reciprocate. Thus, genetic implementation of reciprocity helps to avoid inefficient outcomes due to mutual attempts to exploit others.

If the reciprocal acts V and v, respectively, were not available, the game of figure 1 would simplify to the degenerate Prisoner's Dilemma game shown in table 5. This game has the unique solution

$$s = (s_1, s_2) = (XU, xu)$$

in undominated strategies. According to the proposition, this inefficient result will be avoided if retaliatory acts are possible and players can genetically develop a preference for reciprocity. It is, of course, well known that retaliatory precommitment will resolve the Prisoner's Dilemma (see, e.g., Witt 1986). Here our purpose is to suggest an evolutionary setting and to show that such retaliatory precommitment would, in fact, be evolutionarily stable.

We have restricted ourselves to a very simple model where there is no effort or time cost of punishing that psychic satisfaction from retaliation would have to overcome. Of course, nothing would change if such costs are always smaller than the absolute value of the desire for revenge. But there may be circumstances where this is not true and where cooperation may fail, since retaliation is not self-enforcing. Another restriction of our analysis is that it considers only genetic evolution and not cultural evolution (see, e.g., Boyd and Richerson 1985). One reason is that we feel less confident modeling cultural evolution and speculating about its stability conditions. Since cultural

TABLE 5. Bimatrix Representation of Figure 1 When Moves V and v, Respectively, Are Not Available

	Player 2	
Player 1	xu	fu
XU	(0,0)	(1,0)
FU	(0,1)	(0.5,0.5)

changes are often inspired by other coexisting cultures and not only by rare mutants, the stability properties of evolutionarily stable strategies, for instance, may not be appropriate for cultural evolution.

In the meanwhile, our model has been generalized in two ways (see Güth 1991). First, we have given up the assumption of perfect behavioral control, that is, an unintended action will now also be used due to small mistake probabilities. The more general and complex model allows the investigation of the incentives for developing a better behavioral control. More important, we were also able to generalize our results to situations where there is incomplete information about reciprocal incentives, that is, one knows their own reciprocal incentive but not that of the other individual. In such situations, 'desire for revenge' is also the only evolutionarily stable strategy, as is the case when reciprocal incentives are common knowledge.

Peter Ockenfels (1989) has applied our basic approach to Prisoner's Dilemma games that can be played either simultaneously or sequentially as games of perfect information. Players are assumed to have genetically determined preferences either for using their cooperative strategy or only for mutual cooperation, which strategies are totally unrelated to reproductive success. Unfortunately, such games can have multiple equilibria so that Ockenfels has to rely on equilibrium selection. To justify preferences for cooperation as an evolutionarily stable strategy when one is only incompletely informed about the opponent's preference type, Ockenfels assumes that a defective type will be recognized with positive probability. A similar situation has been analysed by Frank (1987), who assumes that player in Prisoner's Dilemma games can be either honest (reliable cooperators) or dishonest (defecting from cooperation) and that honesty can be signaled perfectly or imperfectly. By comparing the expected payoffs of honest players (who cannot defect) and dishonest players for all possible compositions of the population, Frank derives the evolutionary dynamics and the evolutionarily stable composition of the population.

Final Remarks

The desire for reciprocity is a well-known fact (see, e.g., Gouldner 1960; Young 1986) and can be easily explored experimentally. We do not assume this desire to be exogenously given, but rather we try to derive it by applying the concept of evolutionary stability. Of course, our approach cannot be used to explain momentary human preferences, since biological evolution is very slow in comparison with changes in preferences for consumer products. Only incentives for basic behavioral attitudes such as reciprocity (see Trivers 1971) can be approached through a model of genetic evolution.

Our model shows that reciprocal behavior may help avoid inefficiencies resulting from individual selfishness. One would, therefore, like to explore ways of ensuring efficient results through mechanisms guaranteeing reciprocity. A game in which reciprocity is self-enforcing can be called a reciprocal mechanism. Our own example of a reciprocal mechanism rests on the idea of going back to the "biological game" and demonstrating the evolutionary stability of preferences for reciprocity.

REFERENCES

Boyd, R., and Richerson, P. 1985. *Culture and the Evolutionary Process*. Chicago: University of Chicago Press.
Frank, R. H. 1987. "If Homo Economicus Could Choose His Own Utility Function, Would He Want One with a Conscience?" *American Economic Review* 7:593–604.
Gouldner, A. W. 1960. "The Norm of Reciprocity: A Preliminary Statement." *American Sociological Review* 25:161–78.
Güth, W. 1991. "Incomplete Information about Reciprocal Incentives—An Evolutionary Approach to Explaining Cooperative Behavior." Working Paper. University of Frankfurt. Photocopy.
Maynard Smith, J. 1978. "The Evolution of Behavior." *Scientific American*, September, 136–45.
Maynard Smith, J. 1982. *Evolution and the Theory of Games*. Cambridge: Cambridge University Press.
Maynard Smith, J., and Price, G. R. 1973. "The Logic of Animal Conflict." *Nature* 246:15–18.
Ockenfels, P. 1989. "Cooperation in Prisoner's Dilemma Games—An Evolutionary Approach." Working Paper. University of Frankfurt. Photocopy.
Selten, R. 1983. "Evolutionary Stability in Extensive Two-Person Games." *Mathematical Social Sciences* 5:269–363.
Trivers, R. L. 1971. "The Evolution of Reciprocal Altruism." *Quarterly Review of Biology* 46:35–57.
Van Damme, E. 1987. *Stability and Perfection of Nash Equilibria*. Berlin: Springer-Verlag.
Witt, U. 1986. "Evolution and Stability of Cooperation without Enforceable Contracts." *Kyklos* 39:245–66.
Young, G. A., Jr. 1986. "Patterns of Threat and Punishment Reciprocity in a Conflict Setting." *Journal for Personality of Social Psychology* 51:541–46.

CHAPTER 3

Evolution of a Field of Socioeconomic Forces

Peter Weise

Until recently, linear static and dynamic models have been widely used in economics. In these models, individual behavior is described and analytically treated as if it can be isolated from the society or the economy as a whole. The behavior of a society or of an economy then consists of the additive actions of its members, and thus does not differ from the sum of the individual actions. Moreover, in linear models, the range of different types of behavior is rather limited.

Recently, therefore, there has been a growing interest in nonlinear, dynamic economic models. These models allow the representation of a wider range of different types of behavior and, consequently, are able to depict a more realistic scenario of economic or social behavior. Nonlinear interrelationships have been introduced into some theories of the business cycle, of interdependent preferences, of network externalities, and of evolutionary economics, to mention only a few (see Gaertner 1987; Silverberg 1987; Weise and Kraft 1988; Arthur 1989; Witt 1989).

A unifying concept more or less exactly elaborated pervades all of these approaches; this concept is based on the notions of self-reinforcing processes and of self-organization and is aimed at analyzing different types of collective behavior arising out of individual actions. In order to make an equilibrium state of an unstable system there has to exist a force that reinforces fluctuations around this state, thus eventually initiating a self-reinforcing process; and in order to hold together a system composed of many parts there has to exist a variable that is generated by the components of the total system and that, in turn, conducts the behavior of every individual component, thus sustaining the self-organization of the system.

In this chapter, I will outline an approach that, explicitly utilizing the

---

Critical comments and helpful suggestions by D. von Bargen, W. Brandes, K. Brandt, T. Eger, M. Kraft, J. Lessmann, H. Ursprung, U. Witt, and four anonymous referees are gratefully acknowledged. Responsibility for any errors and omissions is, of course, entirely mine.

notions of self-reinforcing processes and of self-organization, gives a more general and, in some ways, more explicit version of the models cited previously; thence it may be considered as a step toward a general theory of evolutionary processes. This approach is applied to analyzing the behavior of a multitude of individuals acting interdependently and generating a field of socioeconomic forces that determines the behavior of every individual.

Behavior of a Single Person

The core of the neoclassical theory of human behavior is formed by the combined assumptions of stable preferences devoid of any psychological content and of maximization subject to restrictions. In addition, preferences are given, not formed socially.

Yet social interaction is fundamental to life. From time to time, people give up self-oriented activities and engage in activities oriented toward others. When they are together, people may remain more-or-less isolated (simply gazing at one another), may engage in market transactions and exchange goods of equal value, or may respond to other people's actions in various ways. The last mentioned is social interaction—it involves a succession of action and reaction. The dynamic qualities of this chain of action and reaction, its moderate level of unpredictability and partial degree of control, which leads to a certain level of arousal and sensory stimulation, comprise a basic source of satisfaction. Each person stimulate the other and is in turn stimulated; all are valued by the others as a source of social interrelationship.[1]

In a similar vein, some psychologists define social interaction as a field of forces generated by persons who mutually influence one another. These forces are perceived as tensions that motivate human behavior, though they are generated by people's actions. A dynamic, self-produced field of forces determines people's activities.[2]

The generation and evolution of social interaction mediated by a field of forces is the focus of this chapter. The following three points are stressed: (1) configurations of interdependent actors exerting social pressures replace groups of isolated individuals whose behavior is coordinated through markets; (2) social interaction emerges as a succession of actions and reactions leading to a field of forces that determines behavior and is a basic source of satisfaction; and (3) an evolutionary process of the field of social forces gives rise to cyclical, or abruptly changing, social behavior and to certain regularities of mass phenomena.

---

1. See Latané and Hothersall 1974; cf. Eysenck (1965, 85): "[M]ost of our stimulation, after all, derives from concourse with other people." See Jones 1984 for a discussion of some arguments.

2. Cf. Lewin 1951 for a more statically oriented version of this idea.

I make the following three assumptions. First, at each moment, a person is performing an activity (i.e., the person is engaged in a certain state of behavior). Second, all states of behavior are mutually exclusive, and the number of states of behavior is countable. And third, a restriction exists that prevents all behavioral alternatives being simultaneously realized, that is, a given budget of time, income, or the like has to be allocated among the alternatives. Thus, there exists a problem of choice or conflict.

These three assumptions describe human behavior as a transition process between discrete states that goes on in time. Four further assumptions define human behavior as embedded in a field of socioeconomic forces. Fourth, every alternative activity is bound up with facilitating and inhibiting drives or motives that determine the attraction level of an activity. Fifth, inhibition grows over time if an activity is performed uninterruptedly, and the degree of tension is thus increased. Consequently, the attractiveness of an activity diminishes over time. Sixth, maximal individual satisfaction requires that the person choose the transition rates from one activity to another so as to equalize the levels of tension of the states of behavior at the margin. And finally, each person exercises an influence on other people and is, in turn, influenced by other people; thus a field of socioeconomic forces is built up.[3]

To demonstrate the assumptions precisely and to show how the model works, the following special assumptions are made without loss of generality.

1. There are only two alternative states of behavior: activity S_1 and activity S_2. The latter can be regarded as encompassing all other feasible states or activities.
2. There is a time restriction on behavior in that only one interstate transition is feasible within a unit-time interval. Sequences of behavior over time then occur through sequences of this unit-time period.
3. During this unit-time period inhibition grows as a quadratic function of time.

Let $q_{12}t$ ($q_{21}t$) be the marginal increase of tension over time t as long as S_1 (S_2) is performed; this is thus a measure of the diminishing attractiveness of S_1 (S_2) relative to S_2 (S_1) during time t. Therefore, q_{12} (q_{21}) may be designated as tension intensity or transition intensity. Total tension in time is obtained by

---

3. In psychology, two kinds of psychological processes are essentially distinguished: activating and inhibiting processes that are connected to arousal, emotional intensity, excitement, and tension. They activate and inhibit human behavior; activating and inhibiting forces are stimuli, emotions, drives, or motives. See Pribram 1969a, 422–23 and 1969b. Cf. Krelle 1968; Lesourne 1977 and 1979 for similar ideas. See Winston 1987 for a treatment of the choice of time-dependent activities.

$$\int q_{12} t\, dt = \frac{1}{2} q_{12} t^2 \left(\int q_{21} t\, dt = \frac{1}{2} q_{21} t^2 \right).$$

Under assumption 2, only one transition from an activity to the other is allowed. Suppose the person to be in S_1. When will he or she go from S_1 to S_2 and how much time will he or she spend on S_1 if a sequence of unit-time periods is considered? The answer is straightforward. Let t_1 be the time span in which the person is in state S_1 and $(1 - t_1)$ the time span in which he or she is in state S_2, so that t_1 and $(1 - t_1)$ can also be interpreted as proportions of time. If the individual optimizes, he or she will choose the proportions of time spent with S_1 and S_2 that minimize tension. Minimizing tension, T,

$$\min_{0 < t_1 < 1} T = \frac{1}{2} q_{12} t_1^2 + \frac{1}{2} q_{21}(1 - t_1)^2$$

for $q_{12}, q_{21} > 0$ yields

$$\frac{dT}{dt_1} = q_{12} t_1 - q_{21}(1 - t_1) = 0.$$

This condition can be reformulated as $t_1^* = q_{21}/(q_{12} + q_{21})$ and can be interpreted as follows. The optimal time span within the unit-time interval or the optimal proportion of time during a sequence of time intervals t_1^*, is equal to the ratio of the (missed) tension intensities of S_1 and S_2 or, equivalently, the optimal time spans or optimal proportions of time, t_1^*, and $(1 - t_1^*)$, are inversely proportionate to the tension intensities of S_2 and S_1.

This means that, in order to minimize tension, a person has to perform S_1 during the time span t_1^* and then change to S_2 for a time span $(1 - t_1^*)$; if transitions over a sequence of unit-time intervals are allowed, the optimizing person in the long run has to stay in the proportions t_1^* and $(1 - t_1^*)$ in S_1 and S_2, respectively.[4]

The problem of determining the optimal t_1^* can also be reformulated as a problem of minimizing a tension function or maximizing a "utility" function. Because

$$-\frac{dT}{dt_1} = [t_1 + (1 - t_1)] q_{21} - t_1(q_{21} + q_{12}),$$

---

4. Cf. Doob 1953. Transition rates or transition probabilities are defined as the number of switches from one alternative to another per unit-time period; referring to transitions per unit-time period, the transition rates or transition probabilities reflect the combined results of preferences and restrictions. In the model developed here, preferences and restrictions are separated; as a consequence, q_{12} and q_{21} only reflect preferences, while a time restriction determines the number of switches.

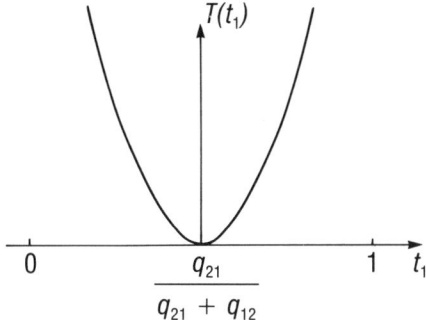

Fig. 1. The tension function

where $0 < t_1 < 1$; you obtain, by integration,

$$T(t_1) = \frac{q_{21} + q_{12}}{2} \left(\frac{q_{21}}{q_{21} + q_{12}} - t_1 \right)^2.$$

This function may be called a tension function—its negative may be called a "utility" function—with $T = 0$ for $t_1^* = q_{21}/(q_{21} + q_{12})$, so that minimization or maximization of this function leads, respectively, to the optimal value of t_1 (see fig. 1). If we define force as the negative derivative of this tension or utility function, namely $F \equiv -dT(t_1)/dt_1$, we notice that force will be minimized for $t_1 = q_{21} (q_{21} + q_{12})$. Therefore, it seems appropriate to regard human behavior as driven by motives, stimuli, drives, and so on, conceived of as a combination or sum of forces. To say a person behaves as if minimizing tension (maximizing "utility") is the same as saying that a person is driven by forces to a state of minimum tension.

A Multitude of Persons and Configurations

Now let us consider a multitude of N persons who exert social pressure and exercise an influence on one another. The result is a change in tension and a corresponding alteration of tension intensities. When we consider a multitude of persons, we have to abandon the deterministic view of behavior and have to assume a stochastic point of view. So let us reinterpret tension intensities q_{12} and q_{21} as individual transition rates $\bar{q}_{12}$ and $\bar{q}_{21}$ describing the probability per unit of time of changing behavior from 1 to 2 and 2 to 1, respectively, in an infinitesimally small time interval. Let us further assume that only one change of behavior is feasible within this small time interval and that the Markovian assumption is fulfilled. Let us finally assume that transitions can occur between adjacent configurations of persons only. Then, the motion of the multitude of persons is described by the equation

$$dx/dt = n_2 \bar{q}_{21} - n_1 \bar{q}_{12},^5 \qquad (1)$$

where N is an even number, with N persons changing activities, N_1 choosing S_1 and N_2 choosing S_2, so that $N_1 + N_2 = N$; define $n_1 = N_1/N$, $n_2 = N_2/N$, $n = N_1 - (N/2) = (N/2) - N_2$, $x = n/(N/2)$, so that $x = 2(n_1 - 1/2) = -2(n_2 - 1/2)$ and $-1 \leq x \geq 1$.

Let us define, for the case that S_1 is preferred, the force of preference as $\bar{q}_{21} = \text{constant} > \bar{q}_{12} = \text{constant}$; the force of conformity as $d\bar{q}_{21}(n_1)/dn_1 > 0$, $d\bar{q}_{12}(n_1)/dn_1 < 0$, and $d(n_2\bar{q}_{21} - n_1\bar{q}_{12})/dn_1 > 0$; and the force of anticonformity as $d\bar{q}_{21}(n_1)/dn_1 < 0$, $d\bar{q}_{12}(n_1)/dn_1 > 0$, and $d(n_2\bar{q}_{21} - n_1\bar{q}_{12})/dn_1 < 0$. The definitions are analogous for the case where S_2 is preferred.

In order to avoid this rather clumsy notation and in order to get an explicit solution, a specific, the forces of preference, conformity, and anticonformity merely approximately representative supposition is

$$\bar{q}_{12}(x) = \exp[-(b + cx + dx^3)],$$

$$\bar{q}_{21}(x) = \exp[(b + cx + dx^3)], \qquad (2)$$

where b is the relative preference of S_1 over S_2; c is the influence of social pressure to conform or the inclination to imitate; d is the opposite force to conformity, that is, either to stand out against the others directly or to prefer deviant behavior when relatively many other individuals act in conformity. We obtain

$$dx/dt = n_2\exp(b + cx + dx^3) - n_1\exp[-(b + cx + dx^3)]$$

$$= \sinh(b + cx = dx^3) - x\cosh(b + cx + dx^3).$$

In equilibrium, $dx/dt = 0$, so that

$$x^* = \tanh(b + cx + dx^3).$$

In order to understand this approach more fully and in order to com-

---

5. This equation is a special case of the so-called master equation; see Weidlich and Haag 1983. In the following we consider the motion equation for the mathematical expectation only.

prehend the socioeconomic content of the model, I will discuss the consequences of different parameter values in terms of tension intensities q_{12} and q_{21} instead of transition rates $\bar{q}_{12}$ and $\bar{q}_{21}$. In the next section, then, I discuss the dynamic behavior of the model by means of transition rates $\bar{q}_{12}$ and $\bar{q}_{21}$.

According to the value of b, the tension intensities q_{12} and q_{21} differ so that one state of behavior is preferred to the other one independently of the behavior of others; b is, therefore, called a preference parameter. According to the value of c, the number of persons choosing one state of behavior determines the relative values of q_{12} and q_{21}, thus, the number of persons influences the attractiveness of S_1 and S_2; c is therefore labeled a conformity parameter. Finally, d stands for the decreasing attractiveness of an activity when chosen by a great majority of persons; thus, d represents the building up of a countervailing power to conformity, and d is called the anticonformity parameter.

If b, c, $d = 0$, then $q_{12} = q_{21}$; neither activity is preferred to the other. If $b \neq 0$, c, $d = 0$, then $q_{12} \neq q_{21}$; this means that S_1 is preferred to S_2 or vice versa. In both cases, if $c = d = 0$, all persons are completely independent of one another, and neither social pressure nor an inclination to anticonformity exists. As a consequence, the behavioral states S_1 and S_2 alone influence the behavior of the persons; the persons themselves do not exert social influence upon one another.

If $c \neq 0$, $d = 0$, the situation changes. In this case, q_{12} and q_{21} vary according to n, that is, the behavior of the majority.[6] The attractiveness of an activity is thus directly dependent on social behavior. The tension intensities q_{12} and q_{21} are determined via parameter c; consequently, the attractiveness of S_1 relative to S_2 varies, and a configuration of persons is generated, via n, who mutually influence one another and thereby reciprocally exert social pressure on each other. If every person is minimizing the tension imposed by S_1 or S_2 and n, an equilibrium may be established.[7]

There is a unique and stable equilibrium for $0 < c < 1$; there are two stable equilibria and one unstable equilibrium if $c > 1$. This means that either an equilibrium, which is determined by preference parameter b only, exists if the inclination to conformity is weak (i.e., $c < 1$), or two equilibria, determined by conformity parameter c and biased by preference parameter b, exist if the inclination to conformity is strong (i.e., $c > 1$). Some typical constellations are illustrated in figures 2a through 2c.

---

6. Or according to a variable varying monotonously with n; examples are a norm, a rumor, an atmosphere, a style, a fashion, and so on.

7. There is a striking similarity of these and subsequent results to a Nash equilibrium in a noncooperative game. In game theory, we think of people as having fixed utility functions that depend upon the actions of every agent, while in the present chapter we think of the aggregate actions of all other agents as influencing the preferences of each individual.

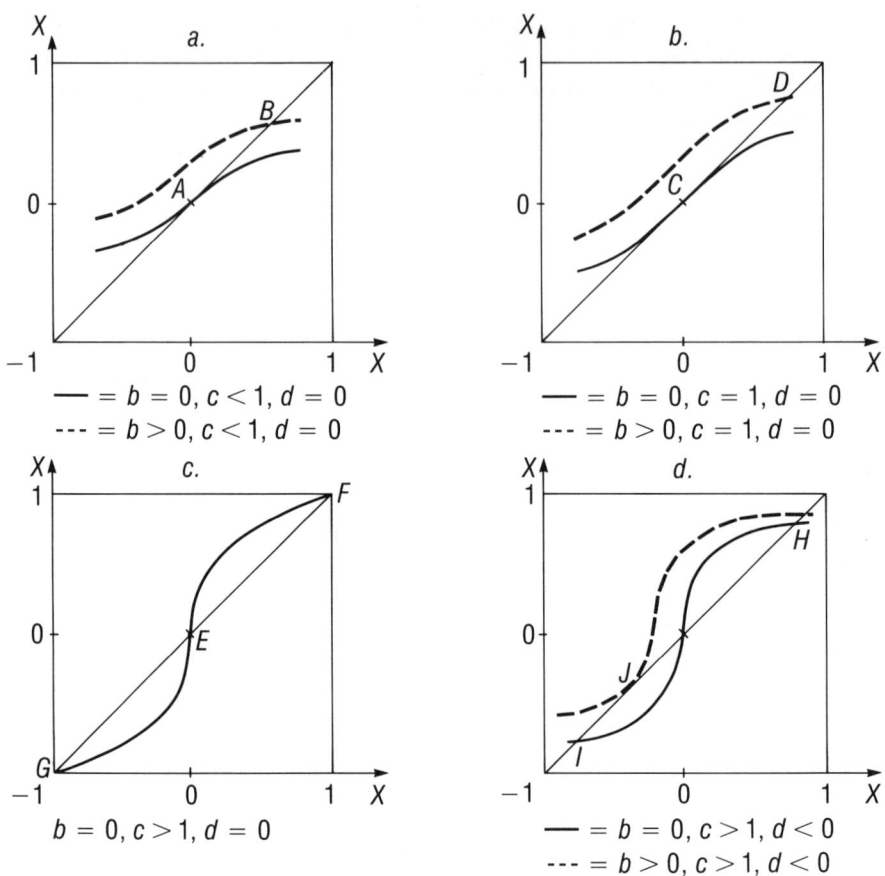

Fig. 2. Typical constellations of the motion equation

In figure 2a, $x = 0$ is an equilibrium for $b = 0$ (point A), and a point $x > 0$ (i.e., S_1 is preferred to S_2) is an equilibrium for $b > 0$ (point B). In figure 2b, a domain around $x = 0$ is an equilibrium for $b = 0$, indicating that conformity forces are exactly offsetting equilibrating forces caused by independently acting persons (around point C); moreover, a point $x > 0$ is an equilibrium for $b > 0$ (i.e., S_1 is strongly preferred to S_2 [point D]). In figure 2c, $x = 0$ is an unstable equilibrium for $b = 0$, indicating that conformity forces prevail over equilibrating forces caused by independently acting people (point E); if conformity is relatively strong, two stable corner equilibrium points exist, $x \to 1$ and $x \to -1$ (points F and G).[8]

---

8. Cf. Granovetter and Soong (1981 and 1986), who derived similar results taking a different approach but disregard the notion of self-organization.

The salient behavioral assumption of our activity choice model is the assumption that an individual, when continuously engaged in one activity, is, in the course of time, exposed to rising tension. An analogous assumption may be made according to the overall effect of conformity: the stronger a tendency to conformity, the less attractive it is. To incorporate this assumption into our model, we have to suppose $d < 0$. Typical constellations are depicted in figure 2d. The study of this diagram reveals that the interpretation is analogous to the case of $d = 0$ with the exception of one important point. Two stable interior equilibria exist that are caused by the equivalence of conformity and anticonformity forces (points H and I). The consequence may be a "catastrophic" jump of social behavior if the parameters take critical values relative to one another (point J); at this point, preference for S_1 just equals conformity to S_2 so that both forces draw in different directions. Moreover, two different modes of behavior may occur under the same set of parameter values. Consequently, a certain degree of tension may abruptly change its value and lead to a discontinuous alteration of social behavior via altered q_{12} and q_{21}, or two different degrees of tension may be produced causing two differently preferred equilibria so that a configuration of people may be locked into the less-preferred equilibrium.[9]

All the cases I have discussed may again be transformed into "utility" or tension functions as shown previously. One obtains

$$T(x) = \frac{1}{2} k_1 x^2$$

with $k_1 > 0$ for the case of $b = 0$, $0 < c < 1$, $d = 0$;

$$T(x) = \frac{1}{2} k_1 x^2 + k_2 x$$

with $k_1 > 0$, $k_2 \neq 0$ for the case of $b \neq 0$, $0 < c < 1$, $d = 0$;

$$T(x) = \frac{1}{4} k_3 x^4 + \frac{1}{2} k_1 x^2$$

with $k_3 > 0$, $k_1 < 0$ for the case of $b = 0$, $c > 1$, $d < 0$; and

$$T(x) = \frac{1}{4} k_3 x^4 + \frac{1}{2} k_1 x^2 + k_2 x$$

with $k_3 > 0$, $k_1 < 0$, $k_2 \neq 0$ for the case of $b \neq 0$, $c > 1$, $d < 0$.

Thus, it is shown how a multitude of interacting people, N, may generate

---

9. See Weise and Eger (1987), Weise and Brandes (1990) for an analysis of the forces of preference, conformity, and anti-conformity in different settings of self-organization. Cf. Zeeman (1977) for an introduction to catastrophe theory.

a field of conformity and anticonformity forces that determine individual behavior. The equilibrium caused by independently acting people and leading to the point $x = 0$ (i.e., $n = 0$) is, on the one hand, biased by a relative preference for S_1 over S_2 or vice versa, expressed by preference parameter b; it is, on the other hand, made unstable by a sufficiently strong conformity force, expressed by conformity parameter c, thus driving the multitude of persons to another stable equilibrium, that is, an equilibrium of an interacting configuration of people in a field of conformity forces. This equilibrium is an interior equilibrium if anticonformity, expressed by anticonformity parameter d, is sufficiently strong. Social interaction as a sequence of actions and reactions builds up forces that stimulate and motivate people to minimize tension. People exert social influence on one another, thereby varying the values of tension intensities q_{12} and q_{21} so that, in order to minimize tension, an altered choice of activity is effected. This altered activity choice, on the other hand, again changes the values of the tension intensities and so forth until an equilibrium has been established.

Evolution in Time

Until now, I have concentrated my analysis on the more static aspects of the model. I have shown how the relative values of tension intensities q_{12} and q_{21} determine the optimal time spans given to S_1 and S_2 via the behavioral postulate of tension minimization. The tension intensities themselves are determined by components that reflect the influence of activities S_1 and S_2 and of the behavior of other persons. But what will happen if we consider the dynamic aspects of the model? To answer this, we have to distinguish between two cases, a case where parameters are constant and a case where they are variable. Consider equation 1 and transition rates 2.

Suppose, first, parameters b, c, and d to be constant. A multitude of persons characterized by a certain set of constant parameters b, c, and d converges in the course of time to a stable equilibrium configuration from whatever constellation it starts. The equilibrium configurations have been discussed above: there may be one stable equilibrium, one unstable equilibrium, and two stable corner equilibria, or one unstable equilibrium and two stable interior equilibria, and various critical cases not mentioned explicitly. Evolution over time is then depicted as a convergence process to an equilibrium state. If $c > 1$, a self-reinforcing process develops. During this process, on the one hand, a field of forces is built up and varied through the actions of people and, on the other hand, this very field of forces determines the behavior of the individual persons, thus sustaining a self-organization process. In equilibrium, this convergence process comes to rest so that nothing further occurs in the course of time (with the exception of minimal fluctuations). The optimal allotment of time to states S_1 and S_2 has been realized; evolution in this sense has come to an end.

Suppose, however, as a second case, parameters b, c, and d to be variable. Two subcases may be distinguished: first, the parameters evolve according to a prescription independent of the history and of the state of the configuration (e.g., $b = b[t]$); or, second, the evolution of the parameters depends on the history and on the state of the configuration (e.g., $b = b[x]$ or $b = b[c]$).

Assume first, for instance, that b varies over time and consider the special case $\bar{q}_{12} = \exp\left[-(b + cx)\right]$, $\bar{q}_{21} = \exp(b + cx)$. The rationale for this may be that an activity performed continuously outgrows its attractiveness not only in the short run, but may also do so in the long run. The repeated choice of an activity may bring about an increasing unattractiveness that, in the course of time, may reverse itself. Hence, variation of preferences over time may eventually generate a cyclical behavior that is strongly intensified by conformity forces. This is the case when b varies sinusoidally and when, because of a high value of conformity parameter c, a strongly cyclical social behavior evolves, brought about by rather moderate cyclical variations of preference parameter b.[10]

Similarly, conformity parameter c may vary over time. Social pressure may change over time or at times. Suppose conformity parameter c changes at a certain time from a subcritical value, $c < 1$, to a critical value, $c > 1$. Though preference parameter b behaves moderately, a strongly fluctuating social behavior occurs because of an abrupt variation in the field of social forces.

In these cases, evolution never converges to an equilibrium state. Because preference and conformity parameters vary over time, the field of forces also varies, so that social behavior evolves accordingly. Moreover, anticonformity parameter d also may vary; then a stronger or weaker tendency to extreme social behavior emerges. In all these cases, evolution is caused by parameters varying in time according to an exogenous law of motion.[11]

Second, parameters may vary endogenously, contingent upon the development of a configuration. Preference, conformity, and anticonformity parameters are then a function of the history and the state of a configuration. At

---

10. For an analysis of economic examples of this result and for references to the psychological literature, see Scitovsky 1976; Hirschman 1982.

11. The forces of conformity and anticonformity seem to be fundamental to socioeconomic processes in general and to self-organizing processes in particular. While the force of conformity gives rise to self-reinforcing processes, the force of anticonformity prevents an ever-increasing growth. Thus, the famous logistic equation $x_{t+1} = ax_t(1 - x_t)$ is composed of a conformity force, a, and an anticonformity force, $(1 - x_t)$. If the forces are relatively strong, chaotic motion may occur (cf. May 1976; Lorenz 1989). Also see Gierer 1981.

every moment of time, parameters take on definite values; via transition rates $\bar{q}_{12}$ and $\bar{q}_{21}$ a contingent social behavior is generated; in turn, social behavior modifies the values of the parameters. A time process evolves in the course of which changes in social behavior occur must faster than changes in parameter values; so, subject to a given parameter value, social behavior is in equilibrium at any time. Eventually, this process would converge to an equilibrium of social behavior and parameter values (see Schlicht 1985 for general results). But assume there is a hierarchy of parameters. Parameters at a lower level converge to equilibrium parameter values contingent on parameters at a higher level. Parameters at a higher level converge more slowly to equilibrium parameter values contingent on parameters at a still higher level, and so forth. Evolution over time, then, is a self-reinforcing and self-organizing process that never stops (cf. Haken 1982; Eger and Weise 1986).

There is a third starting point for representing evolutionary processes that is as important as the assumptions of parameters obeying an exogenous law of motion or of hierarchically ordered parameters varying at different time scales. Even with constant parameters, cyclical, catastrophic, or chaotic behavior may be the consequence if the overall effect caused by the parameters varies. This may be due to a changing constellation of subgroups such that the field of social forces changes too. Suppose there are two subgroups of persons with the distinctive feature that each group's behavior is oriented toward the other, but that the orientations are opposite. Let

$$\bar{q}_{12}{}^1 = \exp\left[-(b^1 + c_1{}^1 x^1 + c_2{}^1 x^2)\right],$$

$$\bar{q}_{21}{}^1 = \exp(b^1 + c_1{}^1 x^1 + c_2{}^1 x^2);$$

$$\bar{q}_{12}{}^2 = \exp\left[-(b^2 + c_1{}^2 x^2 + c_2{}^2 x^1)\right],$$

$$\bar{q}_{21}{}^2 = \exp(b^2 + c_1{}^2 x^2 + c_2{}^2 x^1);$$

where superscripts denote subgroups 1 and 2. Many interesting constellations exist (see Kraft, Landes, and Weise 1986). Assume, for instance, strong conformity forces with regard to behavior of members of the own group, $c_1{}^1$ and $c_1{}^2 > 1$, and a conformity tendency of one group to the other, $c_2{}^1 > 0$, but an anticonformity tendency of the second group to the first one, $c_2{}^2 < 0$. Then a limit cycle may exist (i.e., cyclical behavior occurs). Though parameters are constant, the overall effect varies because of changing proportions of persons acting in a certain way.

Summing up, we see that evolution over time may take place as a time process converging to a stable equilibrium state if parameters are fixed; never approaching an equilibrium state if parameters obey an exogenous law of motion; evolving according to a hierarchy of endogenously varying parameters; or, finally, exhibiting nonconvergent behavior if certain subgroups act appropriately.

Concluding Remarks

The evolutionary, activity-choice model presented here is a stylized and simplified one. It has been assumed that people have only two activities at their disposal, that marginal tension is a linear function in time, and that a behavioral restriction exists whose quality is not exactly specified. It goes without saying that more than two activities may be considered, that nonlinear, marginal tension functions may be assumed, and that a specific behavioral restriction may be stated. Yet the greater generality of the model thus obtained would conceal its salient features. Therefore, rather simplistic suppositions have been made.

I have shown how an individual behaves if he or she minimizes tension rising in time, and I have demonstrated how the activity choices of a multitude of persons generate a field of social forces. The field of forces, on the other hand, gives rise to determinate choices of activities by single persons. In this way, a self-reinforcing and self-organizing process evolves. If parameters are made time dependent in a proper manner, or if at least two subgroups of persons are interacting appropriately, an evolutionary process of the field of social forces emerges and gives rise to cyclical, abruptly changing, or chaotic social behavior, or to certain regularities of mass phenomena.

REFERENCES

Arthur, W. B. 1989. "Competing Technologies, Increasing Returns, and Lock-in by Historical Events." *Economic Journal* 99:116–31.
Doob, J. L. 1953. *Stochastic Processes.* New York: John Wiley and Sons.
Eger, T., and Weise, P. 1986. "Liberalismus und gesellschaftliche Selbstorganisation." In *Liberalismus im Kreuzfeuer,* ed. H. G. Nutzinger, 60–78. Frankfurt am Main: Knecht.
Eysenck, H. J. 1965. *Fact and Fiction in Psychology.* Harmondsworth: Penguin.
Gaertner, W. 1987. "Periodic and Aperiodic Consumer Behavior." *Applied Mathematics and Computation* 22:233–54.
Gierer, A. 1981. "Socioeconomic Inequalities: Effects of Self-Enhancement, Depletion, and Redistriction." *Jahrbücher für Nationalökonomie und Statistik* 196:309–31.
Granovetter, M., and Soong, R. 1981. "Threshold Models of Diffusion and Collective Behavior." In *Modelle für Ausbreitungsprozesse in sozialen Strukturen,* ed. H. J.

Hummel and W. Sodeur, 95–119. Duisberg: Sozialwissenschaftliche Kooperative.
Granovetter, M., and Soong, R. 1986. "Threshold Models of Intertemporal Effects in Consumer Demand." *Journal of Behavior and Organization* 7:83–99.
Haken, H. 1982. *Synergetik.* Berlin: Springer.
Hirschman, A. O. 1982. *Shifting Involvements.* Princeton: Princeton University Press.
Jones, S. 1984. *The Economics of Conformism.* Oxford: Basil Blackwell.
Kraft, M.; Landes, T.; and Weise, P. 1986. "Dynamic Aspects of a Stochastic Business Cycle Model." *Methods of Operations Research* 53:445–53.
Krelle, W. 1968. *Präferenz- und Entscheidungstheorie.* Tübingen: Mohr (Siebeck).
Latané, B., and Hothersall, D. 1974. "Social Attraction in Animals." In *New Horizons in Psychology,* ed. P. C. Dodwell, 2:259–75. Harmondsworth: Penguin.
Lesourne, J. 1977. *A Theory of the Individual for Economic Analysis.* Amsterdam: North-Holland.
Lesourne, J. 1979. "Economic Dynamics and Individual Behavior." In *Sociological Economics,* ed. L. Levy-Garbona, 29–47. Beverly Hills: Sage.
Lewin, K. 1951. *Field Theory in Social Science.* New York: Harper and Row.
Lorenz, H.-W. 1989. *Nonlinear Dynamical Economics and Chaotic Motion.* Berlin: Springer.
May, R. M. 1976. "Simple Mathematical Models with Very Complicated Dynamics." *Nature* 261:459–67.
Pribram, K. H., ed. 1969a. *Brain and Behaviour.* Vol. 1, *Moods, States, and Mind.* Harmondsworth: Penguin.
Pribram, K. H., ed. 1969b. *Brain and Behaviour.* Vol. 4, *Adaptation.* Harmondsworth: Penguin.
Scitovsky, T. 1976. *The Joyless Economy.* New York: Oxford University Press.
Schlicht, E. 1985. *Isolation and Aggregation in Economics.* Berlin: Springer.
Silverberg, G. 1987. "Technical Progress, Capital Accumulation, and Effective Demand: A Self-Organization Model." In *Economic Evolution and Structural Adjustment,* ed. D. Batten, J. Casti, and B. Johansson, 116–44. Berlin: Springer.
Weidlich, W., and Haag, G. 1983. *Concepts and Models of a Quantitative Sociology.* Berlin: Springer.
Weise, P., and Eger, T. 1987. "Das Koordinationsproblem sozialer Gruppen." *European Journal of Political Economy* 3:351–67.
Weise, P., and Kraft, M. 1988. "Cumulative Processes, Disproportionalities, and Spiethoff's Theory of the Business Cycle." In *Recent Approaches to Economic Dynamics,* ed. P. Flaschel and M. Krüger, 3–16. Frankfurt am Main: Lang.
Weise, P., and Brandes, W. 1990. "A Synergetic View of Institutions." *Theory and Decision* 28:173–87.
Winston, G. C. 1987. "Activity Choice: A New Approach to Economic Behavior." *Journal of Economic Behavior and Organization* 8:567–85.
Witt, U. 1989. "The Evolution of Economic Institutions as a Propagation Process." *Public Choice* 62:155–72.
Zeeman, E. 1977. *Catastrophe Theory.* Reading, Mass.: Addison-Wesley.

CHAPTER 4

Imitating Evolution: Collective, Two-Level Learning Processes

Hans-Paul Schwefel

In the early stages of the development of instruments designed to extend human capacities, attempts were frequently made to imitate natural forms. The beginning of the computer revolution was characterized by models based on the way the human brain was thought to work. John von Neumann (1958) and Ross Ashby (1960) are good examples of this kind of hubris. Norbert Wiener (1948), the father of cybernetics, had pointed in the direction of a search for common principles in living and artificial systems. At the time, however, very little was known about how the brain actually works and even now, in the second wave of the search for artificial intelligence, we are not much further forward. Nevertheless, some work was successful enough to encourage hopes about artificial brains and intelligent automata. The coining of the term *artificial intelligence* aroused both far-fetched and fearful expectations. Of course it was the software, not the hardware, that was intelligent— programs became self-controlling by means of skillful hierarchical arrangements. Lower level rules could be changed by higher level rules so that the former could adapt to situations perceived by the latter. Learning machines or learning algorithms became the subject of investigation.

Intelligent behavior is, however, not the exclusive property of individual organisms—in nature, larger subsystems made up of many individuals also appear to behave intelligently. Evolution itself takes place through phylogenetic rather than ontogenetic learning.[1] Although it was recognized that evolution is involved in the development of brains, this was thought to be a stupid, wasteful, trial-and-error process, pointless to try to imitate. Indeed, this view of the matter has still not entirely disappeared.[2]

---

1. Ontogeny is the developmental history of an organism from fertilized egg to adult, whereas phylogeny is the sequence of ancestor-descendant forms created during the evolutionary history of a taxon.

2. No one seemed to have noticed that adjusting 50,000 genes with about 60,000 nucleotides per gene within only 10^{14} generations or iterations (about one hour for yeasts and

Evolution strategies, discussed in this chapter, are both algorithmic macromodels of collective learning processes and parallel processing tools for solving difficult optimization (more modestly, meliorization) problems. Evolutionary achievements have usually been interpreted as simply the result of adaptation or equilibration. The openness of living systems, however, enables them to do more, that is, they can grope for thus far unknown, innovative improvements. With a little optimism, it is possible to see evolution as a permanent, though not necessarily gradual, improvement process during which a population of individuals may even develop an internal model of its environment. This helps to speed up the stupid but powerful motor of "chance."[3] Insight into general development processes, not only macroeconomic ones, may well result from using computer experiments with evolution strategies and giving them an anthropomorphic interpretation.

Blind or Pure Random Search

As early as 1960, right at the beginning of the computer era, organic evolution was used as a paradigm for interindividual learning in the search for algorithmic metamechanisms that could adapt submechanisms. Ashby's proposal for a homeostatic automaton, which had to maintain an internal equilibrium in the face of external disturbances, should have operated according to the principles of mutation and selection. From today's point of view, the mere sequential operation of von Neumann computers prevented the breakthrough of such an idea. The algorithm proved to be extremely inefficient. This fact led to the belief that

>   —evolutionary principles cannot provide a convincing explanation for the remarkable achievements of natural systems: the prohibitive amount of time and effort required to create a book from a collection of letters or a clock from the separate parts by throwing dice—blind chance—has been taken as "proof" for the impossibility of evolution;
>   —stochastic learning processes are always inferior to sophisticated deterministic rules: it can, for example, easily be shown that total enumeration (deterministic or stochastic grid search) is less expensive than a Monte Carlo strategy because repetition is avoided.

---

bacteria) overtaxes even the best deterministic optimization procedures under ideal circumstances such as convexity and noiseless response. One natural trick for escaping from the scarcity of time problem has been parallel processing (the population principle).

3. Evolution principles, observed today, will have evolved "themselves" over time. Recombination of individual knowledge, stored in the set of genes by sexual propagation, is an achievement of that kind, as are polygeny and pleiotropy. These lead to correlated mutations if natural laws must be obeyed with respect to the genetically controlled attributes of an individual.

Decision making aided by chance processes is, therefore, normally considered as the most stupid alternative.[4]

In fact, Ashby's model of organic mechanisms or the principles of mutation and selection are really too simple. His mutations are purely random parameter constellations, which appear according to a uniform probability density within a given interval. For a predetermined coarsegraining (or accuracy request), the effort needed to find the solution—in fact by chance—grows exponentially with the number of parameters involved. The selection in Ashby's algorithm merely means successive comparison of all intermediate solutions and storing only the best result. The same kind of algorithm for optimization purposes was first mentioned by Brooks (1958). There is no backcoupling of the current knowledge to further actions, hence no learning at all. In principle, all trials could be performed simultaneously (in parallel).

Somewhat more "natural" than the blind search is the so-called creeping random search, also mentioned by Brooks (1959).[5] The randomly chosen trials are now concentrated around the current best location, which changes with every improvement. This way of learning could be said to be based on two sayings: "The apple never falls far from the tree" and "survival of the fittest" (or, better, the fitter of the ancestor and the descendant). Mutation and selection are obviously programmed a little more adequately in this model, but only a little.

(1 + 1), or Two-membered Evolution Strategy

More practical relevance for the creeping random search method called two-membered evolution (with one parent and one child per generation/iteration) was achieved by introducing an additional rule for controlling the size of the mutation steps, or the standard deviation of the normally distributed random changes with expectation zero. Rechenberg (1973) put in a simple rule for controlling the size of the mutation steps (for all parameters at the same time) in accordance with the observed success rate. This rule was obtained from two different unimodal, but n-dimensional, response surface models, a hyperspherical one and an inclined ridge one. Figure 1 shows typical graphs for $n = 2$ decision variables x_1 and x_2 and the corresponding objective/fitness function

---

4. If, in the following, the term *at random* is used, this will never be meant in the sense of a cause-and-effect relationship (explicative or Newtonian model) but always in a descriptive, macromodeling way as, for example, in thermodynamics. Indeed, on a digital computer, use is made of only pseudorandom numbers that stem from a discrete, nonlinear, recursive process yielding (largely) aperiodic sequences (nowadays called deterministic chaos).

5. There are a number of variants, most of them obviously developed independently, e.g., by Favreau and Franks (1958), Munson and Rubin (1959), or Rastrigin (1963), sometimes with, and sometimes without, a hint of analogy with organic evolution.

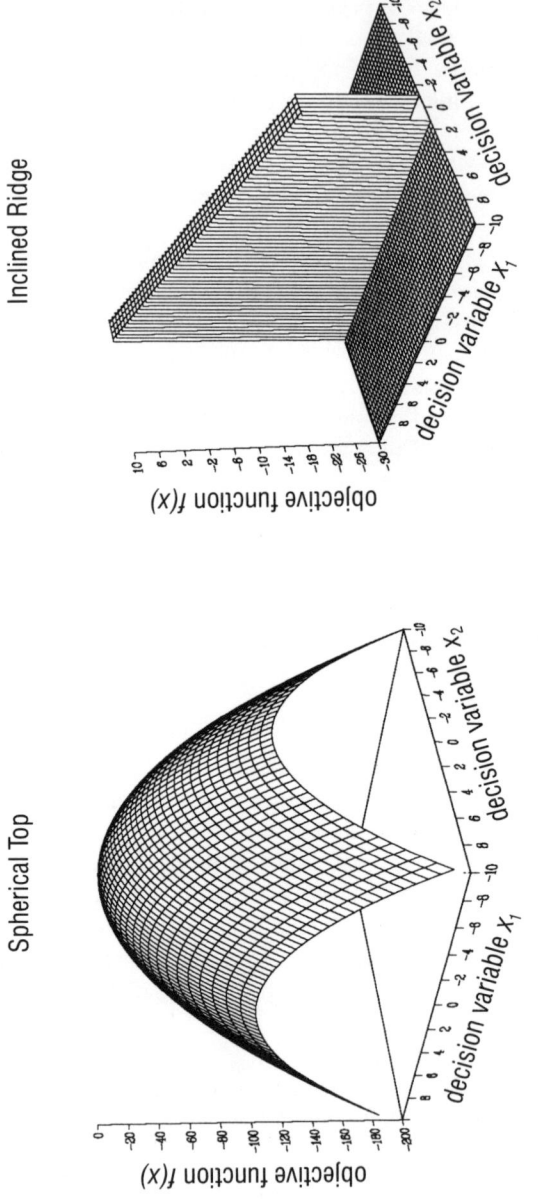

Fig. 1. Two typical response surfaces

$f(x_1,x_2)$. Rechenberg showed that the maximum progress rate corresponds to a success rate of about 20 percent. As soon as successes become more frequent, it should be possible to accelerate the process by increasing the standard deviation; conversely, the mutation rate should be decreased as soon as the success rate is less than one in five. There have been many similar proposals for controlling the mean step-size and sometimes also the direction of the mutations.[6]

This type of exogenously controlled random search comes within the general framework of other deterministic, hill-climbing, optimum-seeking algorithms currently used in many applications, where it is impossible or seems not worthwhile making use of knowledge about first—and, perhaps also, second—partial derivatives of the objective function (and of the constraints functions).[7]

John Holland's genetic algorithms (GA) approach to imitating organic evolution principles should be mentioned too, but will not be presented in detail here. His mutation (and recombination) rules operate on a bitwise representation of numbers and are especially suited for solving combinatorial optimization problems (Holland 1975). With a delay of more than a decade, the genetic algorithms are now attracting much attention (see, e.g., Grefenstette 1985 and 1987; Schaffer 1989). Up until now, GAs have not supported self-adaptive behavior of the simulated individuals, that is, the collective online learning of strategy parameters such as mutation or recombination operators. These parameters may be seen—and are handled only within multimembered evolution strategies (ESs)—as genetically coded internal models of the environment.[8]

Optimum Seeking with an Internal Model

Gradient and Newton methods do have an explicit internal model on the basis of which they interpret the information gathered by function evaluations and

---

6. For a more detailed description, see Schwefel 1977 and 1981.

7. Competitors are, e.g., the strategies of Hooke and Jeeves 1961 (pattern search), Rosenbrock 1960 (rotating coordinates search), Davies, Swann, and Campey (see Box, Davies, and Swann 1969), Nelder and Mead 1965 (simplex search), or M. J. Box 1965 (complex search), or even the conjugate direction search method of M. J. D. Powell (1964), and the derivative-free version of the variable metric method of Davidon, Fletcher, and Powell (Fletcher and Powell 1963) that uses a difference approximation scheme of Stewart (1967) for gaining knowledge about the gradient. One extensive test series, showing the relative merits and shortcomings of the different methods, was performed by Schwefel (1977 and 1981).

8. Recent investigations by Hoffmeister and Bäck (1991), who tried to recombine GAs and ESs, show that the usually adopted selection rules of Genetic Algorithms jeopardize the requisite variety of the internal models and, thus, enhance premature convergence of the evolutionary search process.

corresponding partial derivatives. They then predict the optimum action to be taken from local ascent information or even from the local curvatures as given by the Hessian matrix of second partial derivatives. Gradient methods rely upon a linear model, Newton, quasi-Newton, and conjugate gradient (or direction) methods on a quadratic internal model. The latter still use line search subroutines for finding the minimum or maximum in the predicted direction. Instead of making use of the second derivatives they often, however, use the change in the gradient direction during the iterations as an indicator. Some versions even gather the knowledge needed by small trial steps around the local position. At least n (or, better, $O(n)$, e.g., $2n + 1$) steps are necessary for adjusting the linear model (tangent hyperplane) and $O(n^2)$ for the quadratic model. Whether such effort is worthwhile depends heavily on the real response surface and the validity of the model used. None of these strategies work in the case of a disturbed answer (the slightest form of which is caused by rounding errors) or a drifting extreme. As soon as the anticipated improvement cannot be achieved, the search process normally ends. Pathological situations are sometimes handled by erasing current knowledge or by taking a random step as the "ultima ratio". If there is a discrepancy between reality and the model used, the search may diverge instead of converging, a well-known phenomenon of the Newton-Raphson procedure.

Several proposals have been made for combining concepts of the two-membered evolution strategy with direction adaptation rules that are very efficient in the quadratic case (e.g., Matyas 1965; Marti 1980). This pays off if the objective is a polynomial of the second order, or it can be well approximated by a quadratic function.

Multimembered ($M + L$) and (M, L) Evolution Strategies

Is it possible to achieve such an increase in efficiency by learning an internal model of the environment (here, the topology of the objective function) within natural systems? The immediate reaction is to again think only of individual learning. The key to the answer—which is yes, if the key is found—lies in realizing the possibilities of collective learning. The multimembered evolution strategies are a first step toward using that kind of collective natural intelligence.

At first sight, and on the basis of thinking only of classical, von Neumann computers with strictly sequential operations, it seems wasteful to imitate the principle of population. However, massively parallel machines with hundreds and thousands of processors now appear likely to enter the market fairly soon, and, because of their intrinsic parallelism, evolution strategies will be able to make use of them immediately. Multiple Instructions Multiple

Data (MIMD) computers are especially well suited here. Every processor can now represent an individual and calculate its fitness (i.e., evaluate the objective function) and, if applicable, the constraint functions. Generally, how much time the processor needs for the evaluation will depend on the individual's parameter values. On machines with autonomous, asynchronously operating processors there need not and should not be a synchronization of the generations. They could overlap in time, just as in nature.

In what follows, however, two more lucid synchronous versions will be described, that is, an (M, L) and an $(M + L)$ strategy. M parents of generation g produce L different descendants. In the $(M + L)$ case the M best of all $M + L$ individuals of generation g become ancestors of generation $g + 1$. In principle, parents with very favorable attributes thus may "live" and have children during two or even more consecutive generations. This is not the case in the (M, L) version. Here, only the M best of the L descendants of generation g can become parents of generation $g + 1$, even if these are not better than their ancestors. Now, of course, L must be larger than M in order for the population (or quasi species) not to die out or for it to perform a random walk (for $M = L$).

Choosing $M > 1$, which also means preserving individuals whose fitness is less than the best, once again seems to be at least unnecessary, as does ignoring the parents of the last generation during the selection within the (M, L) strategy version. If L is large enough (e.g., $L > 5*M$) and the mutation rates are well adapted (according to the 20 percent success rate rule from the two-membered strategy), then, in general, each parent will generate one improved descendant. In that case, it would not matter whether the ancestors are "forgotten" or allowed to survive. An $(M + L)$ strategy should only prevent the loss of very good positions already reached. This kind of reasoning, however, is only valid as long as the mutation rates (or mean step-sizes, or standard deviations of the mutations) are not changed individually. Under that condition, it can be shown theoretically (Schwefel 1977 and 1981) that, on sequential machines, the $(1 + 1)$ strategy is the most efficient variant among all plus strategies, and a $(1, 5)$ version is the fastest of the comma algorithms. Incidentally, the latter is slower than the two-membered procedure by a factor of less than five. Per generation (i.e., in the case using a parallel computer), the convergence rate grows monotonically, but sublinearly, with the number of the descendants per parent.[9]

---

9. To be complete, it should be mentioned here that there are two deterministic, optimum-seeking methods that are comparable to the multimembered evolution strategies displayed here. On the one hand, this is the evolutionary operation (EVOP) procedure of G. E. P. Box (1957), which was devised for the design and analysis of experiments and can be classified as some kind of a $(1 + L)$ method. On the other hand, the family of polygonal strategies of Nelder and Mead

Self-learning of Strategy Parameters

The overall purpose of devising a multimembered evolution strategy has been to internalize the adaptation of the step sizes, that is, to allow for online learning of parameters at a higher hierarchical level by mutation and selection, rather than by exogenous control of the success rate. Every individual now carries not only a vector of object parameters, but, simultaneously, a vector of strategy variables that are also mutated. In the most simple case, this concerns only one overall mutation rate for all object parameter changes. More generally, however, both n different variances and $n(n-1)/2$ covariances of a more general n-dimensional normal probability density distribution can now be used. In that case, the equiprobability contours of mutations are hyperellipsoids, the axes of which are no longer parallel to the axes of the object parameters. The direct correspondence between genotype and phenotype is given up. Correlated mutations may occur in the phenotype space (Schwefel 1981).

Genes that control the mutation rate, for example, by means of repair enzymes, are well known, and phenomena like polygeny or pleiotropy, which, in the light of mathematical modeling, are two sides of the same coin (i.e., linear correlation), are also reported from the real world.[10]

Because the evolutionary learning process is based on parallel experiments, it makes use of another important principle, sexual inheritance. Mixing of individually achieved successful parameter sets by recombination is possible within the (M, L) scheme of the multimembered evolution strategy only if M is larger than one. Fortunately, M must not be increased with the number n of the decision variables. Theoretical results for the convergence rate up to now are available only for $M = 1$. That is why experimental mathematics had to be used for further investigations. In the following simulation, the results of a suitable test series will be reported (see also Schwefel 1987).

(1965) and M. J. Box (1965), descendants from EVOP, are, because of their reliability, well known among those who have to solve difficult optimization problems. They are called simplex or complex strategies, respectively, may be termed $(M + 1)$ algorithms in this context, and are available in many numerical procedures libraries today. The simplex algorithm of Nelder and Mead must not be confused, however, with the simplex method of George Dantzig (1963) for linear programming (LP).

10. Allometric growth is just another example of that kind of learning and of applying natural laws by means of correlated actions. This may be seen as online learning of an internal model of the environment. The famous $2^{1/3}$ relationship between the diameters at the branchings of blood vessels, derived from the laws of laminar flow, is just one example of a natural law that was learned by means of mutation and selection and has never been forgotten. Even if the initial "idea" was one individual's mutation, this must, a posteriori, be called a collective achievement.

Learning a Mutation Rate (Test 1)

In the case of $n = 30$ parameters, one common standard deviation for all mutation steps had to be learned and permanently adapted in accordance with the progress toward the extreme of the objective function. The strategy parameter, the standard deviation, may be thought of as representing the radius of a circle (in $n = 2$ dimensions), or of a hypersphere (if $n > 3$), on whose surface all mutations will fall. The center of the circle or sphere is the parent's position in the object parameter space. Comparing a $(1 + 10)$ and a $(1, 10)$ evolution strategy, it was at first surprising to find that, contrary to the previously mentioned theoretical results (which were achieved for constant or exogenously controlled variances), the latter gave a better overall performance. Sometimes a recession occurs where the best of ten descendants is worse than its parent, but this is not as harmful as the stagnation phases which show up in the $(1 + 10)$ case.

The explanation for this phenomenon lies in the forced survival of a good position in the parameter space in the case of nonadapted variance. The indirect selection pressure on the step-size—which is evaluated only according to the success or failure achieved with it—is stronger when accidentally gained good positions can be forgotten. Thus, it is possible to speculate that a 'programmed' finite life span of all individuals is not the result of natural incapacity, but is a proper measure for avoiding stagnation caused by an unsuitable internal model (which easily leads to overadaptation). This is even more important in a disturbed and changing environment than in the simulated static, noiseless case.

Learning a Scaling of the Object Variables (Test 2)

Starting with nonadapted individual variances for the search process, $n = 30$ different mutation rates now had to be scaled and rescaled permanently to achieve a high convergence rate. The circles or hyperspheres mentioned previously as the loci of all possible mutations now can and should be changed into ellipses or hyperellipsoids, respectively. With equal standard deviations for all object parameter variations, the problem would be badly scaled and cause drastically increased search times.

Learning so many strategy parameters at the same time could not be achieved with either a $(1 + 10)$ or with a $(1, 10)$ strategy. Increasing L to 100 or even 1,000 was also no help. On the contrary, the larger L, the more effectively the search process got stuck in a relative (not local) optimum. This, at first shocking, result can be explained.

Since the convergence rate is, in general, inversely proportional to the number of variables, descendants that only operate in a lower dimensional subspace may gain a selection advantage—measured by progress in one generation—by sharply reducing some of the step-sizes. The opportunity principle, "the swifter is the enemy of the better," comes to the fore here and leads, sooner or later, to premature stagnation. A sudden change of the strategy parameters, which would then be necessary, is not excluded in principle, but is a rare event in the multiparametric case.

Two steps are necessary if the opportunity trap is to be avoided. First, of the L descendants, $M > 1$ must be allowed to become parents of the next generation, that is, the selection pressure has to be reduced (this could be called soft selection). Second, the principle of recombination has to be applied by mixing the information stored by the different individuals with respect to the object variables and, in particular, the strategy parameters (variances). With regard to the latter, it looks as if intermediate recombination is preferable to discrete mixing, but that must be confirmed by further experiments.

Synergism of Collective Learning (Test 3)

A third test series was designed to demonstrate how close collective learning, especially of the different variances, which in some way comprise the "internal model of the environment," comes to the prescient knowledge of an "expert." Three strategy variants were compared:

—a (1, 100) strategy with prefixed optimum relations among all variances,
—a (15, 100) strategy under the same conditions, and
—a (15, 100) strategy with variable, initially nonoptimum, step-size relations.

The number of object variables was again taken to be $n = 30$. So 30 different mutation rates had to be permanently adapted. Discrete recombination of the decision variables and intermediate recombination of the strategy parameters—here, among all parents simultaneously—was allowed for in the latter case.

The surprising result of this third test was that the (15, 100) scheme with mutation of the individual step-sizes converged more rapidly than the (15, 100) variant with prefixed optimum relations among the variances. Indeed, in the case of medium selection pressure, it was nearly as fast as a (1, 100) strategy with prefixed optimum scaling.

To investigate that phenomenon more closely—it really should be called "synergistic intelligence amplification" and is achieved by recombining individual myopics—the number M of parents was varied for fixed $L = 100$ descendants per generation within a fourth test series.

The Optimum Selection Pressure (Test 4)

Four strategy variants with $L = 100$ and variable M were confronted with each other. Figure 2 shows the convergence rates (measured in decades with respect to the approximation of the optimum):

- an $(M, 100)$ strategy with prefixed optimum scaling of the relationship among the variances (curve a in fig. 2),
- an $(M, 100)$ strategy with prefixed, nonoptimum scaling (curve b),
- an $(M, 100)$ strategy with online learning of the scaling by means of mutation and recombination of individual step-sizes (curve c), and
- an $(M, 100)$ strategy with online learning by means of recombination only (curve d).

As expected, for prefixed scalings (cases a and b), strong selection (i.e., letting only the best descendant become the parent of the next generation) yields the maximum convergence rates. Increasing $M > 1$, or, in other words, lowering the selection pressure, results in monotonously decreasing convergence rates.

The introduction of recombination without individual mutations of the variances (case d) leads to qualitatively different behavior. If the number of survivors among the 100 descendants is large enough (e.g., $M = 30$), the same progress rate as in the case of prefixed optimum scaling can be achieved. Slightly better results with $M = 20$ survivors are only due to the fact that the more fit individuals should achieve faster average progress. However, increasing the selection pressure beyond $M < 20$ leads to the loss of requisite variety and to overadaptation that, in the long term at least, does not pay.

In principle, curve c shows the same type of unimodal relationship between convergence rates and selection pressure. Now, however, intermediate values of $M = 8$ to $M = 20$ survivors, who learn the scaling of the object variables by means of recombination and individual mutation, lead to even higher progress rates than in the case of prefixed optimum scalings (curve a) under conditions that are otherwise the same, especially where the selection pressure is the same. This is at least counterintuitive and must be interpreted as a synergistic speed-up, since it shows that a group of individuals with imperfect knowledge (here, imperfect internal models of their environment and, thus, nonoptimum individual behavior) together (i.e., by means of recombination) can almost approximate the speed of convergence that a pre-

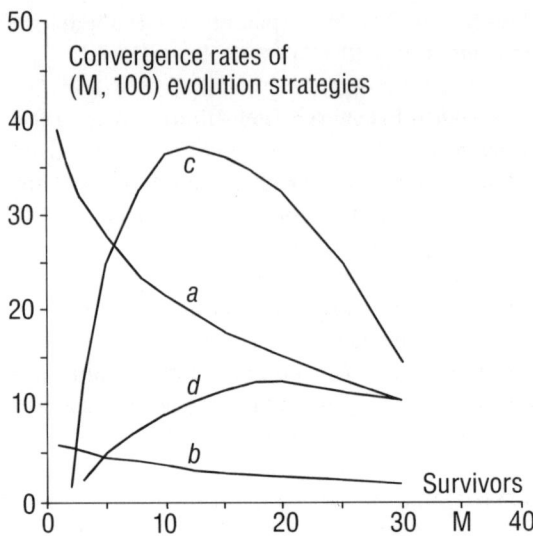

Fig. 2. Comparison among four types of evolutionary learning modes

scient expert (case $M = 1$ of curve *a*) might achieve. In fact, the group of nonexperts as a whole performs better than even the best individual member, or, in other words, the whole is greater than the sum of its parts.

There are many optimization problems for which the proper scaling of the variables is not sufficient for speeding up the convergence rate, since progress can primarily be achieved only in directions that are not parallel to the axes of the object parameters. In these cases, covariances must also be included in the set of strategy parameters, and this will lead to correlated mutations. The "mutation ellipsoids" are allowed to revolve in the n-dimensional object parameter space. It has been demonstrated elsewhere (Schwefel 1987), that this is possible and helps in speeding up the search, but nothing else has to be done. If the rules learned from the scaling experiments are obeyed, multimembered evolution may be able to handle two-level learning under even more difficult circumstances.

Collective, online learning of strategy parameters, that is, the interindividual building up of a model of the environment, works without exogenous supervision if and only if

—in the course of the experimental trial-and-error process forgetting is allowed for, where intermediate improvements were achieved with nonadapted strategy parameters not well suited for further progress,

—the selection pressure is moderate, that is, not only the fittest individual is taken as the ancestor of the following generation (iteration), and
—recombinations of individually achieved parameter positions are enhanced, both with respect to the decision variables describing the object to be optimized and with respect to the strategy parameters that represent an interpretation of the local environment—even if an imperfect one.

The best options for further progress are not congruent with the interpretation of the current situation by the "specialist" who currently has optimum position; rather, they are to be found in the collective pool of experiences and aspirations. Rigorously adopting the slogan "survival of the fittest" as a problem-solving strategy, that is, making use of a $(1 + L)$ evolution algorithm, has turned out to be doubly unsuitable advice for optimum-seeking or meliorization processes. Neither individual survival over more than one generation nor predesignating only the currently fittest to be a parent appear to be good for the whole system.

The loss of the belief that extrapolating current knowledge and choosing the steepest ascent in accordance with the mostly linear models of the real world provide a simple, manageable path to the future means that a new strategy or paradigm is needed.

What has been emphasized previously is diversity (or requisite variety), not only with respect to individual actions, but also with respect to individual internal models of "the world." This measure is necessary to keep exploration and evaluation going in a groping-in-the-dark situation, and thus the vitality of the whole system. It has been rather hard to accept the fact that some ideas have to die so that new ones can emerge. In a socioeconomic setting, however, this does not mean that the producers have to leave the market, only their products do, if these have not proved to be acceptable. Solidarity should help those who have not been successful, but nevertheless contributed to the necessary exploration.

A warning was given with respect to opportunist behavior: too strong competition leads to stagnation in the long term by favoring the swifter, not the better. Attempts to maximize the success rate (e.g., in R&D), result in zero mutation rates and no progress at all. We should learn to live with failures, but this should not be too difficult. An error-free system cannot evolve. Simple deduction and processing of facts only helps in situations with complete knowledge, not in finding a path toward an open future.

Many potentially useful experiments with different versions of evolutionary strategies have yet to be performed. Some of these might lead to a better understanding of collective phenomena in areas of human affairs. However, readiness to perform systems analysis of one's own system has sometimes been rather poor, to say the least. Prejudices are comfortable and systems thinking is especially uncomfortable when there is the danger that a person's own way of acting may have to be revised. Last but not least, diversity of prejudices may at least be useful epistemologically.

The evolution strategy presented here is a first and still very simple model of evolutionary processes—a first approximation only toward a quantified hypothesis. Others have come to similar conclusions, however, by using different approaches to modeling collective behavior, for example, Allen and McGlade (1987), Kwasnicka and Kwasnicki (1986), and Schull (1990), to mention only a few.

REFERENCES

Allen, P. M., and McGlade, J. M. 1987. "Evolutionary Drive: The Effect of Microscopic Diversity, Error Making, and Noise." *Foundations of Physics* 17:723–38.
Ashby, W. R. 1960. *Design for a Brain*. 2d ed. New York: Chapman and Hall.
Box, G. E. P. 1957. "Evolutionary Operation: A Method for Increasing Industrial Productivity." *Applied Statistics* 6:81–101.
Box, M. J. 1965. "A New Method of Constrained Optimization and a Comparison with Other Methods." *Computer Journal* 8:42–52.
Box, M. J.; Davies, D.; and Swann, W. H. 1969. *Nonlinear Optimization Techniques*. ICI Monograph, no. 5. Edinburgh: Oliver and Boyd.
Brooks, S. H. 1958. "A Discussion of Random Methods for Seeking Maxima." *Operations Research* 6:244–51.
Brooks, S. H. 1959. "A Comparison of Maximum-Seeking Methods." *Operations Research* 7:430–57.
Dantzig, G. B. 1963. *Linear Programming and Extensions*. Princeton, N.J.: Princeton University Press.
Favreau, R. F., and Franks, R. 1958. "Random Optimization by Analogue Techniques." In *Proceedings of the 2d Analogue Comp. Meeting, Strasbourg*, 437–43.
Fletcher, R., and Powell, M. J. D. 1963. "A Rapidly Convergent Descent Method for Minimization." *Computer Journal* 6:163–68.
Grefenstette, J. J., ed. 1985. *Proceedings of the First International Conference on Genetic Algorithms*. Hillsdale, N.J.: Lawrence Erlbaum.
Grefenstette, J. J., ed. 1987. *Proceedings of the Second International Conference on Genetic Algorithms and Their Applications*. Hillsdale, N.J.: Lawrence Erlbaum.
Hoffmeister, F., and Bäck, T. 1990. *Genetic Algorithms and Evolution Strategies: Similarities and Differences*. University of Dortmund, Department of Computer Science, Internal Report no. 365.
Holland, J. H. 1975. *Adaptation in Natural and Artificial Systems*. Ann Arbor: University of Michigan Press.
Hooke, R., and Jeeves, T. A. 1961. "Direct Search Solution of Numerical and Statistical Problems." *Journal of the ACM* 8:212–29.

Kwasnicka, H., and Kwasnicki, W. 1986. "Diversity and Development: Tempo and Mode of Evolutionary Processes." *Technological Forecasting and Social Change* 30:223–43.

Marti, K. 1980. "On Accelerations of the Convergence in Random Search Methods." *Methods of Operations Research* 37:391–406.

Matyas, J. 1965. "Random Optimization." *Automation and Remote Control* 26:244–51.

Munson, J. K., and Rubin, A. I. 1959. "Optimization by Random Search on the Analogue Computer." *IRE Transactions EC* 8:200–203.

Nelder, J. A., and Mead, R. 1965. "A Simplex Method for Function Minimization." *Computer Journal* 7:308–13.

Neumann, John von. 1958. *The Computer and the Brain.* New Haven: Yale University Press.

Powell, M. J. D. 1964. "An Efficient Method for Finding the Minimum of a Function of Several Variables without Calculating Derivatives." *Computer Journal* 7:155–62.

Rastrigin, L. A. 1963. "The Convergence of the Random Search Method in the Extremal Control of a Many-Parameter System." *Automation and Remote Control* 24:1337–42.

Rechenberg, I. 1973. *Evolutionsstrategie: Optimierung technischer Systeme nach Prinzipien der biologischen Evolution.* Stuttgart: Frommann-Holzboog.

Rosenbrock, H. H. 1960. "An Automatic Method for Finding the Greatest or Least Value of a Function." *Computer Journal* 3:175–84.

Schaffer, J. D., ed. 1989. *Proceedings of the Third International Conference on Genetic Algorithms.* San Mateo, Calif.: Morgan Kaufmann.

Schull, J. 1990. "Are Species Intelligent?" *Behavioral and Brain Sciences* 13:63–108.

Schwefel, H.-P. 1977. *Numerische Optimierung von Computer-Modellen mittels der Evolutionsstrategie.* Basel: Birkhäuser.

Schwefel, H.-P. 1981. *Numerical Optimization of Computer Models.* Chichester: Wiley.

Schwefel, H.-P. 1987. "Collective Phenomena in Evolutionary Systems." In *Papers Presented at the International Conference on "Problems of Constancy and Change," 31st Annual Meeting of the International Society for General Systems Research, Budapest,* 2:1025–32.

Stewart, G. W. 1967. "A Modification of Davidon's Minimization Method to Accept Difference Approximations of Derivatives." *Journal of the ACM* 14:72–83.

Wiener, N. 1948. *Cybernetics, or Control and Communication in the Animal and the Machine.* New York: Wiley.

Part 3
Socioeconomic Evolution and Economic Growth

CHAPTER 5

The Factors of Production of Evolutionary Economics

Joseph A. Weissmahr

The factors of production—land, labor, and capital—are considered to be fundamental concepts in economic thinking. Their original purpose was to explain the production of wealth in the economy. The history of economic thought, however, shows that they did not fulfill this purpose because the restrictive way in which they were interpreted led to the labor theory of value. That the labor theory of value is conceptually false has long been recognized, but the criticism of the factors of production as explanatory variables is relatively recent. Criticism of the factors of production started in the 1950s, when, as a result of the empirical work of Simon Kuznets, attention of economists returned to the evolutionary ideas of economic growth.

Evolutionary thinking has a long history in economics, but so far it has not developed into a coherent theoretical framework. Its development was handicapped by the gradual elimination of the effect of natural forces from economic theory. An evolutionary economic theory, however, cannot be constructed without including the effect of natural forces that are necessary for the evolution of humans in the first place and continue to be the physical basis of their survival and multiplication.

Economic evolution means change through the appearance of novelty and the increase of human wealth. The factors of production of evolutionary economics, therefore, should be considered not only as building blocks of the economy, but also as variables that can explain why and how the economy evolves.

The History of the Factors of Production

The idea of the factors of production can be traced to Aristotle, who believed that genuine wealth, which was in limited supply, derived from productive activity in agriculture and mining.

Very similar ideas were proposed by the Physiocrats in France in the eighteenth century. According to their leading exponent, François Quesnay, wealth came from the *produit net,* consisting of the surplus over the cost of production produced in agriculture and mining. The Physiocrats regarded the *produit net* as a gift of nature. This idea came from the observation that from one grain sown, ten grains were produced in agriculture; whereas, in manufacturing, human work only transformed materials without producing anything new. They concluded that only agriculture was productive and other occupations did not produce wealth (Kuczynski 1971, XLV–LI).

In seventeenth-century England, thinking developed in other directions. The ideas of William Petty and especially those of John Locke had a decisive influence on further economic theorizing. Petty believed that "while labour is the father and active principle of wealth, earth is the mother." Locke disagreed with Petty and maintained that land yielded wealth only due to the application of labor, and that capital was labor stored up in tools and equipment. This amounted to saying that the only determining factor in the production of wealth was human labor. Locke's formulation, which later became known as the labor theory of value, was not intended as an economic theory, but served as a justification for his theory of private property.

In the traditional view, the ownership of property involved social obligations; property and labor were social functions. Locke began from the dictum of the Scriptures that the earth and its fruits were originally given to mankind in common. Then, by postulating that men have a right to preserve their life and have a right to their own labor, he justified private appropriation. He published these ideas in 1690 in *Two Treatises of Government.* In the fourth edition (1713), Locke added a new, and more convincing argument.

> To which let me add, that he who appropriates land to himself by his labour, does not lessen but increase the common stock of mankind. For the provisions serving to the support of humane life, produced by one acre of inclosed and cultivated land, are (to speak much within compasse) ten times more, than those, which are yielded by an acre of Land, of an equal richnesse, lyeing wast in common. And therefore he, that incloses Land and has a greater plenty of the conveniencys of life from ten acres, than he could have from an hundred left to Nature, may truly be said, to give ninety acres to Mankind. For his labour now supplys him with provisions out of ten acres, which were but the product of an hundred lying in common. (Locke 1960, 312)

The major religious and philosophical argument against acquisitiveness derived from the opinion that it may impoverish others. By showing that the appropriation of land is not a zero-sum game, in which every gain is someone else's loss, but a positive-sum process in which both the appropriator and mankind gains, Locke succeeded in making acquisitive behavior morally acceptable and even praiseworthy. However, by attributing *all* the production increase to human physical labor used in improving the enclosed land, he also laid the foundations of the labor theory of value and unwittingly reinterpreted the positive-sum game between men and nature, to a zero-sum game between men only.

Now it is interesting to follow the development of the thinking of Adam Smith, because he was familiar with the writings of Locke and also knew Quesnay personally. Adam Smith wrote an early draft (ED) for the *Wealth of Nations* about 1763, in which he included the "economic" material from his jurisprudence lectures. Parts of this ED were found by W. R. Scott. He published them in 1937, and they are also reproduced in the appendix to *Lectures on Jurisprudence* of the collected works of Adam Smith (1978, 561–81). The ED contains several passages in which the effect of natural forces on the economy is acknowledged; these passages, however, were not included in the *Wealth of Nations* (*WN*) published in 1776. There are three passages where there are substantial differences between the ED and *WN*.

The first passage in the ED reads as follows:

Every body must be sensible how much labour is abridged and facilitated by the application of proper machinery. By means of the plough two men, with the assistance of three horses, will cultivate more ground than twenty could do with the spade. A miller and his servant, with a wind or water mill, will at their ease grind more corn than eight men could do, with the severest labour, by hand mills. (Smith 1978, 569)

The corresponding passage in *WN* is much shorter.

Thirdly and lastly, every body must be sensible how much labour is facilitated and abridged by the application of proper machinery. It is unnecessary to give any example. (Smith 1976, 19)

The second passage in the ED initially refers to a corn grinding mill.

He who first thought of substituting, in the room of the crank or handle, an outer wheel which was to be turned round by a stream of water, and much more, he who first thought of employing a stream of wind for the same purpose, was probably no work man of any kind, but a philosopher or meer man of speculation; . . . It was a real philosopher only who could invent the fire engine, and first form the idea of producing so great an effect by a power in nature which had never before been thought of. . . . It must have been a philosopher who, in the same manner, first

> invented those now common and therefore disregarded machines, wind and water mill. . . . In philosophy as in every other business this subdivision of employment improves dexterity and saves time. (Smith 1978, 570)

In a note to this passage, W. R. Scott suggested that the "real philosopher who could invent the fire engine" was a reference to James Watt.

The corresponding passage appears in *WN* in a much abbreviated form.

> Only the division of labor of philosophers is discussed without mentioning any examples. (Smith 1976, 21–22)

The third passage in the ED refers to the use of fire engines (steam engines), which, at the time of Smith, were mainly used for pumping water out of coal mines, and the use of water and wind mills used for grinding corn.

> If the speculations of philosophers have been turned towards the improvement of the mechanic arts, the benefit of them may evidently descend to the meanest of people. Whoever burns coals has them at a better bargain by means of the inventor of the fire engine. Whoever eats bread receives a much greater advantage of the same kind from the inventors and improvers of wind and water mills. (Smith 1978, 574)

This passage is entirely omitted in *WN*.

The only reference in *WN* to the "labours of nature" expressing ideas similar to those of the Physiocrats is to be found, not in book 4, chapter 9 on agricultural systems where the theory of the Physiocrats is being criticized, but in book 2, chapter 5, "Of the Different Employment of Capitals." Here Smith acknowledges that "in agriculture nature labours along with man . . . [at] . . . no expence," but claims that, in manufacturing, the situation is different: "In them nature does nothing; man does all" (Smith 1976, 363–64).

Smith seems to have forgotten his own references in the ED to water and wind power and to the new powers of the steam engine.

It is interesting to note that David Ricardo also has cited this passage from *WN*, in a footnote, in the chapter of his *Principles* on rent. Ricardo has this comment.

> Does nature nothing for man in manufacturing? Are the powers of wind and water, which move our machinery, and assist navigation, nothing? The pressure of the atmosphere and the elasticity of steam, which enable us to work the most stupendous engines—are they not the gifts of nature? To say nothing of the effects of the matter of heat in softening and

melting metals, of the decomposition of the atmosphere in the process of dyeing and fermentation. There is not a manufacture which can be mentioned, in which nature does not give her assistance to man, and give it too, generously and gratuitously. (Ricardo 1951, 76)

These references show that both Smith and Ricardo were aware of the influence of natural forces on the economy, but it seems that the anthropocentric view, which served Locke to make private property socially acceptable, had taken such a strong hold in their minds that no contrary argument could modify their unshakeable belief in the labor theory of value.

Marx took over the labor theory of value from Smith and Ricardo. He then combined it with the idea of the *produit net* of the Physiocrats and drew the eminently logical conclusion that, if all value comes from the work of men, the profit going to the capitalist must correspond to the surplus value produced by the workers. Marx's conclusion that profit comes from the exploitation of workers was the logical endpoint to which the labor theory of value was leading. Of course, Marx was wrong. He was wrong because the labor theory of value is conceptually false, a point that I will address in more detail in my discussion of the role of energy in evolutionary economics.

In the hundred years after Marx, the factors of production were used by the Marginalist school as a basis for justifying the distribution of income as rent, wages, and interest. Profit got lost in the shuffle, which was fortunate because it eliminated the need to answer a fundamental question: where does profit come from?

The attention of economists focused on the inadequacy of the factors of production for explaining the production of wealth when, in the 1950s, Kuznets's empirical analysis of the input-output statistics of the United States from 1870 to 1950 showed that more than 70 percent of the per capita economic growth could not be explained by increases in the factors of production. The unexplained residual was aptly called "the measure of ignorance" on the important subject of economic growth (Abramovitz 1956; a recent discussion of the connection between economic growth and technical progress from an evolutionary point of view can be found in Nelson 1987).

The most original of the critics of the factors of production—land, labor, and capital—was Kenneth Boulding, who stated that they "are extremely heterogeneous aggregates [that] have all the scientific validity of the medieval elements of earth, air, fire, and water." Starting from the proposition that "all processes of production involve the direction of energy by some know-how structure toward the selection, transportation, and transformation of materials into products," Boulding arrived at the conclusion that all three factors are composed of varying combinations of Know-how, Energy, and Materials, which he proposed as more suitable alternatives (Boulding 1981, 27–28).

Boulding analysed the factors of production from the point of view of their composition. He asked what they are composed of or what they consist of. In the next section I will analyse them from the point of view of the driving force behind them by asking the question: What makes them productive?

The Driving Forces and Factors of Production

Driving force analysis is similar to motivation analysis in psychology. However, whereas the latter focuses on psychological explanations, driving force analysis focuses on all other forces that are important for the achievement of economic results. Driving force analysis does not deny the existence of psychological motivational forces, but takes them for granted in the sense of Popper, who postulated that all living beings are problem solvers by nature, and in the sense of Adam Smith, who took it for granted that the desire of humans to try to improve their condition is a fundamental propensity of human nature.

My analysis of the driving forces behind the factors of production—land, labor, and capital—will consider the human influences and also the influence of the forces of nature on the economy that were neglected by Adam Smith in his final version of *WN*.

The land production factor includes, in a narrow sense, agricultural land and, in a wider sense, all raw materials entering the economic process. Agricultural land is productive because of the produce that can be grown on it. Agricultural production, however, would not be possible without energy flow, which, therefore, can be considered as the driving force behind the agricultural land production factor. The validity of this conclusion is not weakened by the counterargument that, besides the sun, water and fertilizers are needed for raising crops, because rain is due to solar heating of the oceans and artificial fertilizers are produced with fossil energy. All raw materials have to be mined or prepared before they can qualify as suitable raw materials for manufacturing. The land production factor, in its wider sense of raw materials, is, therefore, dependent on the driving force of energy. It can be concluded that the driving force behind the production factor Land, both in its narrow and wider sense, is energy flow in various forms.

Labor is a more complex notion. As a factor of production it can be subdivided into the physical energy of human muscles and the creativity of the human mind. Of these two, only the creativity of the human mind is a fundamental driving force. The human mind has the unique capability of generating knowledge, which enables humans to capture more energy than is needed for their survival, and thus qualifies the human mind as a fundamental driving force. The physical energy of human muscles relies, through the food chain, on the driving force of solar energy and can, therefore, be regarded as a rather inefficient form of solar energy.

Capital is formed when new knowledge and energy inputs produce more wealth in the economy than is consumed. Capital has several forms. In the form of productive equipment, capital can be used in combination with new energy for producing additional wealth. As a store of value, capital can be regarded as a human invention providing an alternative method for storing energy. The driving forces that enable the accumulation of all forms of capital are human creativity and energy in various forms.

There are, therefore, two fundamental driving forces behind the economic process: *human creativity* and *energy flow*. Human creativity is the source of knowledge, which enables humans to capture increasing amounts of energy, and thereby improve the use of human time.

The word energy is used in this chapter in a much wider sense than is customary in economics. Included are all forms of energy that can be used, directly or indirectly, for performing work. Energy here means not only the customary fuels such as wood, coal, and oil, but also solar energy that has no price, but is nevertheless indispensable for the production of food (a chemical form of energy), draft animals and slaves (living forms of mechanical energy), and water and wind power. All these forms of energy are derived from present or past solar energy flow.

There is another important distinction to be made between material forms of energy and other materials. Commercially available material forms of energy, such as coal or oil, are classified in economics together with other materials as commodities. Material forms of energy, however, are very different from other materials used in the economic process. Material forms of energy belong to a special category because they can be used only once for performing work, whereas other materials can be (at least potentially) recycled and used over and over again.

The preceding analysis of the driving forces behind the traditional factors of production leads to the identification of the factors of production of evolutionary economics: *knowledge, energy,* and *time*.

These factors can be used to give a reasonable description of the production process, which, in Boulding's words, "involve[s] the direction of energy by some know-how structure toward the transformation of materials into products" (1981, 27). What is even more important, the knowledge, energy, and time factors are essential components for increasing human productivity in the economy and can be used for explaining the creation of wealth. The difficulty of measuring knowledge, energy, and time inputs might seem to decrease their usefulness. This, however, is not the case. What is important is not the influence of any one factor separately, but their combined effect, which is measurable in the increase of productivity and per capita wealth.

The conclusions of the present analysis, that the factors of production are knowledge, energy, and time, seem to be very similar to the conclusions of Boulding, who names know-how, energy, and materials, but mentions space-time separately. There are, however, two substantial differences that must be emphasized. Boulding follows the anthropocentric tradition and considers energy as a factor only in the sense of a limitation on human action. But energy is not only a limitation. The novelty of my approach consists in considering energy as an additional, independent driving force that has a similar effect in the economy as human action.

The other difference consists in not including materials among the factors of production. It is true that materials are needed for producing products, but since materials can be recycled they will not be scarce, provided that the necessary knowledge and pollution-free energy is available. This utopian-sounding situation has been actually achieved by biological evolution. Nature used only pollution-free solar energy and time for the development of genetic knowledge that enabled the utilization and recycling of materials over millions of years. Learning from nature will solve the problem of pollution and assure the long term viability of the human economy.

Knowledge

Neoclassical equilibrium theory does not consider knowledge as an important factor in the economy. After all, new knowledge is a nuisance, it disturbs the equilibrium.

The Austrian school of economics, on the other hand, always emphasized the importance of knowledge. Its founder, Carl Menger (1871), suggested that the economic progress of mankind will be commensurate with the progress of human knowledge. In 1912, Schumpeter proposed a mechanism of knowledge application through the entrepreneur, indicating the way new knowledge is introduced into the economy (Schumpeter 1934). He could not integrate this insight into the Walrasian equilibrium framework because the dynamic concept of new knowledge application is incompatible with equilibrium. Another reason knowledge could not be integrated by the Austrian school into economic theory, was its insistence that new knowledge cannot be predicted and, therefore, the future is unknowable.

That new knowledge cannot be predicted in detail is, of course, true. But, to have a fairly good idea about the future, one does not have to predict all the new knowledge that might be developed in detail. It is sufficient to identify, in general terms, the small number of variables that have had an important influence in the past 10,000 years. Then it is safe to assume that they will also influence the next hundred years. The review of economic history shows two such important influences: one is knowledge about energy use, the other is knowledge about the improvement of human time.

All short statements are likely to be misunderstood, so it is useful to describe in more detail how wealth was created in the past. It was done by:

—increasing the availability of energy for doing work at diminishing costs,
—substituting knowledge for energy,
—improving the use of human time by material means, and
—improving the use of human time by immaterial means.

An important step in the creation of wealth over the ages consisted of increasing the availability of converted solar energy per capita for doing work at diminishing costs. Primitive man used 1 MWH, agricultural man used 3 MWH, and industrial man in developed countries uses 100 MWH (megawatt-hours) of energy per capita per year.[1]

Substitution of knowledge for energy is another way of creating wealth. Biotechnology and microelectronics are recent examples, but the process has been going on for a long time, as the invention of the wheel and the sailing ship demonstrate. When the efficiency of machines is increased by better design or better materials, knowledge has been substituted for energy. New knowledge, which leads to the decrease in the cost of energy, is another way of improving productivity. Decreasing the cost of energy is important for the economy because it leads to lower cost products even in those industries that do not invest in new machines.

Improving the use of human time by material means is the third way to create wealth. Obvious examples are new products that create new markets, new employment, and additional purchasing power. Some new products have an important part in the development of industrial expansion cycles; examples are the steam locomotive, the electric motor, and the automobile. The introduction of robots, which eliminate repetitive human work, can also be cited in this category because they give the opportunity to use human time in more creative ways.

Improving the use of human time by immaterial means is still another way of creating wealth. The following means are of particular importance for the economy: the price system, the political system, the educational system, all of which influence economic results from the outside, and the economic organizational system, which acts from the inside of the economy.

---

1. The energy used by primitive man is calculated on the basis of the required food per capita (2.300 KCal/day) plus a small amount of wood used for cooking and camp fires. Agricultural man's energy use is calculated on the same basis as that for primitive man, plus the energy available in the form of draft animals, slaves, and a small amount of water or wind power. Industrial man's energy use is an average of the actual energy used per capita in Europe and the United States in the 1970s, consisting mainly of fossil fuels such as coal, oil, and natural gas. All energy figures stated in the text are approximations. (1 megawatt-hour = 1 million watt hours).

Energy

The reason energy must be a factor of production in evolutionary economics requires some explanation. As long as it is believed that the only important actor in the economic universe is Homo economicus, one cannot appreciate the real importance of energy for the economy. The first step in understanding the importance of energy consists of the realization that Homo economicus—at least as far as his physical energy is concerned—can be substituted in the economy by the lowly commodity called energy. If, however, energy is a substitute for human physical labor—the only wealth-producing factor according to the labor theory of value—then one can start thinking about energy as a wealth-producing factor in its own right. The next step in appreciating the importance of energy is the realization that energy can be substituted for human physical work, because it can do work—applied through machines—at a lower cost. It is this cost saving, compared to the cost of doing the same work by physical labor, that produces profit in the economic process.

The possibility of substituting human physical energy by lower cost forms of energy also explains why Marx's theory that profit comes from the exploitation of labor is false. As the following quotation shows, Marx came very close to giving a correct explanation for the origin of profits, but finally chose the formulation that reinforced his cherished theory of exploitation.

> It is the difference between the price of machinery and the price of the labour-power replaced by that machinery that determines the cost, to the capitalist, of producing a commodity and through the pressure of competition influences his action. Hence the invention now-a-days of machines in England, that are employed only in North America; . . . In the older countries, machinery, when employed in some branches of industry, creates such a redundancy of labour in other branches that in these latter the fall of wages below the value of labour-power impedes the use of machinery, and from the standpoint of the capitalist, whose profit comes, not from a diminution of the labour employed, but of the labour payed for, renders that use superfluous and often impossible. (Marx 1867, 393)

The first sentence shows that Marx correctly identified one of the major ways productivity is increased in the industrial economy: the substitution of expensive energy (labor-power) with lower cost energy that drives the machine. The last sentence also shows how close Marx came to identifying one of the important sources of profit, the "diminution of the labour employed." Marx nevertheless concludes that "the capitalist[s] . . . profit comes, not from a diminution of the labour employed, but of the labour payed for." Marx could not recognize the real source of profit because it would have invalidated his theory of exploitation. If Marx had admitted that profit comes from "diminution of labour employed," he would have had to abandon his theory of exploitation because not even the most wicked capitalist can exploit laborers who have been dismissed.

Profit is additional wealth that was not there before. Unless one believes in magic, it is reasonable to assume that profit must come from something that is added to the economic system from the outside. The importance of the introduction of energy flow from the outside as an additional driving force consists above all in that it transforms the economy from an isolated system into an open system, in which the zero-sum game of the fight for supposedly fixed resources is transformed into a potentially cooperative, positive-sum game. By the introduction of new energy from the outside, new wealth is created by the exploitation of energy, so that exploitation of human labor becomes not only unnecessary, but harmful for economic results.

If one recognizes that one source of profit is the substitution of human physical energy by cheaper sources of energy, it is clear that the best source is one that is a free good, such as solar energy flow. It is a preposterous idea to include among the factors of production solar energy flow, precisely because it has no price. One of the self-imposed taboos of neoclassical thinking is that the term *factor of production* is limited to inputs that command a price. Sunlight would become a factor of production only if it could be bottled and sold. Fortunately, the Physiocrats did not have this taboo. They instinctively recognized that agricultural productivity has something to do with a "gift of nature." Today it is known that this "gift" consists of photosynthesis, in which the energy of solar photons enables plants to combine carbon from carbon dioxide in the air with hydrogen from water to produce chemical molecules, commonly called food. Locke and Quesnay were both partially right, human action and energy flow are both needed for increasing economic wealth. Both are not only cost factors, but also profit factors in the economy.

There is, of course, an even more compelling reason for including energy flow among the factors of production of evolutionary economics. All the learned philosophers who did not see the importance of energy flow would not have had the opportunity of voicing their mistaken ideas if the prior existence of the sun had not made evolution in nature—and the existence of said philosophers—possible. Energy is both an independent variable, because solar radiation made the evolution of humans possible and continues to be an essential contributor to their survival, and also a dependent variable, because human action can increase the amount of energy used in the economy.

Time

Time is a complex notion and it is important in the economy in various ways. The economic process is historical, it develops in time. Time also has quantitative implications in the economy. If the time required for a process can be reduced, quantitative economic gain may result.

The French philosopher Bergson distinguished between mathematical time and the subjective experience of the passage of time, which he called *la durée*, meaning experienced or real time. From the point of view of economics, real time has two important features: irreversibility and dynamic continuity.

Real time is irreversible because it is the subjective experience of an individual whose life is an irreversible process. Real time is scarce because it is irreversible and limited in total amount by the life span of each individual. Therefore, real time has a subjective value to each individual regardless of his or her economic status. This is the reason medicine men were always in high esteem, and why people are willing to pay a high price for small pieces of matter called pharmaceuticals. In effect the pharmaceutical industry sells improvements in human time.

Real time also has an objective value for the community. This is measured by the productivity of human time. The more productivity increases, the higher the value of human time.

Real time has a dynamic structure. The present is linked with the past and the future through the perceptions of the individual memory of the past and expectations of the future. Inclusion of the future in economic considerations leads to enlightened, self-interested behavior. Herbert Simon speaks of enlightened self-interest when an individual sacrifices some of his or her short-run interest but receives long-run rewards that more than compensate for the immediate sacrifice (Simon 1983, 58, 105–7). The inclusion of the future in economic considerations is an essential requirement for turning the economy into a positive-sum game.

Conclusions

Evolutionary economic theory must be able to explain why and how the economy evolves. To do that, it must consider all the essential factors that influence economic results, both within the socioeconomic system and outside of it in the natural environment.

Neoclassical economic theory focused its attention on the decisions and actions of human participants in the exchange economy. The price it had to pay was that it could not explain why and how the economy evolves.

The unilateral emphasis on the importance of the human element in the economy has also limited the development of an evolutionary economic theory thus far. In nature, biological evolution proceeded for millions of years by using the energy and time factors for generating genetic knowledge, while recycling materials continuously. It is, therefore, not unreasonable to suggest that similar factors are also at work in the evolution of the economy.

It must be recognized that the desires and habitual actions of human agents alone are insufficient for explaining the quantitative increase of wealth in the economy. There are two driving forces behind the economic process: human creativity and various forms of energy flow. It is knowledge from human brains, in combination with new energy, that is necessary, and in combination also sufficient, for achieving the ultimate purpose of the economic process: the improvement of human time.

REFERENCES

Abramovitz, Moses. 1956. "Resource and Output Trends in the United States since 1870," *American Economic Review* 46:5–23.
Boulding, Kenneth E. 1981. *Evolutionary Economics*. Beverly Hills, Calif.: Sage.
Kuczynski, Marguerite. 1971. *François Quesnay ökonomische Schriften*. Berlin: Akademia Verlag.
Locke, John. 1960. *Two Treatises of Government*. Critical ed. by Peter Laslett. Cambridge: Cambridge University Press.
Marx, Karl. 1867. *Capital*. Vol. 1. New York: International Publishers.
Menger, Carl. 1871. *Grundsätze der Volkswirtschaftslehre*. Vienna: Braumüller.
Nelson, Richard R. 1987. *Understanding Technical Change as an Evolutionary Process*. Amsterdam: North-Holland.
Ricardo, David. 1951. *On the Principles of Political Economy and Taxation*. Ed. Piero Sraffa. Cambridge: Cambridge University Press.
Schumpeter, Joseph A. 1934. *The Theory of Economic Development*. Cambridge, Mass.: Harvard University Press.
Simon, Herbert A. 1983. *Reason in Human Affairs*. Stanford: Stanford University Press.
Smith, Adam. 1976. *An Inquiry into the Nature and Causes of the Wealth of Nations*. Collected Works, The Glasgow Edition, book 2, ed. R. H. Campbell et al. Oxford: Clarendon Press.
Smith, Adam. 1978. "Early Draft of Part of the Wealth of Nations, 1763." In *Lectures on Jurisprudence*, Collected Works, The Glasgow Edition, book 5, ed. R. L. Meek et al. Oxford: Clarendon Press.

CHAPTER 6

A New Theory of "Modern Economic Growth"

Günter Hesse

The term *modern economic growth* (Kuznets 1966 and 1971) is used to characterize an economy with sustained structural transformation and a marked increase in real Gross Domestic Product (GDP) per capita. It is now a commonplace that the central feature of this structural transformation is "the shift of resources from agriculture to industry" (Lewis 1976, 136; Chenery, Robinson, and Syrquin 1986, ix). Industrialization is the heart of modern economic growth.

Industrialization is usually measured by the ratio of agricultural to total labor force (Hayami and Ruttan 1985, 129; Hesse 1989, 139). Figure 1 illustrates the development of the ratio of agricultural to total labor force (LA) over the last five hundred years in those parts of the world that were already relatively densely populated by about 1500.[1]

The standard explanation (e.g., IBRD 1987, chap. 3) of a decreasing LA, the central feature of modern economic growth, is simple. According to Engel's law, which states that the income elasticity of demand for food is less than one, the structure of demand changes as real per capita income rises. If, on the supply side, we have at least average labor productivity in agriculture, the LA is decreasing in the long run. Above average or increasing labor productivity in agriculture accelerates the process of structural change. Although the division of labor is generally mentioned too, the main force creating increasing real per capita income is technical progress. Increasing agricultural productivity is a part of this technical progress, working via increasing real per capita income and Engel's law on the demand side and by lowering the labor input requirements per unit of output on the supply side. An implication of this standard explanation is that technical progress was sufficient in the now developed, industrialized countries and that, in the

---

1. See Boserup 1981, 12; Braudel 1985, 1:52–53; Thornton 1987, xvii. The lines in fig. 1 indicate rough trends; country LA values move around these trends within limits. Because of limited space it is not possible to go into the details of the estimation (see Hesse 1989, 140–46).

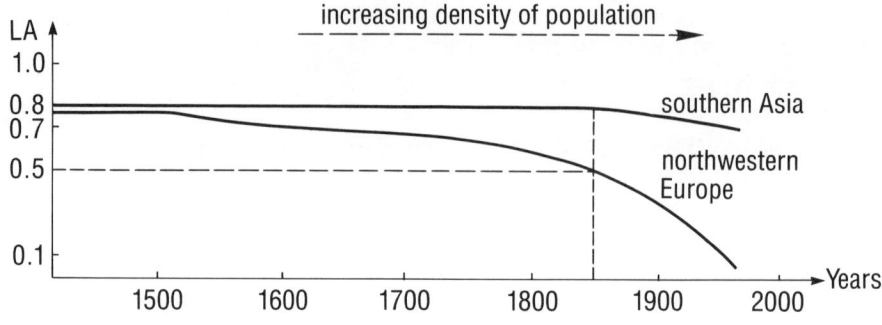

Fig. 1. Ratio of agricultural to total labor force

developing world, containing almost three-fourths of the world's population, it was insufficient or nonexistent.

Although the standard explanation seems straightforward and intelligible, its foundations are dubious on at least two grounds. First, the basic assumption of the standard explanation, that is, increasing real per capita income, is seriously at variance with the empirical facts during the early phase of industrialization. What is now known about the development of the standard of living between the middle of the fifteenth century and the first decades of the nineteenth century in the relevant parts of Europe, points to a decreasing rather than increasing tendency.[2] The index of the real wage rate of a building craftsman in southern England (Phelps-Brown and Hopkins 1981, 28ff.) was about 100 during the fifteenth century (123 in 1477). As population density rose (see Wrigley and Schofield 1981), the index fell for over a hundred years and dropped below 40 in the early decades of the seventeenth century. Stagnating and even gently diminishing population in the third quarter of the seventeenth century, the import of human and financial capital from the continent caused by the religious wars, the decline of some continental competitors, and a sequence of good harvests as a result of favorable weather (Manley 1974) all contributed to a recovery of the index to a value of about 68 between 1740 and 1749. Then, however, with population density again rising markedly, the index fell until the first decade of the nineteenth century (to an average of 44). This was the period formerly associated with the onset of the Industrial Revolution.

---

2. This is admitted by Fourastie and Schneider 1989, 92–93, 103. I call the years from the first decades of the sixteenth century to the first decades of the nineteenth century (when LA was about 0.5 in Northwest Europe) the early phase of industrialization because, up to the middle of the nineteenth century, industrial motive power gained from burning fossil fuels was of minor (Britain) or almost no importance (continent) to the industrializing economies (Musson 1976; Humphrey and Stanislaw 1979; Kanefsky 1980; Greenberg 1982; Cameron 1985).

A completely new age (Braudel 1985, 3:691) began in the third decade of the nineteenth century when, in spite of rising population density but with increasing per capita industrial energy consumption, the real wage rate index increased. However, we have to wait until 1886 (index = 129) for the previous peak year (1477, index = 123) to be surpassed (Phelps-Brown and Hopkins 1981, 31).[3]

Thus, it appears that the basic feature of modern economic growth, a decreasing LA, does not follow increasing abstract real per capita income but precedes increasing per capita material production.

Second, the underlying notion of technical progress (TP) simply presents, as if it were a miracle, something that actually requires explanation. If you introduce TP to explain the existence of modern economic growth in a small part of the world at a certain time, you have to answer the question of why there was no, or insufficient, TP at other times and places. This question usually is left to noneconomic approaches, for example, religion, n-achievement, institutions, all of which, it may be claimed, have been unable to give convincing answers (Hesse 1989, 146–50). An important step on the way to a serious analysis of modern economic growth, therefore, is to abandon the "neoclassical" notion of TP and to focus instead on a sober analysis of innovation and creativity.

Innovations can be divided into two groups, those that increase the economic effectiveness of a transformation process[4] and those that open up

---

3. Of course, there are a lot of questions concerning the calculation of the index and the representativeness of southern England builders' wage rates (Loschky 1980), but the broad trends are consistent with other relevant data. Working hours per person and year probably more than doubled between the fifteenth and the nineteenth century (cf. Slicher van Bath 1963, 183, 302; Freudenberger 1974; Freudenberger and Cummins 1976 for the data). Around the middle of the nineteenth century the peak load of 3,200–3,800 hours (Clark 1960) was realized, and people in the more densely populated parts of Europe, the great majority illiterates (Graff 1987), were literally working themselves to death just to make a living. Life expectancy in this alm and workhouse society was lower than in the poorest third world countries today (IBRD 1974, 68, 296). Stature declined and diet worsened. An inquiry about body heights in Central Germany covering more than a thousand years locates the absolute minimum of the average stature of women in the middle of the nineteenth century (Kunter 1984, 74ff.). The per capita and annual meat consumption in middle Europe declined from more than 100 kg at the end of the fifteenth to less than 20 kg in the middle of the nineteenth century (Abel 1981). There is a strong positive correlation between meat consumption and per capita GDP (Abel 1966). The bulk of studies on the standard of living is for the eighteenth and the nineteenth centuries and confirms the declining trend up to the first decades of the nineteenth century (Cage 1983; Lindert and Williamson 1983; Braudel 1985, 3:637ff.; Schwarz 1985; Olsson 1986, Mokyr 1988). Stature declined in Britain (Fogel et al. 1983) and elsewhere (Komlos 1985), and annual working hours increased (Thomas 1964; Reid 1976; Tranter 1981).

4. Increasing economic effectiveness of a given transformation process (a fixed set of input and output goods) results from a declining share of waste in the overall outcome of this process. Increasing economic effectiveness can be demonstrated in a quantity diagram, like neoclassical

new access to resources (Hesse 1986, 86ff.). The vast majority of innovations open up new access to resources by introducing new goods on the input and/or output side. It is important to distinguish between "access" and "resources" because confounding these can lead to the statement that man is able to create resources (De Gregori 1987). It should be noted that since the sets of input/output goods now are changed, we cannot use one quantity diagram to represent this kind of innovation.

Increasing effectiveness, such as neoclassical TP, is easy to evaluate. It is good, by definition, because it reduces the problems of scarcity to a limited degree. Innovations that open up new access to resources are mainly shifting problems, and it is almost impossible to get an intersubjectively and, if we have a nonreproducible process, intergenerationally valid evaluation. If there had only been increasing effectiveness since the middle of the nineteenth century, there would be no additional problems today. However, because there was also the kind of innovation that simply opened up new access to resources, we do have many new problems today, for instance pollution. In economic development, we permanently have both consequences of innovations: increasing effectiveness (up to a limit) in treating known problems and entirely new, sometimes more severe, problems.

The economic problem is not solved; it merely changes its appearance. It is not solved because the creativity of modern man is limited, and it appears in new forms because he is creative.

There is creativity in our economic world. The human brain permanently creates perceptions that are of limited duration and that are spontaneously replaced by other actively constituted perceptions, but this is only cognitive creativity. This creativity creates new cognitive systems, new ways of combining new elements, but not quantities of goods from nothing. This creativity is consistent with recent scientific knowledge (Pöppel 1971, 1985, and 1988) and is a general feature of modern man's brain; it is something like an anthropological constant (Hesse 1986).

When man's creative capacity is acknowledged, economic development in the long run will be explained as the result of innovative adaptation to some basic invariable constraints (Hesse 1987a). This is the basic, nonbiological evolutionary process in economics.

The appropriate time period to be considered by a nonbiological theory of long-term development are the last 30,000 to 40,000 years, when the biological constitution of mankind was constant.

In the next section, the framework of this long-run development will be

---

TP, but, in accordance with the now known laws of nature, the effectiveness (quantity of given input goods to quantity of given output goods) cannot grow beyond unity. Increasing effectiveness is a special kind of learning by doing.

briefly outlined (for a more detailed discussion, see Hesse 1988). Roughly speaking, the development reflects the permanent struggle of modern man to make the best of the perceived situation and his very limited ability to solve or eliminate basic problems. Cognitive creativity is used mainly to shift problems, and the theory of long-term development reconstructs a long chain consisting of problem–creative response; problem shift–creative response; problem shift again–creative response; and so on.

The third section of this chapter then turns to the constraint that, in historical perspective, seems to have been crucial for the fact that industrialization occurred only in one part of the world, that is, the invariable restriction on the temporal allocation of elementary production processes in agricultural production due to the marked seasonal variation of temperature in northern Europe (Hesse 1982 and 1984). Compared to the advanced tropical civilizations, an additional crucial innovative adaptation was induced in this part of the world, which at the time was the only larger, relatively densely populated region with severe seasonal temperature swings. The constraint, and the creative response to it, may also explain why an early phase of industrialization arose at all.

The fourth section reviews some of the empirical evidence for the theory suggested in the third section. In the last section, some tentative conclusions are drawn.

The Framework of Long-Term Development

To be alive is to consume energy—to make entropy. Since creativity is limited to cognitive creativity, people cannot create matter or energy. They have to take this energy and matter from their environment and to turn it into a usable form. Acquiring and transforming energy needs input energy or labor. Cognitive creativity can increase the effectiveness of this input energy by designing means of production that change the point of application of human labor or make additional parts or forces of nature available. Production of technical means of production is a well-known innovative adaptation that has important consequences. Probably of much more importance is another form of "production of means of production" and that is the procreation and education of controlled offspring to increase the availability of human labor, or its product, to the deciding generation of parents.

According to this non-Malthusian investment theory of demographic behavior, the process of procreation and child rearing is not instinctive or quasi-natural, but a result of decision making and deliberate action. This investment theory of child rearing is not new (Müller 1924 and 1927), and people all over the world seem to behave according to the theory. To the farmer in Europe, "begetting farm hands, whom he needn't pay" (Beckman

1779, 99ff.) was a matter of course. Caldwell (1982), Boserup (1986), and others rediscovered this wealth-flow theory of population (Caldwell 1982) after intensive research in third world countries. The optimal number of spaced children in each family is where the discounted net flow of income is maximal. (For further details, cf. Caldwell 1982). If we neglect inputs, the level of the net flow of income, which includes benefits of all sorts, depends on two variables: the level of income that a child can earn and the degree to which parents can share the child's earnings. A high level of child earnings and a high degree of control will, ceteris paribus, lead to high optimal numbers of children and, other things being equal, high rates of population growth. Today, in both Eastern and Western industrialized countries, the optimal number of offspring is very low in spite of very high levels of earnings of offspring because the degree of control approximates zero. Almost the same pattern is found when the access to an essential resource, such as land, is free because population density is so low that land is not a scarce good. The rate of population growth may then be very low despite a high level of labor productivity, because parents' control of the earnings of the offspring is very limited. Let us assume this to be the "hunter-gatherer pattern." We can now start economic development with low rates of population growth and high levels of the marginal product of labor in food production.

The next step is to introduce another very important invariable constraint: the generalized law of *diminishing marginal returns* in the production of organic matter, which is the origin of many innovative adaptations and the corresponding technical and institutional achievements. This law can be derived very briefly as follows: a food producer has to transform four basic resources (solar energy, water, carbon dioxide, and minerals) into an edible form, as desired by human beings (see Hesse 1987b for more details and literature). To this end, humans modify and manipulate ecological systems. Two components of this intervention can be distinguished.

(*a*) Intervention in the biological component by
—arranging food chains to their own purpose
—changing the length of the food chain,
(*b*) Manipulation of the physical environment by
—fertilization, soil improvement,
—irrigation projects

The content of carbon dioxide in the atmosphere is difficult to control and humans can in no way influence the amount of solar energy that falls per time unit on a given surface unit. The flow of solar energy is thus the central, but uncontrollable resource in this production process. It is the fixed factor in agricultural production.

On this elementary level of consideration of agricultural production, we have, on the input side, the nonproduced flow of solar energy and the amount of labor necessary to manipulate the biological and physical components of the ecological system. On the output side, we have a flow of foodstuff energy, which enables life to exist. At this basic level, a generalized law of agricultural production is valid.

As the share in the flow of solar energy per surface unit, which humans can use in the form of food energy, is increased, the input of produced energy increases faster than the energy yield.

For preindustrial forms of agricultural production in which the flow of solar energy is the only energy source, the law means that the time, or work hours, spent making life possible increases. But the law is valid for both preindustrial and industrialized forms of agricultural production. The latter is characterized by intensive use of stocks of energy. The energy efficiency is often, to a very large degree, smaller than in the so-called primitive systems (Leach 1976; Stanhill 1984).

Over a very long time period, it was possible, despite a rising population, to avoid, on average, a decline in the marginal productivity of labor by changing places and occupying new territories, thus simply increasing the geographic range but not economic population density.[5] Because hunter-gatherers try to keep a minimum group size ("security in numbers") even if bad luck is cumulative, the rate of population growth is positive under average conditions.

---

5. Given the generalized law of the production of organic matter, we can explain permanent "mobility," a basic feature of a hunter-gatherer socioeconomic system, as an innovative adaptation to this constraint. By migrating (changing ranges within territories) hunter-gatherers keep the total working time spent in foodstuff production out of a given stream of solar energy (time and surface area) at a constant and very low level and maintain a remarkably high, and on average constant, level of the marginal product of labor (Sahlins 1974; Winterhalder and Smith 1981). Hunter-gatherers can also maintain a constant technology, even with rising population, if they divide their groups from time to time and occupy new territories hitherto not inhabited. Geographic population density in this case is so low that even with a very extensive land use system (hunting and gathering) the existing groups use only a small part of the surface of the world. Increasing population and an increasing number of groups do not increase economic population density under these conditions. Therefore, no new problems arise, and we have constant technology, not because there is no creativity, but because the best solutions to the existing and unchanging problems have already been invented. This is the simplest case of a nonstationary economy. According to Cassel (1918), it can be called a "proportionally growing economy" (*gleichmäßig fortschreitende Wirtschaft*), and can be described by basic neoclassical growth theory (Hesse 1988). In some regions of the earth, this theoretically very simple phase was passed ten thousand years ago.

However, even if the rate of growth of population is very low, the time will eventually come when the old methods, used over millenia to cope with the generalized law and to postpone diminishing marginal returns to labor, have to be abandoned because economic population density rises.

With increasing population density, output per surface/time unit—per unit of solar energy—has to increase. According to the generalized law, increasing yield per surface unit, usually called agricultural productivity, is unavoidably accompanied by diminishing marginal returns to labor input.

There remains just one type of creative answer—innovations that slow down the rate of decline of marginal productivity of labor. The way to slow down the rate of decline of marginal productivity of labor while increasing agricultural productivity is to change land use systems (Salehi-Isfahani 1988). One of the earliest steps in the observable, long chain of systems with ever-increasing intensity of land use and declining productivity (e.g., Thünen 1842; Boserup 1965) is the broadening of the number of items used by hunter-gatherers (see Dennell 1983, 149–92) exploiting "tropical pyramids" (Odum 1983, 128) and one of the most recent steps in this long chain, which has innumerable ingenious links, is multicropping, with three to four main crops in some tropical parts of the world. (On the ingenuity of old and recent tropical land use systems, compare, e.g., Perkins 1969; Ruthenberg 1971; Bray 1984.) Of course, intensity of land use and population density is still low under conditions extremely hostile to agricultural production, for example very low average yearly temperature, deserts, or very poor soil.

It should be emphasized that agricultural productivity, beyond a minimum level sufficient for medium population density, is anything but decisive to the evolution of modern economic growth (i.e., industrialization). To give just one illustration: yields (in wheat units) per hectare, surface/time unit, in Bangladesh today are three times higher than in the United States (Hayami and Ruttan 1985, 120; cf. Kravis 1976, 28). Other things, for example, soil characteristics or mineral and water input, being equal, organic dry matter production per hectare and year in high radiation tropical areas is two to three times higher than in "moderate," cold climates (Cooper 1986, 120–21, Holliday 1976, 140, 142).

The long chain of land use systems that embodies technological change is the result of an innovative adaptation to the invariant constraint given by the generalized law of agricultural production under increasing economic population density, which, according to the wealth-flow theory of demographic behavior, is itself an innovative adaptation to a more basic invariable constraint, namely limited (cognitive) creativity.

It should also be emphasized that, in this regard, there was no difference between the South and the North even in the early phase of industrialization, but, as I will discuss in the next section, the capital intensity, that is, the ratio of indirect to direct labor, in agriculture was markedly higher in the North. There, more implements produced by craft or industry were used, thus contributing to different contents of learning by doing processes and different contents of human and real capital formation in the economy.[6]

In these agrarian high cultures there is substantial trade, division of labor, private property rights, and markets as well as money, banking, capital formation, and many innovations.[7] In other words, a fully developed economy ready to be analysed by classical political economy (e.g., Adam Smith).

These agrarian high cultures are not static economies, there is some variation, but one basic feature does not change. The LA remains at a high level for centuries and there is no argument available for showing why there should be something like a natural path leading to industrialization.

A New Theory of Industrialization

After the exogenous mortality shocks of the Black Plague era, European population rose sharply in the fifteenth and sixteenth centuries. Real wages decreased, and the food chain became shorter to adapt to the generalized law of agricultural production. Production and consumption of meat sank, while that of vegetable foodstuffs, especially grain, rose. The sixteenth century was, according to Abel, "the century of grains" (1981, 33). "Livestock farming was crowded out by arable farming" (41). In this respect, northwestern Europe did not differ, at the time, from other regions of the world with increasing population density, such as India or central and southern China.

There was, however, one crucial difference. Northwestern Europe was the first and only large region of the world that faced a high and increasing

---

6. There are still other similarities in problem shifts and creative answers accompanying the formation of so-called advanced civilizations. A very important sequence starts with the growing investment in land that itself is a part of the creative answer to the growing demand for food per surface/time unit. "Immovables" admit, to a certain degree, permanent exaction from the investors, they permit taxes and "states." To ensure this source of revenue, both the "sword" (military) and the "word" (state religions, legitimating hierarchy) are employed, with a lot of new problems and creative answers. Another sequence of problems and creative responses emerges in connection with gathering and spending of taxes and supplying the growing capitol cities with food and with luxury goods from remote places. Writing (Graff 1987), transportation equipment (Boserup 1981) and technics of far distant trade (Curtin 1984) are solutions to some of these problems (Jones 1988, 62–63). More exclusive property rights in land are granted to give an additional incentive to invest in land (Wagner 1870) and hereditary rights support the status of the parents in the family. Together with a "family morality" (Caldwell 1982) this contributes to the growing controlability of the younger by the older family members. Procreation and education remain profitable to the primary demographic decision makers, that is, the families, in spite of decreasing marginal returns of labor of their offspring.

7. According to Chao (1986, 2ff.), China was an atomistic market economy with private property in land for more than two millenia before the 1950s.

population density and an additional unavoidable restriction, a limitation on the temporal allocation of the "elementary processes" in vegetable agricultural production, which was becoming more important; that is, the seasonal fluctuation of the mean daily or monthly temperature.[8] Seasonal temperature swings play a less important role in extensive land use systems such as livestock farming with nonproduced feed or hunting. The constraint becomes relevant as the agricultural economy begins to depend on the production of vegetable foodstuffs.

To assess the consequences of this unavoidable constraint in agricultural production conditions (Hesse 1984, 56), consider figure 2. The horizontal axis represents the maximum work days in a year. The left vertical axis shows the structural change of agricultural production (CSA) and the right axis shows yearly work hours per person (LHY). Both values will change with an increasing population density. Work hours will increase and the share of meat in the diet will decrease.

With a given maximum number of daily work hours (e.g.: ten hours, $\tan\alpha = 10$), the minimum work days per person must increase if the annual amount of work hours is to be expanded. This means that points above the line $LmMm$ are unattainable. Below this line, there are a multitude of possibilities for distributing a given number of annual work hours over the work days during the year. Under the circumstances just mentioned, however, because of the constraint on the temporal allocation of elementary processes in vegetable food production, the temporary inactivity in agricultural production increases, as the structure of agricultural production changes. The curve LS symbolizes this unavoidable inactivity. Thus, a second factor restricts the distribution of direct agricultural work hours over more days in the year, and it is not possible to meet this demand by increasing the daily work hours, which are already at a maximum. The result is a period $(0N)$ of extremely intensive, directly productive activity and a period $(360 - 0N)$ of unavoidable inactivity in agricultural production. John Law ([1705] 1966, 98) for example, observed that, in England, those "that labour the Ground were idle one half of their time."

The shift of the curve LS to LS^* and beyond indicates the existence of the seasonality of agricultural employment in tropical savannah regions, which could initially be the result of a seasonal distribution of precipitation. This restriction can be overcome, as population density increases, by the construction of irrigation facilities, that is, investment in land can neutralize the seasonality of rainfall. Indeed, this has been occurring in all tropical countries for millennia. Bangladesh, for example, has a single monsoon season and pronounced periods of drought, but a great deal of the land is irrigated and the

---

8. See Georgescu-Roegen 1976, chap. 4, on the theory of production using the concept of "elementary processes."

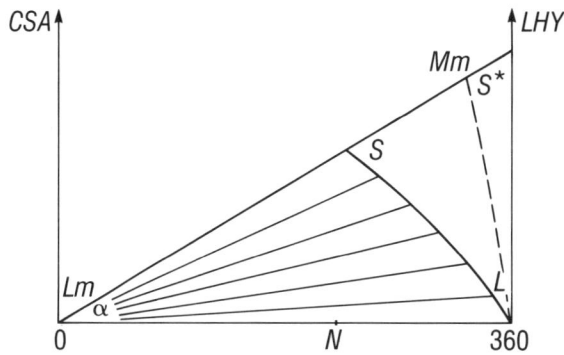

Fig. 2. Increasing length and decreasing number of agricultural working days

country has one of the highest degrees of arable land utilization in the world, taking a country average of about two main harvests per year and unit of arable land. In contrast, in the densely populated, nontropical region of Europe, we have the initial emergence of a unique *coexistence* of

—seasonally very scarce agricultural labor, which farmers must hire at premium summer wages, and
—seasonal surplus of labor, which can only find employment at very low wages in non agricultural production (LI = L [I + S] − LS).

In figure 3, LA is the percentage of the workforce employed in the agricultural sector, which fluctuates greatly throughout the year because of the unavoidable parallel organization of the basic process. Employment in nonagricultural sectors, in industrial production (LI) and in service industries (LS), is a mirror image of LA. While service industry employment remains relatively constant throughout the year, LI (the area between the two lower curves, L [I + S] and LS) is subject to great fluctuations. LI is greatest when industrial wages reach their minimum (For historical evidence, see, e.g., Smith [1776] 1963; Nebel 1909; Weber-Kellerman 1987, 378).

This lasting coexistence of seasonally scarce agricultural labor receiving premium wages and surplus industrial labor receiving very low wages had consequences for the utilization of industrially produced farm implements in agricultural production. By expanding the utilization of less expensive winter labor for tool production (capital as previously accomplished labor), expensive summer labor can be replaced, and the capital intensity at the minimal cost combination is increased. Farm laborers are increasingly equipped with industrially produced tools, thus increasing production per worker. In this

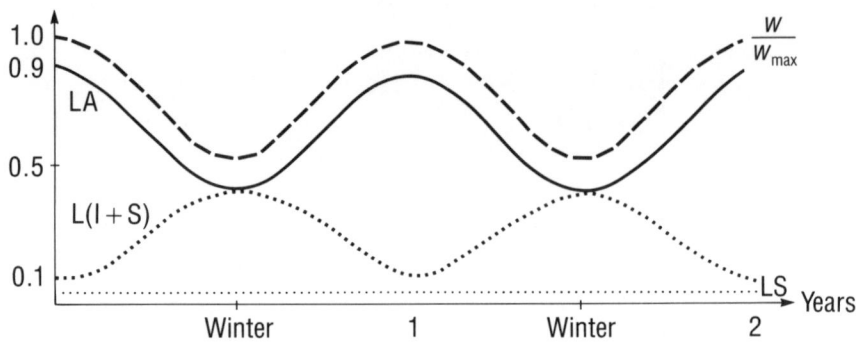

Fig. 3. Seasonal variation of the sectoral distribution of work force and the wage rate percentage of the top wage rate

way, gross production per agricultural worker can increase, although the marginal product of an additional, direct or indirect, labor unit in the agricultural sector tends to fall. This conclusion is supported by the most recent research. "Factor endowments per worker emerge as more important sources of higher output per worker in British agriculture than total factor productivity" (Crafts 1989, 421). The percentage of the work force employed in the agricultural sector falls.

This lasting coexistence also has consequences for the prices of simple, nonagricultural consumer goods and for the intermediate products for urban craftsmen, who process these goods into finished products (putting-out system, protoindustrialization, see Mendels 1972). There is enormous pressure on the prices of these goods due to the relative increase in the labor potential, which is, to some extent, a by-product of agricultural production (Beckman 1779, 83ff.) and which can only be utilized in nonagricultural production.

Under these conditions, lower classes who must purchase food can be forced to expand their nonagricultural production as a matter of survival in spite of sinking real wages. Small farmers, rural craftsmen, and land-poor and landless rural inhabitants all belong to these lower classes. The percentage of rural lower classes climbed rapidly as population rose rapidly in the early phase of industrialization. For Germany, the figures are 53 percent (12.2 million) in 1800 and 57 percent (19.4 million) in 1845 (Saalfeld 1984).

The emergence of a land-poor class as population density rises is not a unique development of northwestern Europe. The difference, however, compared with tropical regions, is that these land-poor laborers can find work throughout almost the entire year in agriculture in the tropics, but in northwestern Europe, they must find nonagricultural employment for at least part of the year. As would be expected, the number of hours worked annually tends to rise.

Stated briefly, the percentage of the entire work force employed in the agricultural sector decreased in the early phase of industrialization as a result of innovative adaptation to the unavoidable seasonal constraint. Worsening nutrition, deteriorating physical stature, and emigration all attest to the fact that this adaptation occurred under the severe pressure of the need to maintain survival. Life expectancy was lower in the then industrializing countries than in the poorest third world countries today (World Bank 1984, 68, 296). Tropical regions do not face this additional, unavoidable restriction. Until the nineteenth century, the nontropical industrializing countries can in no circumstances be considered a role model for economic policy in tropical countries.

In the framework of the evolutionary model, the decisive difference (compared with the tropical regions) is that a growing part of the labor potential is forced to work and to learn in the nonagricultural sector. Thus, different contents of economic human and real capital emerge in tropical and nontropical regions of the world, despite given, universally equal levels of human cognitive creativity. It must be emphasized that the *content* of economic human and real capital formation is much more important than its level, because this was a crucial but unintentionally generated "precondition" to the controlled employment of additional energy produced from stocks.[9]

The importance of the breadth of these areas of nonagricultural activity becomes clear when one considers that each technological innovation results from a long chain of small changes and is based on a multitude of complementary production processes and qualifications. Innovation first gains economic relevance when the initial high costs and prices are drastically reduced by learning by producing and, especially, by competition (Heuß 1965).

It is not possible to demonstrate in detail how production methods, production organization, and goods are changed under strong competitive pressure, that is, when they are no longer controllable by craft guilds, and how markets for industrial goods arose, goods that were later produced by factories. It is in the factories that economies of scale can be realized, that is, in the transition from home industrial production with parallel organization and a high capital coefficient to in-line, "factory organization," with a lower capital coefficient. Secondly, new "power engines," improved by more than a century of learning by producing, could be used in these factories with decreasing average fixed costs and limited illiquidity risk because large and

---

9. If we use the usual residual concept of productivity as a proxy for the importance of the content, we can use the various "sources of growth" calculation to illustrate this point. The most recent researches on U.S. long-term growth, for example, "lead to the conclusion that productivity changes accounted for almost six-tenths of the growth of per capita NNP in the (second half) of the nineteenth century" and for 77.5 percent of per capita NNP growth between 1900 and 1960 (Gallman 1986, 190). During this period, there was a forty-fivefold increase in the energy per labor hour in the manufacturing sector in the United States gained from using up stocks (Schurr, Sonenblum, and Wood 1983, 440).

94   Explaining Process and Change

relatively secure markets existed. The drawback of this increasing material production per factory worker, resulting from economies of scale and increasing industrial energy use per worker, is the deindustrialization of rural areas, which initially brings considerable social problems.

The economic preconditions, among other factors, a particular content of human and real capital accumulation, were created for the utilization of energy sources other than the fixed flow of solar energy. These preconditions arose in the process of innovative adaptation to an additional specific and extremely relevant constraint that did not exist in the tropics.

Utilization of a flow or a stock of energy, roughly speaking at extraction rather than reproduction cost, is the central point when considering the divergent development in the second phase of industrialization. This fact is clearly brought out by correlating per capita GNP as a measure of economic development with the percentage of the entire work force employed in the agricultural sector (LA) and per capita commercial energy consumption, measured by per capita kg oil units (p.c. CEC kg oil units). In figure 4, five country groups are shown with their average GNP per capita in 1983 U.S. dollars on the horizontal axis.[10] For these country groups (classified in 1983), the additional characteristics are shown on the vertical axis, percentage of the entire work force employed in the agricultural sector (LA) is given on the left axis and per capita energy consumption on the right axis. Two values are given to each of the two variables: percentage of work force employed in agriculture in 1965 (line 1) and 1981 (line 2) and per capita energy consumption in 1965 (line 3) and 1983 (line 4).

Figure 4 clearly demonstrates that high LA values (low level of industrialization) and low per capita energy consumption, where the economy depends primarily on the flow of solar energy, necessitate low per capita GNP values. Conversely, low LA values (high level of industrialization) and high per capita energy consumption accompany high per capita GNP values.

Some Empirical Evidence

In this section some empirical evidence for the theory suggested in the previous section will be briefly reviewed.

I begin with the correlation between the percentage of the work force employed in the agricultural sector (LA) and a measure of seasonality (S) for a

---

10. The groups are World Bank country groups:
A = Low income countries, $260 per capita GNP (GNP/c), average;
B = Middle income countries of the lower category, $750 GNP/c, average;
C = Middle income countries of the upper category, $2,050 GNP/c, average;
D = Eastern European centrally planned economies, $2,620 GDP/c, average; and
E = Industrialized market economies, $11,060 GNP/c, average.

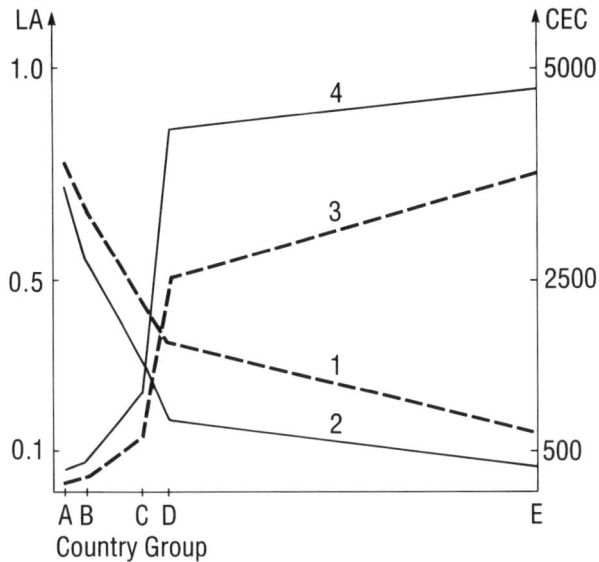

Fig. 4. Labor force in agriculture, per capita commercial energy consumption, and per capita GNP. (Data from: IBRD 1985, tables 1, 8, 21; National Accounts Statistics 1988, table 1.)

series of countries comprising 90 percent of the world population. The measure $S = w \times g$, where w is the warmth sum, the sum of the average monthly temperatures, and g is the thermal growing season, the fraction of the year with average monthly temperatures above 5°C, expresses the seasonal opportunity costs of producing nonagricultural goods.[11]

The theory in the previous section suggests that the higher these opportunity costs are, the higher LA will be. This hypothesis is clearly supported by the data depicted in the scatter diagram in figure 5.[12] An S-shaped curve, as expected, illustrates the relationship between LA and S. In regions with very short thermal growing seasons, the extreme North and South, S plays a less important role because of very low population density. In regions with a thermal growing season of 1, tropical countries, rising values of the warmth sum do not change opportunity costs significantly.

As indicated by the vertical lines for the countries in figure 5, there is a

---

11. The data for the warmth sum and the thermal growing season were taken from Walter and Lieth 1967. Several climatic diagrams were used for each country, where possible from the most densely populated areas.

12. The population of various countries is indicated in the diagram by circles of differing sizes. Two values, connected with a vertical line, for each country show LA in 1960 and in 1980. The shaded circles indicate values for 1980.

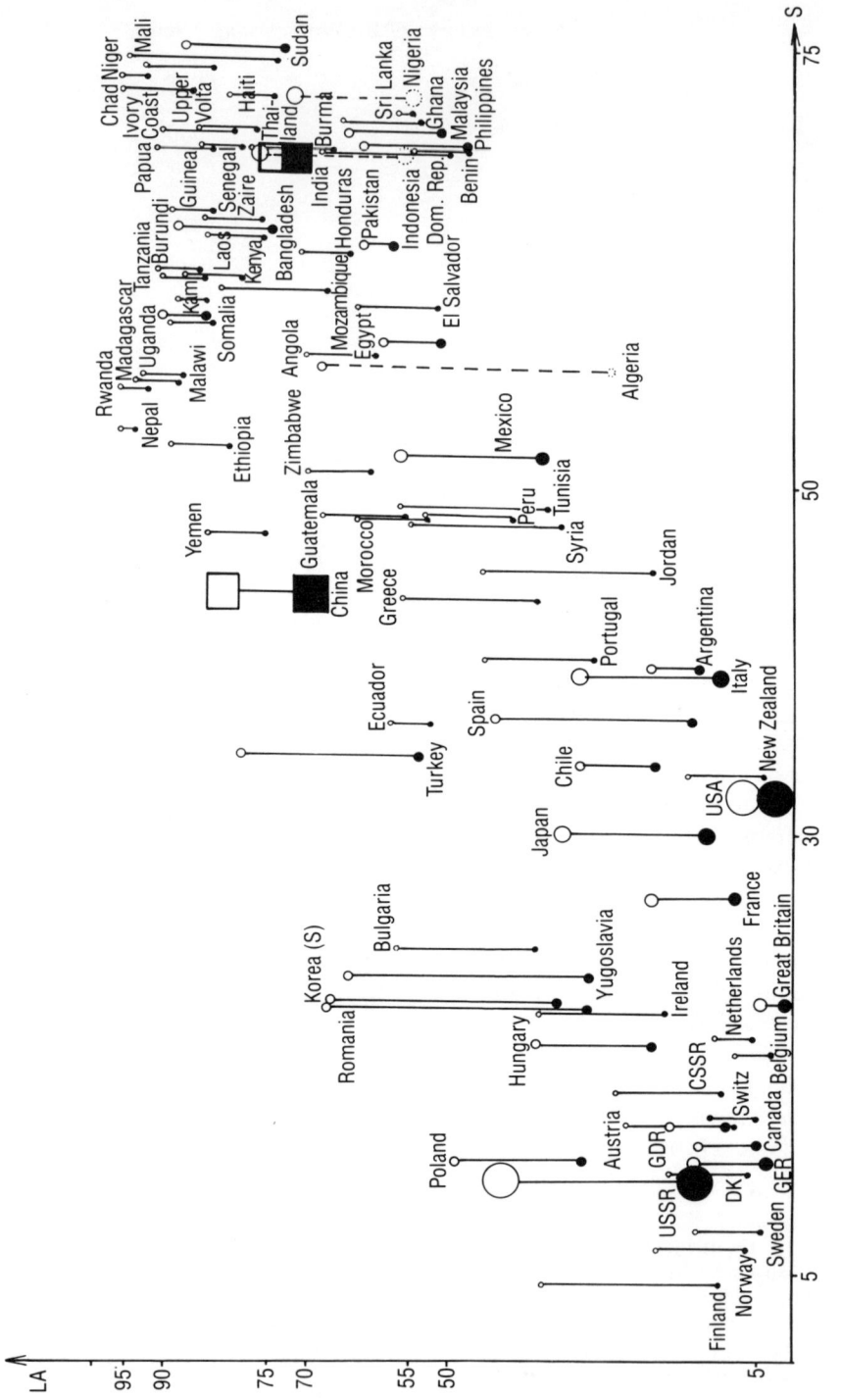

Fig. 5. LA and seasonality

clear decrease in the LA values everywhere from 1960 to 1980. This expresses a general trend, but does not alter the positive, cross-country correlation predicted by the theory. Using, for instance, the 1980 data in figure 5, a regression function LA $= 25.09 - 2.38$ S $+ 0.10$ S$^2 - 0.0008$ S^3 can be estimated on the basis of OLS for which $R^2 = $ o.70 with a confidence level of 99.9 percent.

The systematic decrease in LA for a given S since 1850 (cf. fig. 1) has been attributed primarily to the differences in the development of per capita industrial energy consumption. These differences, however, are partially a result of the different incentive structures, expressed by S values. Furthermore, an accelerating element within the various economies also played a role. This was a result of the different contents of human and real capital accumulation in the face of heavy competition. In the industrializing economies, all parameters of competition, especially the invention of new products for producing or applying industrial energy, were used.

Per capita commercial energy consumption (CEC) should, therefore, be included in empirical tests. This has been achieved here by forming a new variable (S/CEC). The theory in the previous section implies that LA rises with rising S values and rising (1/CEC). The S value reflects the incentive structure and (1/CEC) indicates the dependence on the flow of solar energy, given among other factors a certain content of human and real capital accumulation. Unlike the S variable, which is exogenous, the CEC variable is an endogenous outcome of economic and technological choices. But these choices are strongly influenced by the incentive structure (S variable).

The farm economy is the "factory" in which the flow of solar energy is transformed into an energy source usable by human beings. A lower CEC value produces a greater dependence on this flow of solar energy and a larger LA. This conjecture is strongly supported by the empirical data. The data for CEC values were taken from the World Tables of the World Bank and arranged into a scatter diagram in figure 6 (LA values for 1980 only).

Using the data in this figure, a regression function, LA $= 31.89 - 20.67$ (ln [S/CEC $\times$ 100] $+ 5.11$ (ln [S/CEC $\times$ 100])$^2 - 0.25$ (ln [S/CEC $\times$ 100])^3, can be estimated on the basis of OLS for which $R^2 = 0.86$ with a level of confidence of 99.9 percent. This means that up to 86 percent of the variance of fundamental economic structures (LA) of the countries of the world can be explained highly significantly by the logarithm of the compound variable S/CEC as suggested by the theory proposed here.

Conclusion

In this chapter, I have briefly outlined a new evolutionary theory of modern economic growth. In development economics, a host of possible influential

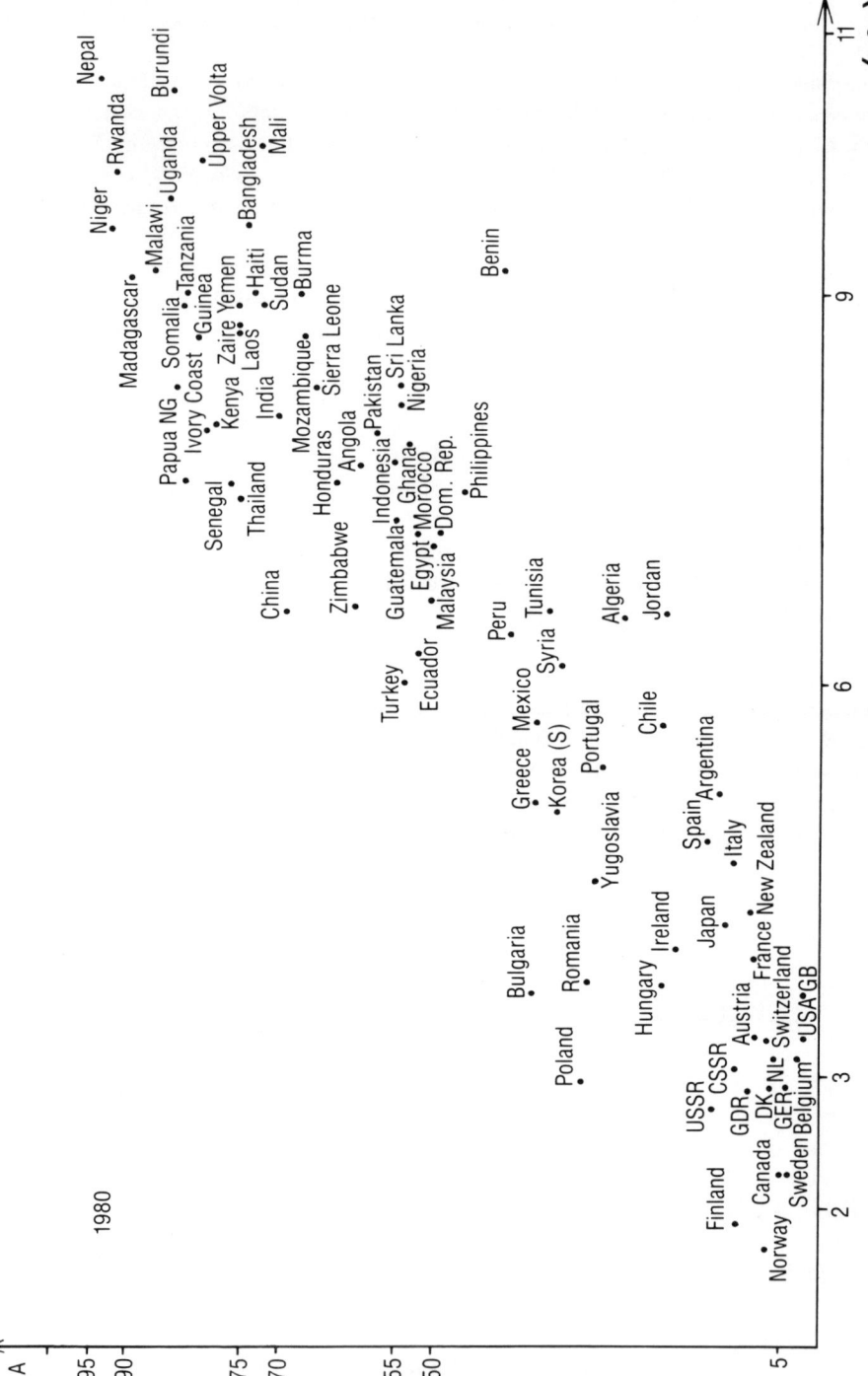

Fig. 6. LA, seasonality, and per capita commercial energy consumption

factors for economic development have been discussed in recent decades. The present theory attempts to determine the truly fundamental factor, that is, human creativity in the face of some basic invariable constraints, one of them geographically determined. The introduction of additional factors with which economic development could be explained in a still more differentiated form offers no insurmountable difficulties in the general framework of the suggested theory. The general concept, innovative adaptation, will, however, not be changed by this. It is compatible with our background knowledge in modern science and philosophy and with the empirical data.

REFERENCES

Abel, Wilhelm. 1966. *Agrarkrisen und Agrarkonjunktur: Eine Geschichte der Land- und Ernährungswirtschaft Mitteleuropas.* Hamburg: Parey.
Abel, Wilhelm. 1981. *Stufen der Ernährung.* Göttingen: Vandenhoeck und Ruprecht.
Beckmann, Johann. 1779. *Beyträge zur Ökonomie, Technologie, Polizey, und Cameralwissenschaft.* Göttingen: Vandenhoeck.
Boserup, Ester. 1965. *The Conditions of Agricultural Growth.* New York: Aldine.
Boserup, Ester. 1981. *Population and Technological Change.* Chicago: University of Chicago Press.
Boserup, Ester. 1986. "Shifts in the Determinants of Fertility in the Developing World." In *The State of Population Theory,* ed. D. Coleman and R. Schofield, 239–55. London: Basil Blackwell.
Braudel, Fernand. 1985. *Sozialgeschichte des 15.–18. Jahrhunderts.* 3 vols. Munich: Kindler.
Bray, Franceska. 1984. "Agriculture." Vol. 6, part 2 of *Science and Civilization in China,* ed. J. Needham. Cambridge: Cambridge University Press.
Cage, R. A. 1983. "The Standard of Living Debate: Glasgow, 1800–1850." *Journal of Economic History* 43:175–82.
Caldwell, John C. 1982. *Theory of Fertility Decline.* London: Academic Press.
Cameron, Rondo. 1985. "A New View of European Industrialization." *Economic History Review* 38:1–23.
Cassel, Gustav. 1918. *Theoretische Sozialökonomie.* Leipzig: Scholl.
Chao, Kang. 1986. *Man and Land in Chinese History: An Economic Analysis.* Stanford: Stanford University Press.
Chenery, Hollis; Robinson, Sherman; and Syrquin, Moshe. 1986. *Industrialization and Growth: A Comparative Study.* New York: Oxford University Press.
Clark, Colin. 1960. *Conditions of Economic Progress.* 3d ed. London: Macmillan.
Cooper, J. P. 1986. "Whole Plant Solar Energy Conversion." In *Food Production and Consumption,* ed. A. N. Duckham, I. G. W. Jones, and E. H. Roberts. Amsterdam: North-Holland.
Crafts, N. F. R. 1989. "British Industrialization in an International Context." *Journal of Interdisciplinary History* 19:415–28.

Curtin, Philip D. 1984. *Cross-cultural Trade in World History.* Cambridge: Cambridge University Press.
De Gregori, Thomas R. 1987. "Resources Are Not, They Become: An Institutional Theory." *Journal of Economic Issues* 21:1241–63.
Dennell, Robin. 1983. *European Economic Prehistory: A New Approach.* London: Academic Press.
Fogel, Robert W.; Engerman, Stanley C.; Floud, Roderick; Friedman, Gerald; Margo, Robert A.; Sokoloff, Kenneth; Steckel, Richard H.; Trussell, T. James; Villaflor, Georgia; and Wachter, Kenneth W. 1983. "Secular Changes in American and British Stature and Nutrition." *Journal of Interdisciplinary History* 14:445–81.
Fourastie, Jean, and Schneider, Jan. 1989. *Warum die Preise sinken? Produktivität und Kaufkraft seit dem Mittelalter.* Frankfurt: Campus.
Freudenberger, Herman. 1974. "Das Arbeitsjahr." In *Wirtschaftliche und soziale Strukturen im säkularen Wandel,* ed. Ingomar Bog, Günter Franz, Karl-Heinrich Kaufhold, Herrmann Kellenbenz, and Wolfgang Zorn, 307–20. Hannover: M. und H. Schaper.
Freudenberger, Herman, and Cummins, Gaylord. 1976. "Health, Work, and Leisure before the Industrial Revolution." *Explorations in Economic History* 13:1–12.
Gallman, Robert E. 1986. "The United States Capital Stock in the Nineteenth Century." In *Long Term Factors in American Economic Growth,* ed. Stanley L. Engerman and Robert E. Gallman, 165–212. Chicago: University of Chicago Press.
Georgescu-Roegen, Nicholas. 1976. *Energy and Economic Myths.* New York: Pergamon.
Graff, Harvey J. 1987. *The Legacies of Literature.* Bloomington: Indiana University Press.
Greenberg, Dolores. 1982. "Reassessing the Power Patterns of the Industrial Revolution: An Anglo-American Comparison." *American History Review* 88:1237–61.
Hayami, Yujiro, and Ruttan, Vernon W. 1985. *Agricultural Development: An International Perspective.* Baltimore: John Hopkins University Press.
Hesse, Günter. 1982. *Die Entstehung industrialisierter Volkswirtschaften: Ein Beitrag zur theoretischen und empirischen Analyse der langfristigen wirtschaftlichen Entwicklung.* Tübingen: Mohr.
Hesse, Günter. 1984. "Industrialisierung in tropischen Regionen." In *Folgekosten von Entwicklungsprojekten Probleme und Konsequenzen für eine effizientere Entwicklungspolitik,* ed. W. A. S. Koch, 33–103. Berlin: Duncker und Humblot.
Hesse, Günter. 1986. "Liberale Wirtschaftspolitik im evolutorischen Prozess." In *Liberalismus im Kreuzfeuer,* ed. H. G. Nutzinger, 79–102. Frankfurt: Knecht.
Hesse, Günter. 1987a. "Innovationen und Restriktionen: Zum Ansatz der Theorie der langfristigen wirtschaftlichen Entwicklung." In *Markt und Wettbewerb,* ed. M. Borchert, U. Fehl, and P. Oberender, 195–226. Bern: Haupt.
Hesse, Günter. 1987b. *Intensivierung der Landnutzung und Arbeitsproduktivität.* Münster: DVV.
Hesse, Günter. 1988. "Innovative Anpassung." University of Würzburg. Typescript.
Hesse, Günter. 1989. "Die frühe Phase der Industrialisierung in der Theorie der langfristigen wirtschaftlichen Entwicklung." In *Landwirtschaft und industrielle Entwicklung,* ed. T. Pierenkämper, 139–59. Stuttgart: Steiner.

Heuß, Ernst. 1965. *Allgemeine Markttheorie*. Tübingen: Mohr.
Holliday, R. H. 1976. "The Efficiency of Solar Energy Conversion by the Whole Crop." In *Food Production and Consumption*, ed. A. N. Duckham, I. G. W. Jones, and E. H. Roberts, 127–45. Amsterdam: North-Holland.
Humphrey, W. S., and Stanislaw, J. A. 1979. "Economic Growth and Energy Consumption in the United Kingdom: 1700–1975." *Energy Policy* 7:29–42.
International Bank for Reconstruction and Development (IBRD). 1974. *World Development Report 1974*. Washington, D.C.: IRBD.
IBRD. 1984. *World Development Report 1984*. Washington, D.C.: IRBD.
IBRD. 1985. *World Development Report 1985*. Washington, D.C.: IBRD.
IBRD. 1987. *World Development Report 1987*. Washington, D.C.: IBRD.
Jones, Eric L. 1988. *Growth Recurring*. Oxford: Clarendon Press.
Kanefsky, John W. 1980. "Steam Engines in 18th Century Britain: A Quantitative Assessment." *Technology and Culture* 21 (2): 161–86.
Komlos, John. 1985. "Stature and Nutrition in the Habsburg Monarchy." *American Historical Review* 90:1149–61.
Kravis, Irving B. 1976. "A Survey of International Comparisons of Productivity." *Economic Journal* 86:1–44.
Kunter, Manfred. 1984. "Zur Anthropologie der frühmittelalterlichen Bevölkerung Hessens." In *Hessen im Frühmittelalter*, ed. H. Roth and E. Wamers, 74–78. Sigmaringen: Thorbecke.
Kuznets, Simon. 1966. *Modern Economic Growth*. New Haven: Yale University Press.
Kuznets, Simon. 1971. *Economic Growth of Nations: Total Output and Production Structure*. Cambridge, Mass.: Harvard University Press.
Law, John. [1705] 1966. *Money and Trade Considered with a Proposal for Supplying the Nation With Money*. New York: Sentry Press.
Leach, G. L. 1976. "Industrial Energy in Human Food Chains." In *Food Production and Consumption*, ed. A. N. Duckham, 371–82. Amsterdam: North-Holland.
Lewis, Arthur W. 1976. "The Diffusion of Development." In *The Market and the State: Essays in Honor of Adam Smith*, ed. Th. Wilson and A. S. Skinner, 135–63. Oxford: Clarendon Press.
Lindert, Peter H., and Williamson, Jeffrey G. 1983. "English Worker's Living Standards during the Industrial Revolution: A New Look." *Economic History Review* 36 (1): 1–25.
Loschky, D. 1980. "Seven Centuries of Real Income per Wage Earner Reconsidered." *Economica* 47:185–88.
Manley, Gordon. 1974. "Central England Temperatures: Monthly Means, 1659–1973." *Quarterly Journal of the Royal Meteorological Society* 100:389–405.
Mendels, Franklin F. 1972. "Proto-Industrialization: The First Phases of the Industrialization Process." *Journal of Economic History* 32:241–61.
Mokyr, Joel. 1988. "Is There Still Life in the Pessimist Case? Consumption during the Industrial Revolution, 1790–1850." *Journal of Economic History* 48:69–92.
Müller, J. 1924. *Der Geburtenrückgang*. Jena: Fischer.
Müller, J. 1927. "Geburtenrückgang." In *Handwörterbuch der Staatswissenschaftten*, 4th ed, 641–47. Jena: Fischer.

Musson, Albert E. 1976. "Industrial Motive Power in the United Kingdom, 1800–1870." *Economic History Review* 24:415–39.
National Accounts Statistics 1988. New York: United Nations.
Nebel, Adolf. 1909. *Die ländlichen Arbeitsverhältnisse in Kurhessen.* Fulda: Actiendruckerei.
Odum, Eugene P. 1983. *Grundlagen der Ökologie.* Bd. 1, Stuttgart: Thieme.
Olsson, Ulf. 1986. "Recent Research in Sweden on the Standard of Living during the Eighteenth and Nineteenth Centuries." *Economic History Review* 34:153–59.
Perkins, Dwight H. 1969. *Agricultural Development in China 1368–1968.* Baltimore: John Hopkins University Press.
Phelps-Brown, Henry, and Hopkins, Sheila. 1981. *Perspectives of Wages and Prices.* New York: Methuen.
Pöppel, Ernst. 1971. "Oscillations as a Possible Basis for Time Perception." *Studium Generale* 24:85–107.
Pöppel, Ernst. 1985. *Grenzen des Bewußtseins.* Munich: Deutsche Verlagsanstalt.
Pöppel, Ernst. 1988. "Taxonomie des Subjektiven auf der Grundlage eines pragmatischen Monismus." In *Aktuelle Kernfragen in der Psychiatrie,* ed. F. Böcker and W. Weig, 24–36. Berlin: Springer.
Raychaudhuri, Tapan, and Habib, Irfan, eds. 1982. *The Cambridge Economic History of India Volume 1: 1200–1750.* Cambridge: Cambridge University Press.
Reid, D. A. 1976. "The Decline of Saint Monday, 1766–1876." *Past and Present* 71:76–101.
Ruthenberg, Hans. 1971. *Farming Systems in the Tropics.* Oxford: Clarendon Press.
Saalfeld, Diedrich. 1984. "Lebensverhältnisse der deutschen Unterschicht im 19. Jahrhundert." *International Review of Social History* 29:215–53.
Salehi-Isfahani, Djavad. 1988. "Technology and Preferences in the Boserup Model of Agricultural Growth." *Journal of Development Economics* 28:175–91.
Sahlins, Marshall. 1974. *Stone Age Economics.* Chicago: Aldine.
Schurr, Sam H.; Sonenblum, Sidney; and Wood, David O., eds. 1983. *Energy, Productivity, and Economic Growth.* Cambridge, Mass.: Oelgeschlager, Gunn and Hain.
Schwarz, L. D. 1985. "The Standard of Living in the Long Run: London 1700–1860." *Economic History Review* 38 (1): 24–41.
Slicher van Bath, Bernard H. 1963. *The Agrarian History of Western Europe 500–1850.* London: Arnold.
Smith, Adam. [1776] 1963. *An Inquiry into the Nature and the Causes of the Wealth of Nations.* Reprint. New York: Random House.
Stanhill, G., ed. 1984. *Energy and Agriculture.* Berlin: Springer.
Thomas, Keith. 1964. "Work and Leisure." *Past and Present* 29:50–66.
Thornton, Russel. 1987. *American Indian Holocaust and Survival: A Population History since 1492.* Norman: University of Oklahoma Press.
Thünen, Johann Heinrich von. 1842. *Der isolierte Staat in Beziehung auf Landwirtschaft und Nationalökonomie.* Rostock: Wiegandt, Hempel und Paren.
Tranter, N. L. 1981. "The Labour Supply, 1780–1860." In *The Economic History of Britain since 1700,* ed. R. Floud and D. McCloskey, 1:204–26. Cambridge: Cambridge University Press.

Wagner, Adolph. 1870. *Die Abschaffung des privaten Grundeigentums*. Leipzig: Duncker und Humblot.
Walter, H., and Lieth, H. 1967. *Klimadiagramm—Weltatlas*. Jena: Fischer.
Weber-Kellermann, Ingeborg. 1987. *Landleben im 19. Jahrhundert*. Munich: Beck.
Winterhalder, Bruce, and Smith, Eric, eds. 1981. *Hunter-Gatherer Foraging Strategies*. Chicago: University of Chicago Press.
Wrigley, Anthony E., and Schofield, R. S. 1981. *The Population History of England, 1541–1871*. London: Academic Press.

CHAPTER 7

Innovation, Cultural Evolution, and Economic Growth

Viktor Vanberg

The interrelation between innovation and economic growth is a subject so multifariously and pervasively studied that it would be presumptuous to try to summarize and discuss, within the scope of a single chapter, even the most pertinent and prominent views and conjectures that have been advanced on this subject. I certainly do not claim to make any such effort here. The purpose of this chapter is the much more limited one of drawing attention to an issue that plays a central role in N. Rosenberg's and L. E. Birdzell's argument on *How the West Grew Rich,* namely the importance for economic growth of the opportunity to experiment in technology and organization (1986, 333).[1]

The fact that *innovations,* both technological and organizational/institutional, are the principal wellspring of economic growth is well recognized (Ruttan 1978, 347). It is also widely recognized that *freedom,* based on secure rights, is an essential prerequisite for the promotion of innovation and the

---

Helpful comments and suggestions from Ulrich Witt and an anonymous referee are gratefully acknowledged.

1. The concept of economic growth is by no means free from ambiguity, and I should note at the outset that the interpretation of "growth" that underlies my argument is not necessarily the same as that used by Rosenberg and Birdzell or, for that matter, by other authors referred to here. I use the notion of economic growth in a subjectivist rather than an objectivist sense: Growth is not the augmentation of some objectively defined product or output of a community. It is, instead, whatever better satisfies the interests and wants of the human individuals who constitute the community, whatever these interests and wants may be. The objection may be raised that a consistent subjectivism is unable to speak meaningfully of growth as a socially desirable process, but can only resort to the tautology that any decision made by any individual is automatically "best" for him or her, under the circumstances. The question of whether—and, if so, in what sense—a consistent subjectivist individualism can come up with a meaningful normative criterion for the comparative evaluation of social outcomes is, indeed, a serious issue, but one that I cannot address in any detail in the present context, except for a brief discussion at the end of the third section, where a distinction is drawn between an internal and an external criterion for growth. I have, however, addressed this issue with greater care in Vanberg 1986a.

105

increase in wealth that results from it (North 1988b, 3ff). The purpose here is to take a closer look at the nature of the *experimental process* in which potentially wealth-enhancing innovations are generated and evaluated, and to examine, in particular, the characteristics that distinguish, in this regard, *organizational/institutional* experiments from those that are *technological* in the ordinary sense of the term.

The chapter is organized as follows. In the second section the concept of innovation is defined in reference to the notion of routines, in the sense of standard solutions to recurring problems of a technological or organizational/institutional nature. The third section outlines a Darwinian evolutionary interpretation of the process in which problem-solving routines change over time, an interpretation that is suggested, for instance, by F. A. Hayek's theory of cultural evolution. The fourth and fifth sections critically examine such an evolutionary interpretation with regard to the role the political-institutional environment plays in conditioning the terms of competition among potential alternative routines, and with regard to relevant differences that not only distinguish the "social-organizational dimension" of cultural evolution from the "technological dimension," but also exist between different kinds of rules and institutions. The sixth section briefly discusses some issues concerning the constitutional foundations of an innovative, open society, and a conclusion is drawn in the final section.

The Knowledge Problem, Routines, and Innovation

In his seminal paper on "The Use of Knowledge in Society" (1948), F. A. Hayek argues that the economic problem of society is, in essence, a *knowledge problem:* The problem of finding a method that not only best utilizes the knowledge dispersed among the individual members of society but also best uses their abilities of discovering and exploring new things (Hayek 1979, 190). And the solution to this problem is, as Hayek puts it, "always a voyage of exploration into the unknown, an attempt to discover new ways of doing things better than they have been done before" (1948, 101).

The phrase "exploration into the unknown" alludes to the fact that the knowledge problem involves two aspects that can be conceptually separated even though, in reality, they are largely intertwined. There is, first, the "crosssectional" problem of communicating knowledge dispersed among the multitude of contemporaneously living individuals. And there is, second, the intertemporal problem of utilizing knowledge and experience that accumulate over time as "new ways of doing things" are discovered and tried out (Hayek 1960, 27).

What we call innovation obviously involves novelty, but it is not novelty per se that constitutes innovation. It is novelty in comparison to some previously practiced standard way of doing certain things, of handling certain kinds of problems. When we call something an innovation we typically (at least implicitly) do so in reference to some existing *routine,* some standard way of dealing with a recurrent problem.[2] An innovation can be viewed as a conjectural new, and potentially superior, routine, compared to the received way of dealing with the problem in question.

With regard to technological innovations, the suggested interpretation in terms of routine solutions to recurrent problems should be quite straightforward. The "technical" instruments or devices that we call *tools* clearly serve as standard solutions to certain kinds of recurrent problems. And it seems appropriate to interpret the term *tool* in this context widely enough so as to include not only the material instruments, as such, but also the routine ways of employing them for certain kinds of tasks. In this sense, technological innovations can be viewed as conjectures for how existing tools may be improved upon or be replaced by better tools, including changes in both, in material instruments and in the standard ways in which they are employed. That a similar interpretation may also apply to organizational/institutional innovations is suggested by Hayek when he refers to rules and institutions as *social tools* (1960, 27). Rules, he argues, are like "general purpose tools" in that they are "adapted to the solution of recurring problem situations and thereby help to make the members of the society in which they prevail more effective in the pursuit of their aims" (1976, 21).[3]

To subsume technological devices and routines as well as organizational/institutional rules under the general notion of tools obviously suggests, as far as the theme of this chapter is concerned, that the mechanisms and processes by which innovations are generated and evaluated can be expected to be essentially of the same nature in both arenas, the technological as well as the institutional. This assumption apparently underlies Hayek's theory of cultural evolution, a theory according to which the "process of innovation" can best be understood as an *evolutionary* process. In the remaining sections of this chapter the evolutionary interpretation of technological and institutional innovation, as suggested by Hayek and others, will be critically exam-

---

2. "Growth depends on the introduction of innovations. Its essence is to go counter to the maintenance of routine practices" (Leibenstein 1980, 106). Nelson and Winter (1982, 41) make the notion of "innovation as deviation from routine behavior" a central ingredient of their "Evolutionary Theory of Economic Change."

3. Hayek continues: "Like a knife or a hammer they have been shaped not with a particular purpose in view but because . . . they have proved serviceable in a great variety of situations. . . . The knowledge which has given them their shape is . . . knowledge of the recurrence of certain problem situations or tasks" (1976, 21). See also Hayek 1973, 4, 113; 1979, 163.

ined, in particular with regard to the similarities and differences that exist between the technological and the organizational/institutional dimensions of cultural evolution.

Innovation and Cultural Evolution

The conceptualization of innovation in reference to routines and tools allows for a straightforward Darwinian interpretation of the process of generation and evaluation of innovations. A Darwinian theory explains change on an aggregate level, namely in the distribution of characteristics in some population, in terms of the interaction of principally two processes operating on the microlevel, that is, on the individuals that constitute the population:

(*a*) a process by which variation and novelty is constantly generated; and
(*b*) a process of systematic selection among the variants generated.

In the case of biological evolution, the change to be explained is that which takes place on the species level; process *a* concerns the genetic variation generated in the process of reproduction; and process *b* concerns the mechanism of selection that operates through differential reproductive success. In the present context, the aggregate-level phenomenon to be explained is that of technological and institutional change, and the two crucial microlevel processes are:

(*a*) the process whereby individuals, in their (separate and joined) efforts to improve their situation, experiment with potential new solutions to recurrent problems; and
(*b*) the process whereby individuals adopt, from among the multitude of conjectural solutions, those that they experience as the more successful ones.

Such a Darwinian, evolutionary interpretation of the role of innovation shifts the focus of interest away from the more spectacular but rare inventions that are the favored subject of much popular discussion on the issue, and, instead, draws attention to the steady stream of small and incremental changes that are constantly generated by innumerable individuals' efforts, separately and jointly, to cope better with the problems they are facing.[4] Human problem-solving behavior always proceeds by the method of trial and error. It constantly generates tentative solutions—new tools, new modes of behavior,

---

4. For a more detailed discussion of various issues of and contributions to an evolutionary economic perspective on innovation, see Witt 1987.

new hypotheses—that are then subjected to systematic selection (Popper 1972, 242ff.).

The central argument in Hayek's theory of cultural evolution is that "the various institutions and habits, tools and methods of doing things, which . . . constitute our inherited civilization" (1960, 62) can be understood as the cumulative result of an evolutionary trial-and-error process, an interpretation which, as Hayek points out, can be traced back to the pre-Darwinian evolutionist approach of the eighteenth-century Scottish moral philosophers.[5] The driving force behind the cumulative process of civilization is, in the Scottish philosophers' as well as in Hayek's view, the continuous experimenting of individuals who, in pursuit of their own purposes, constantly adjust to new circumstances and modify—deliberately as well as unintentionally—the ways in which they go about doing things. As, in the course of such intentional and incidental experimenting, individuals happen to find better "tools" or practices for solving recurrent problems, they will tend to retain these superior solutions and others will tend to imitate their successful innovation (Hayek 1960, 28, 32ff.).

The prospects for this experimental "process of adaptation and learning" (Hayek 1960, 40) to generate wealth-enhancing cumulative improvements in tools and routines depend, for obvious reasons, on the number of—and latitude for—independent trials, an insight that provides an essential argument for the *expediency* of liberty. The greater the number and variety of things that individuals are free to try out, the greater are, if only for statistical reasons, the chances that new, and potentially better, ways of dealing with recurrent problems in the technological as well as in the organizational/institutional arena will be discovered. The essential role of individual liberty in this perspective—independent of considerations concerning its intrinsic moral value—lies, as Hayek puts it, in leaving "room for the unforeseeable and unpredictable" (1960, 29). Whenever we are dealing with problems for which we cannot know in advance what the best solutions may be, he argues, the most promising strategy is to rely on the "independent and competitive efforts of many to induce the emergence of what we shall want when we see it" (29). And it is in this context that Hayek's (1978) argument on *competition as discovery process* has its systematic place.

The trial-and-error process of cultural evolution is "driven from behind," it "consists in the discovery of the not yet known" (Hayek 1960, 40) and, by necessity, "always leads into the unknown" (40). To speak of this open-ended

---

5. "(T)he evolutionists made it clear that civilization was the accumulated hard-earned result of trial and error; that it was the sum of experience, in part handed from generation to generation as explicit knowledge, but to a larger extent embodied in tools and institutions . . ." (Hayek, 1960, 59–60).

evolutionary process in terms such as *cumulative growth* or *improvement* implies, of course, a value judgement. Potential criteria for such judgement fall basically into two categories that I distinguish here as *internal* and *external*. The latter category includes criteria that are conceptually separate from—and can be determined independently of—the evaluations of the individuals themselves who are involved in the process under study. An internal criterion, by contrast, is one that is defined precisely in terms of those evaluations. It is such an internal criterion that is implied when the terms *growth* and *improvement* are used in this chapter. And, though Hayek is not entirely unambiguous about it (Vanberg 1986b), it is such a criterion that is systematically most consistent with his concept of cultural evolution as a process in which individuals, by their very choices of adopting or not adopting, of imitating or not imitating, particular practices constantly select among the various alternatives that are tried out—by themselves as well as others—those which to them, at any given time and measured against whatever purposes and interests they pursue, appear to be the most advantageous ones.

What has been defined here as an internal criterion for growth and improvement in the evolutionary process is in need of further clarification in several regards. First, it needs to take into account that the constraints—in particular those embodied in the institutional framework—under which individuals are able to choose, critically condition the dynamics of the process. This aspect will be discussed in more detail in the next section. Second, in situations in which relevant externalities—generalized Prisoner's Dilemma problems or public good problems—are involved, separate individual choices of preferred alternatives do not produce an aggregate outcome that qualifies as "improvement" in the individuals' own terms of evaluation. The externality issue points to the need to extend the analysis to the level of constitutional choice, the choice among alternative rules for dealing with the externality problem (Vanberg 1986a, 123ff.). Some aspects of this issue will be discussed in subsequent sections. Further, it may be questioned whether the suggested internal criterion for improvement can be meaningfully applied if the individuals' standard of evaluation are themselves subject to change in the course of the evolutionary process. That such change of evaluative standards occurs seems to be an unquestionable fact. Yet, this does not mean that some external standard could or ought to be invoked that transcends the individuals' own and changing standards. It means that human evaluations are an inextricable part of the dynamics and the open-ended nature of the process of evolutionary change. For any point in this process the question can be meaningfully asked of which ones among feasible alternatives the individuals involved may prefer and what, in this sense, constitutes improvement or growth. Yet there is no meaningful way in which we could step out of this process and ask whether individuals living today would have been "happier" living in some earlier stage, or vice versa (Hayek 1960, 41). Such alternatives simply do not present themselves as meaningful objects of choice.

Economic Experiments and Western Growth

The explanation that Rosenberg and Birdzell propose for "how the West grew rich" fits very well the evolutionary interpretation of the process of innovation and economic growth that I have outlined. At the same time, their explanation makes apparent that, in order for such an evolutionary dynamics of cumulative growth to operate, certain preconditions are required that by no means can be assumed to be universally given. In this sense, the arguments of the previous section need to be qualified, and it is the purpose of the present and the following section to discuss some relevant qualifications.

As my discussion suggests, the wealth-creating qualities of the process of cultural evolution will critically depend on two conditions, namely:

(a) whether potentially wealth-enhancing innovations can be and are likely to be tried out; and
(b) whether the mechanism of selective retention reliably operates as an error-eliminating mechanism, that is, that it reliably selects *against* less efficient practices (tools, routines) and *for* wealth-increasing practices.

From this, two obvious conclusions follow. First, circumstances that tend to decrease the number and variety of things that are tried out—either by limiting the range of what *may be* tried out and/or by reducing the incentives for such trials—will tend to reduce the wealth-creating dynamics of the process, and vice versa.[6] Second, circumstances that tend to decrease the reliability of the selection mechanism will also tend to decrease the wealth-enhancing potential of the evolutionary process, and vice versa.

These two principles should be expected to be of crucial importance in any attempt to understand observed differences in economic growth between different economies as well as intertemporal changes in their wealth-creating potential. It is precisely these two principles that play a central role in the analysis of Rosenberg and Birdzell. Summarizing the thrust of their argument, they state:

> Our general conclusion is that the underlying source of the West's ability to attract the lightning of economic revolutions was a unique use of

---
6. This conclusion is, to be sure, subject to the previously mentioned qualifications regarding externality. For a more detailed discussion, see Witt 1987.

experiment in technology and organization to harness resources to the satisfaction of human wants. The key elements of the system were the wide diffusion of the authority and resources necessary to experiment; an absence of more than rudimentary political and religious restrictions on experiment; and incentives which combine ample rewards for success, defined as the widespread economic use of the results of experiments, with a risk of severe penalties for failing to experiment. (1986, 33)

Alluding to the evolutionary analogy, they add: "This diversity in the forms of economic life, like the diversity of biosystems, is important not for its own sake but because it is an earmark of successful adaptation and full utilization of the resources available. The thematic terms are thus *autonomy, experiment,* and *diversity*" (33).

The most fundamental problem in the environmental conditioning of the wealth-creating potential of the process of evolutionary change results from the fact that, in order for economic activity and trade to extend beyond the narrowly confined networks of personal relations and transactions that can be informally or spontaneously monitored, the organized enforcement apparatus of the *state* becomes a necessity. This fact poses a fundamental problem because, as D. C. North puts it, "while such a state is a necessary condition for realizing the gains from trade, it obviously is not sufficient. With a state inevitably comes a struggle to control it in the interests of one of the parties" (1987, 425). Because of the systematic change that occurs in the transition from the close networks of personal exchange to the open, extended networks of impersonal exchange we cannot assume, North points out, a smooth evolutionary process to automatically "develop more and more complex institutions that will enable us to handle more complex interdependence. . . . The rise of impersonal rules and contracts means the rise of the state and with it an unequal distribution of coercive power" (1987, 421). This situation provides obvious opportunities for—and, therefore, invites attempts to—using the coercive apparatus of government to secure differential advantages at the expense of the overall wealth-creating potential of the system.[7]

Fundamental and essential aspects of the environment in which the process of cultural evolution unwinds are shaped by political forces.[8] These forces can never extinguish human individuals' inventiveness and their endeavor to improve their situation.[9] Nor can they prevent the incessant com-

---

7. The various issues that arise in this context are the subject of the growing literature on rent seeking. For a survey, see Tollison 1982.

8. "What distinguishes humans from animals is that the political decision processes are a feedback loop in the chain by which to alter (but not eliminate) the essential characteristics of the competitive-evolutionary process" (North 1988a, 26).

9. As Adam Ferguson put it in his 1767 "Essay on the History of Civil Society" (1980, 6): "[Man] . . . is destined, from the first age of his being, to invent and contrive. He applies the

petition for scarce resources. But they can discourage the willingness to try out new things, they can condition the directions that the endeavor to improve one's lot will take, and they can mold the terms and the form of competition. In other words, the politically controlled framework conditions can induce wealth-creating as well as wealth-destroying competition, they can promote or impede the wealth-increasing potential of the competitive evolutionary process. Or, in the terminology of game theory, it will critically depend on the nature of the political environment to what extent the socioeconomic game will have the characteristics of a positive-sum, rather than a zero-sum or negative-sum game.[10]

In Rosenberg's and Birdzell's analysis of the particular historical constellation of circumstances that allowed the West to organize the socioeconomic game as a positive-sum game and to grow rich, the recurrent themes are diffusion of authority and decentralization. As the crucial ingredients of Western growth, they cite the "breakdown and diffusion of political and religious authority in postfeudal Europe" (1986, 261), the "overall decentralization of authority in Western societies" (326), the "division of political authority" (265), and the "fragmentation of Europe into a multitude of states and principalities" (136), into "individual centers of competing political power" (137). These political framework conditions—this is the basic thrust of their argument—allowed for the competition among a multiplicity of independent decision centers that is the crucial ingredient for economic growth. It is a source of diversity in experiments and it is a mechanism of error elimination, a mechanism that induces as well as disciplines innovation, that generates and selects upon a variety of trials (272, 276).

It is worth mentioning that Rosenberg's and Birdzell's argument on the role of competition among multiple, independent decision centers for Western economic growth is not only confirmed by such studies as E. L. Jones' *The European Miracle* (1987), but is also paralleled by arguments that have been made on the role of competition in the development of Western law and science. The core argument of Jones's study is that one of the "prime conditions of growth and development" in Europe has been a "competitive political arena" (1987, xxxi). "Political decentralization and competition" (xxx), the "competitive nature of the states system" (45) provided, as Jones argues, for protection from arbitrary government and for a freedom of movement among political units that made the development and diffusion of ideas, technology, and economic activity relatively independent from obstacles faced in any one

---

same talents to a variety of purposes, and acts nearly the same part in very different scenes. He would be always improving on his subject, and he carries this intention where-ever he moves, through the streets of the populous city, or the wilds of the forest."

10. From a subjectivist standpoint, the terms *zero-sum* and *positive-* or *negative-sum* can be used to mark the distinction between "games" that do and do not allow for mutual improvement of the players involved. This distinction can be made without the need to sum up payoffs.

nation-state: "The multicell system possessed a built-in ability to replace its local losses, a vigorous recombination, regrowth, or substitution effect" (124).

In his much acclaimed study on the Western legal tradition, H. J. Berman cites the "coexistence and competition within the same community of diverse jurisdictions and diverse legal systems' as "[p]erhaps the most distinctive characteristic of the Western legal tradition" (1983, 10). And he suggests that this "plurality of jurisdictions and legal systems," the "pluralism of Western law," has been a crucial "source of freedom" and a "source of development, or growth—legal growth as well as political and economic growth" (10). And, emphasizing the structural similarities between the process of economic growth and the growth of scientific knowledge, Albert (1987, 157ff.) argues that the *"institutionalization of competition and critique"* has been the crucial ingredient for the unique Western development. In science no less than in the economic sphere it is, as Albert says, the disciplining force of competition that is essential for cumulative growth.

Institutional Experiments

The preceding discussion of the role of the political-institutional framework in conditioning the competitive evolutionary process raises the general question of how the process of institutional innovation and change itself can best be understood. The "rules as tools" analogy emphasized in Hayek's theory of cultural evolution seems to suggest that the dynamics of trial and error are ultimately the same for both, technological as well as organizational/institutional change. More precisely, this analogy makes it appear as if the experimenting with and selecting among potential alternatives is essentially a matter of separate individual choices in both cases, for tools as well as for rules.

Whether such a notion of individualized experimenting and selecting is applicable to the technological realm in general may be a debatable issue in itself, but it can be left aside here. It seems obvious, however, that it is not generally applicable in the realm of rules and institutions. Certainly, there are rules for which an individualized process of innovation and change can be imagined. This is apparently true for rules that Hayek calls "voluntary rules" and about which he says: "It is this flexibility of voluntary rules which . . . makes gradual evolution and spontaneous growth possible, which allows further experience to lead to modifications and improvements. Such evolution is possible only with rules which . . . can be broken by individuals who feel that they have strong enough reasons to brave the censure of their fellows" (1960, 63). For such rules one can imagine an experimental process in which individuals try out new forms of conduct, and a selection process in which individuals choose to imitate or not imitate, to adopt or not adopt new practices, dependent on perceived benefits.[11]

However, there are other kinds of rules for which such flexibility cannot be assumed to exist to the same extent, or at all. To mention only two particular obvious examples: It is hardly possible for an individual driver to experiment with a "left-driving rule" in a community where driving on the right side of the road is the rule; and it is simply unfeasible for an individual citizen to try out a new rule for electing a parliament—even if such individuals would firmly believe in the superiority of an alternative practice.

Where rules can, indeed, be tried out and selected upon in an individualized, trial-and-error fashion, we have reasons to expect the kind of cumulative evolutionary growth I described previously. Where such individualized trial and error is unfeasible, some experimental evolutionary dynamics may still be at work. However, this cannot simply be postulated. A separate argument would be needed, specifying the particular working properties of the supposed evolutionary process. Without such specification, no conclusions can be legitimately drawn concerning the cumulative nature of its results. That more cautious reasoning is, indeed, warranted with regard to processes that lie beyond the realm of strictly individualized trial and error is recognized by Hayek. Immediately following his remarks on "voluntary rules," Hayek acknowledges that the situation is different with "rules which can be changed only discontinuously and for all at the same time."[12] Yet, instead of discussing the particular characteristics that distinguish evolutionary processes on the level where rules can only be collectively experimented with, Hayek simply invokes the questionable concept of "group selection' (Vanberg 1986b).[13]

A matrix may help to facilitate discussion of some of the issues that are relevant in this context. The two dimensions reflect the different modes in which the experimenting with and the selecting among potential alternative rules can be and/or are in fact made. The distinction here is between separate individualized and collective choice, the latter mode being further distin-

---

11. Hayek obviously has such an individualized selection process in mind when he talks about "rules which have been practiced by a few and then imitated by many" (1979, 166) and when he argues that "the success of an innovation by a rule breaker" depends on the new rules obtaining "the approval of society at large . . . by gradually spreading acceptance" (1979, 167).

12. "Unlike any deliberately imposed coercive rules, which can be changed only discontinuously and for all at the same time, rules of this kind allow for gradual and experimental change. The existence of individuals and groups simultaneously observing partially different rules provides the opportunity for the selection of the more effective ones" (Hayek 1960, 63). See also 1960, 110ff. and 1979, 163.

13. Though Hayek severally refers to the problems resulting from "coercive interference in the process of cultural evolution" (1988, 20; see also 1979, 163), he does not systematically account for the role of politically orchestrated "experiments" in his theory of cultural evolution.

guished into a private and a public variety. The private-public distinction concerns the nature of the experimenting/selecting unit: public essentially means political entities (commune, state, nation), while private means any other kind of organized group (firm, club, family, etc.).[14]

What the matrix (fig. 1) is supposed to illustrate is that the modes of experimenting and of selecting can, to some extent, vary independently, and that the different combinations that are possible may have significantly different implications for the nature of the process by which institutions/rules change or evolve. As one moves from the northwestern cell (1) to the southeastern cell (9), the flexibility that Hayek attributes to voluntary rules is bound to decrease. Note that the placement of rules/institutions within this matrix is not only determined by their "nature," but is also a matter of choice. Rules that, per se, would allow for individualized or private collective experimenting (e.g., rules for personal health-care provisions, or rules for the operation of a business corporation) may well be shifted, through the political process, into the realm of public collective experimenting. The extent to which rules and practices are shifted from the individual and private collective realm into the public collective realm can be viewed as an indicator for the difference between more or less free-market, as opposed to more or less socialist regimes.

Rules for the organization of collective political decision-making processes are, by their very nature, a matter of collective public experimentation. They obviously cannot be experimented with individually. But they can be selected upon collectively as well as individually. By the decision of a political body (cell 9), by the locational choices of corporations (cell 8), or by individuals' decisions to migrate between polities (cell 7). Rules for the organization of business firms can be experimented with in a collective private fashion; and they can, again, be selected upon collectively or individually. Collectively, by a corporation's decision to adopt or not to adopt a certain organizational scheme (cell 5). Individually, by individual employees' or stockholders' decisions to join *one* rather than some *other* organizational experiment (cell 4). And, finally, rules of life-style and personal conduct allow, by their nature, for individual experimenting and selecting (cell 1).

Using A. O. Hirschman's (1970) familiar distinction, there are basically

---

14. The distinctions drawn here are not dissimilar to the distinction between internal and external institutions, suggested by Lachmann (1963). Lachmann's distinction is concerned with whether or not a change in the respective institution/rules has to be orchestrated through the political process. External institutions constitute the politically determined framework within which private experimentation takes place. This framework itself can only be altered through collective political action. Internal institutions, in contrast, are all those rules and arrangements that individuals can experiment with and innovate upon in their private capacities, within the range allowed for by the external institutions.

selecting experimenting	individual	collective private	collective public
individual	1	2	3
collective private	4	5	6
collective public	7	8	9

Fig. 1. **Institutional experiments**

two ways, *exit* and *voice,* in which individuals can respond if they are dissatisfied with a collective experiment that they participate in, be it as stockholder in a corporation, as citizens in a political entity, or as members of a sports club. The use of voice would mean an attempt to bring about change within the experiment itself, change that had to be orchestrated simultaneously for all persons involved. The use of exit would mean a withdrawal from the experiment, something that a person can do individually and separately. Whatever may be said about differences in the prospects of using the voice option in the two settings, the most obvious difference between collective private and collective public experiments lies in their respective properties regarding the exit option. The costs to an individual of switching among alternative experiments tends, in general, to be significantly higher for the latter than for the former. Collective public experiments typically have a "territorial basis," that is, any choice of participating in or withdrawing from a particular experiment has implications for one's choice of residency.[15] In simpler terms, if one wants to change between alternative experiments, say, for the organization of private clubs, all that is normally required is a change in one's membership. By comparison, if one wants to change between alternative experiments for the organization of political systems, one typically faces the necessity to migrate from one territory or jurisdiction to some other, with all the consequences that migration implies for many other aspects of a person's life.

For the reasons indicated, it is at the level of collective public experiments that the competitive evolutionary process can be least expected to

---

15. For an interesting discussion on the "territoriality of the law" with regard to the issue of an international legal order, see Schmidtchen and Schmidt-Trenz 1990.

reflect the kind of cumulative growth that may be reasonably attributed to processes closer to the northwestern corner (cell 1) of the matrix. It is at the collective public level, more than anywhere else, that proper safeguards are essential in order to secure the adaptive capacity of a trial-and-error process that is responsive to the principals', the individual citizens' wants. While constitutional provisions securing the responsiveness to voice are important, what may well be more important are provisions that allow for effective, separate, individual choice among experiments, that is, provisions that allow individuals to effectively use the exit option. And the essential method of securing low-cost exit options on this level is decentralization.[16]

Here lies, of course, the main virtue of federalism as a general principle of political organization that tends to enhance governments' responsiveness to their constituents' wants.[17]

Constitutional Foundations of an Open Society

If, as suggested in this chapter, the essence of the process of civilization—or, in less mundane terms, the process of social and economic development—lies in its *experimental* character, in its open-endedness, then a society's current and future wealth-creating potential will critically depend on its capacity for trial-and-error learning and adaptation in the technological as well as in the organizational/institutional realm. An open, "experimenting society" (Campbell 1988), one that—in terms of the matrix shown in figure 1—leaves room for experiments on the individual and private collective level, and that submits public collective experiments to the discipline of competition, such a society should promise to be a richer society, richer in terms of whatever it is that its individual members seek to achieve. If this is true, such a societal order could be expected to be agreeable and preferable to almost everybody, compared to alternative regimes. And one may wonder why historical evidence shows that the emergence and continued existence of such orders has been a rare exception, rather than the rule.

The reason for such discrepancy between what seems to be preferable and what is realized lies, here just as in many other instances, in the fact that agreement in constitutional interests—that is, agreement concerning the kind of society one would want to live in—is not a sufficient condition to bring

---

16. Hayek stresses this aspect when he argues, in reference to local government, that "people can escape exploitation by voting with their feet" (1979, 16), or, when he says about the liberals' preference for local government over central government that it is based on "a hope that competition between the different local authorities would effectively control and direct the development . . . on desirable lines" (1978, 144).

17. For a discussion of some aspects of this issue, see Wiseman 1990 and the chapter on "Open Economy, Federalism, and Taxing Authority" in Brennan and Buchanan 1980.

about the desired state of affairs. As the discussion on public goods and on generalized Prisoner's Dilemma problems has amply shown, a group of individuals can easily produce—in separate pursuit of their interests—an aggregate outcome that nobody likes. In such dilemma constellations, special measures may be necessary in order to secure the generation of what is mutually preferred. This is, in brief, the underlying rationale of the kind of *constitutional* and other constraints on the political process that appear to have been a critical ingredient of Western growth.

The problem that exists with regard to the freedom to innovate is comparable to the problem of free trade. The fact that, in a free-trade world, individual prosperity will, in general, be higher than in a world of abundant protective regulation, does not provide an incentive for special interests to abstain from seeking protection for their particular trade. In a parallel way, the fact that individuals will, in general, be wealthier in an open, experimental society than in one immobilized by pervasive restrictions on innovation, does not provide an incentive for special interests to abstain from seeking protection against innovations that would tend to devalue their particular human and physical capital. In both cases, the benefits that general openness promises can not be expected to be automatically guaranteed through the separate pursuit of individual interests. It may, and often will, require special precautionary devices implemented at the constitutional level.

As Schumpeter's classical notion of the "process of creative destruction" (1975, 83) pointedly suggests, innovations always pose a threat to vested interests. And those who are threatened are likely to resist in various ways (132). Such resistance hardly reflects a desire to live in a world without change, no more, anyway, than a thief's behavior reflects his or her desire to live in a dishonest world. It simply reflects the desire to prevent those changes that are perceived as harmful to one's special interests, a desire that is perfectly compatible with the desire to enjoy the benefits from other innovations.

Conclusion

As Rosenberg and Birdzell show in their study, an essential clue to the West's capacity to grow rich has been its capability to overcome "the formidable social forces opposed to change, growth, and innovation" (1986, 24). And they emphasize, in this context again, the central relevance of decentralization and diffusion of authority for the West's past success (1986, 30, 265) as well as for its prospects of future prosperity (1986, 138, 334). If there is one conclusion that is singularly supported by the historical evidence of Western development and by the general arguments discussed above, it is the insoluble interconnection between growth and decentralization. In the words of Rosenberg and Birdzell (1986, 267): "It is evident that there is no way to imitate the

Western organization of innovation without also imitating the Western decentralization of enterprise, with the authority to make economic decisions diffused into a multitude of enterprises of diverse size, ownership, internal structure, objectives, and situs."

REFERENCES

Albert, Hans. 1987. *Kritik der reinen Erkenntnislehre.* Tübingen: J. C. B. Mohr.
Berman, Harold J. 1983. *Law and Revolution: The Formation of the Western Legal Tradition.* Cambridge, Mass.: Harvard University Press.
Brennan, Geoffrey, and Buchanan, James M. 1980. *The Power to Tax: Analytical Foundations of a Fiscal Constitution.* Cambridge: Cambridge University Press.
Campbell, Donald T. 1988. "The Experimenting Society." In *Methodology and Epistemology for Social Science: Selected Papers.* Chicago: University of Chicago Press.
Ferguson, Adam. [1767] 1980. *An Essay on the History of Civil Society.* Reprint. New Brunswick, N.J.: Transaction Books.
Hayek, F. A. 1948. "The Use of Knowledge in Society." In *Individualism and Economic Order,* 77–91. Chicago: University of Chicago Press.
Hayek, F. A. 1960. *The Constitution of Liberty.* Chicago: University of Chicago Press.
Hayek, F. A. 1973. *Law, Legislation, and Liberty.* Vol. 1, *Rules and Order.* London: Routledge and Kegan Paul.
Hayek, F. A. 1976. *Law, Legislation, and Liberty.* Vol. 2, *The Mirage of Social Justice.* London: Routledge and Kegan Paul.
Hayek, F. A. 1978. "Competition as a Discovery Process." In *New Studies in Philosophy, Politics, Economics, and the History of Ideas,* 179–90. Chicago: University of Chicago Press.
Hayek, F. A. 1979. *Law, Legislation, and Liberty.* Vol. 3, *The Political Order of a Free People.* London: Routledge and Kegan Paul.
Hayek, F. A. 1988. *The Fatal Conceit: The Errors of Socialism.* London: Routledge and Kegan Paul.
Hirschman, Albert O. 1970. *Exit, Voice, and Loyalty: Responses to Decline in Firms, Organizations, and States.* Cambridge, Mass.: Harvard University Press.
Jones, E. L. 1987. *The European Miracle: Environments, Economies, and Geopolitics in the History of Europe and Asia.* 2d ed. Cambridge: Cambridge University Press.
Lachmann, Ludwig. 1963. "Wirtschaftsordnung und wirtschaftliche Institutionen." *ORDO* 14:63–77.
Leibenstein, Harvey. 1980. "Microeconomics and X-Efficiency Theory: If There Is No Crisis, There Ought to Be." *Public Interest* Special Issue, *The Crisis in Economic Theory:* 97–110.
Nelson, Richard R., and Winter, Sidney G. 1982. *An Evolutionary Theory of Economic Change.* Cambridge, Mass.: Harvard University Press.

North, Douglass C. 1987. "Institutions, Transaction Costs, and Economic Growth." *Economic Inquiry* 25:419–28.
North, Douglass C. 1988a. "Ideology and Political/Economic Institutions." *Cato Journal* 8:15–28.
North, Douglass C. 1988b. "Institutions, Economic Growth, and Freedom: A Historical Introduction." In *Freedom, Democracy, and Economic Welfare*, ed. M. A. Walker, 3–25. Vancouver: The Fraser Institute.
Popper, Karl R. 1972. *Objective Knowledge: An Evolutionary Approach*. Oxford: Clarendon Press.
Rosenberg, Nathan, and Birdzell, L. E., Jr. 1986. *How the West Grew Rich: The Economic Transformation of the Industrial World*. New York: Basic Books.
Ruttan, Vernon W. 1978. "Induced Institutional Change." In *Induced Innovation*, ed. H. P. Binswanger and V. W. Ruttan, 327–57. Baltimore: Johns Hopkins University Press.
Schmidtchen, Dieter, and Hans-Jörg Schmidt-Trenz. 1990. "The Division of Labour is Limited by the Extent of the Law: A Constitutional Economics Approach to International Private Law." *Constitutional Political Economy* 1 (Fall): 49–71.
Schumpeter, Joseph A. 1975. *Capitalism, Socialism, and Democracy*. New York: Harper and Row.
Tollison, Robert D. 1982. "Rent Seeking: A Survey." *Kyklos* 35:575–602.
Vanberg, Viktor. 1986a. "Individual Choice and Institutional Constraints." *Analyse & Kritik* 8:113–49.
Vanberg, Viktor. 1986b. "Spontaneous Market Order and Social Rules: A Critical Examination of F. A. Hayek's Theory of Cultural Evolution." *Economics and Philosophy* 2:75–100.
Wiseman, Jack. 1990. "Principles of Political Economy: An Outline Proposal, Illustrated by Application to Fiscal Federalism." *Constitutional Political Economy* 1 (Winter): 101–24.
Witt, Ulrich. 1987. "How Transaction Rights Are Shaped to Channel Innovations." *Journal of Institutional and Theoretical Economics* 143:180–95.

Part 4
Conceptual Problems and Policy Implications

CHAPTER 8

Information, Transactions, and Catallaxy: Reflections on Some Key Concepts of Evolutionary Market Theory

Manfred E. Streit and Gerhard Wegner

> But let us be honest. How much more do we know about market process than Adam Smith knew that is of practical relevance?
> —J. M. Buchanan (1980)

In the present chapter, we argue that the acquisition and diffusion of information relevant to market transactions represent a theoretical challenge that cannot be properly answered within the framework of Walrasian equilibrium theory. As a first step, it is useful to refer to early theoretical insights provided by Hayek in his criticism of equilibrium theory. His criticism is information oriented. From this perspective, the market process has to be considered as a process of communication, and competition is a procedure to discover knowledge dispersed among individual agents and to test its economic relevance. Which knowledge will be discovered and used successfully is unpredictable. Furthermore, under evolutionary conditions, knowledge in society cannot be considered as a given stock. In view of human inventiveness, knowledge must be treated instead as ever-changing in an unpredictable way.

Hayek's criticism has induced us to tackle the problem of the discovery and use of knowledge in a market system by reconsidering transaction costs. Applying an informational concept of transaction costs similar to that developed by Coase, the limitations of equilibrium theory can be further substantiated. And it is possible to show that these limitations are fundamental. They cannot be overcome by simply extending the basic method of analysis without reducing the problem of knowledge in a totally inadequate way. Equally, transaction costs lend themselves to a better understanding of Hayek's argument that the economic order that is permanently established through market

---

We would like to thank P. Golz, H. Lohmann, and H. Wenzel for helpful criticism and suggestions.

transactions must be considered as an unplanned or spontaneous order that differs fundamentally from a planned order or organization. And we hope to strengthen Hayek's argument that the most important deficiency of equilibrium theory consists in its treating the market system, analytically, like a planned order.

An Unanswered Theoretical Challenge

Although Walrasian equilibrium theory has become firmly established as the centerpiece of neoclassical, mainstream economics, in some branches of economic thinking evolutionary concepts continue to receive analytical attention. This is particularly true of the so-called Austrian school.[1] It was mainly Hayek who challenged the Walrasian equilibrium and welfare theory by stressing the problem of information in coordinating decentralized decisions among specialized economic agents under evolutionary conditions. However, his challenge of the 1930s was not taken up. Even where it was considered, only lip service was paid to his concept of "competition as a discovery procedure," and the theoretical intricacies involved were not investigated.

Equilibrium and Evolution

As Hayek argued (1937), the basic idea of the general equilibrium model was to reconstruct the allocation process, given the conditions of supply and demand in all markets. In this way, it became possible to ensure the stability properties of the equilibrium model. Individual preferences, factor endowments, and production functions were treated as data to which allocational adjustments were required. This also allowed one to define the task of welfare theory, namely to analyze the quality of adjustment through the market process to the exogenously defined economic circumstances when judged by the stationary criterion of Pareto efficiency.

---

1. Lachmann and Kirzner in particular encouraged new evolutionary approaches like those of O'Driscoll, Rizzo and Langlois. However, whereas Lachmann departed to a large extent from general equilibrium theory, these new approaches are still in line with the equilibrium-oriented tradition going back to Mises (e.g., the corresponding contributions to Kirzner 1986, particularly the critical analysis by Fehl in the same volume).

The uneasiness about the way in which mainstream economics tends to ignore or reduce evolutionary problems has also been frequently and trenchantly expressed by Boulding (1981) and Georgescu-Roegen (1976), but their criticisms and suggestions did not stir up much curiosity among younger U.S. economists.

Among German economists, evolutionary thinking has received considerable attention. This is particularly due to efforts by Röpke (1977), Fehl (1983), Blaseio (1986), Hutter (1989), and Witt (1992) as well as by authors of the ordo-liberal school of thinking like Heuß (1965), Krüsselberg (1969) and Hoppmann (1980).

Given the basic idea of the general equilibrium model, Hayek was able to show that the combinations of prices and quantities that characterize a general equilibrium have to be considered as periodically reproducible. In equilibrium, the economic plans of all market participants are mutually consistent. Hence, the economic agents have no incentive to revise their plans. Under these conditions, it is only possible to initiate changes in the pattern of allocation by introducing exogenous shocks that, in turn, would require an adjustment to a new equilibrium.

The important feature of this familiar kind of reasoning is that the pattern of allocation is not considered temporary or transient from the outset. Thus, changes in the pattern must be explained by exogenous shocks that, by definition, remain unexplained. Hayek rejected this view because, he argued, the process of coordination through competitive market actions itself contains a capacity to generate shocks that are reflected in a change in the pattern of allocation. The reorientation away from the neoclassical theory of competition that is necessary to cope with this problem has been described by Hayek (1978, 181) as follows: ". . . economic theory sometimes appears at the outset to bar its way to a true appreciation of the character of the process of competition, because it starts from the assumption of the 'given' supply of scarce goods. But which goods are scarce goods, or which things are goods, and how scarce or valuable they are—these are precisely the things which competition has to discover."

Information and Coordination

With regard to the question of knowledge, for a formal proof of the existence of a general equilibrium it is crucial to assume that the economic agents are perfectly informed about their own preferences as well as about the market prices for all those goods that enter their preference function. Under these knowledge conditions and by assuming maximizing behavior, it becomes theoretically possible to construct plans of production and exchange that are mutually consistent and conform to the economically relevant data. The assumption of perfect knowledge is subject to a quite common criticism. However, this kind of criticism can be answered by introducing imperfect knowledge without giving up the basic concept.

Such a response is not possible in the case of Hayek's objection to the knowledge assumption, which went far beyond a simple criticism of assumptions. He did not conceive imperfect information as a deviation from an ideal situation. For him, imperfect information was endemic to the exchange system that results from a division of labor between autonomous economic agents. It must be considered as a starting point when developing an explanatory model and not as a special case among other extensions of a basic model. The latter applies to equilibrium theory, where it is, in fact, a systematic necessity. Given its analytical structure, the information problem can only be introduced as a deviation from the initially ideal situation of perfect information.

Coordination through market transactions as conceived by Hayek not only reflects a division of labor, but also a "division of knowledge" (1937, 49). Imperfect information has to be considered as a concomitant of the division of labor and not as an obstacle to it that can be removed in a thought experiment without giving up a salient feature of the object of analytical inquiry. From an informational point of view, market processes reflect a communicative interaction of individuals based on their own personal knowledge, the sum of which will never be given to anyone in its totality. This implies a view of the information problem that differs irreconcilably from equilibrium theory. To quote Hayek again:

> The problem is thus in no way solved if we can show that all the facts, if they were known to a single mind (as we hypothetically assume them to be given to the observing economist), would uniquely determine the solution; instead, we must show how a solution is produced by the interactions of people each of whom possesses only partial knowledge. To assume all the knowledge to be given to a single mind in the same manner in which we assume it to be given to us as the explaining economists is to assume the problem away. . . . (1945, 530)

Hayek's challenge implied an uncompromising denial of general equilibrium theory as a theory explaining the coordination of decentralized, autonomous, economic decision making. The fundamental difference between his view of the market process and the view implied by equilibrium theory is the way in which the result of the coordination of decentralized economic decisions (the pattern of allocation or the economic order) is brought about. The attempt by equilibrium theory to show what the pattern would be if all the relevant facts were known to a single mind means that no distinction is made between

—the problem of how an individual agent should coordinate his or her economic activities efficiently, and
—the problem of how the economic activities of autonomous individual agents are coordinated through market transactions.[2]

---

2. It is possible to modify this objection somewhat by emphasizing that neoclassical theory makes no serious effort to demonstrate how consistency of individual plans is brought about. Neoclassical modeling always requires an assumption of prior consistency among equilibrium plans. If this assumption is made, the knowledge problem is abstracted irrespective of how

The first problem is clearly a problem of an agent who tries to develop a design or plan that allows him or her to coordinate his or her own economic activities according to his or her individual objectives. And it is characteristic of the neoclassical equilibrium approach that the second problem is also solved as a problem of organization, as if the equilibrium resulted from human actions executed according to a human design that embraces all the objectives (the welfare function) and the economic activities of the individual agents. Hayek, however, denies that the same concept of order is applicable in both cases. Taking up a classical concept, he argues that the allocation patterns produced by the market process are, in fact, "the result of human action, but not the execution of any human design" (Hayek 1967, 96).

The neglect of a conceptual difference between the organization as a source of order governing individual action and "catallaxy" as a spontaneous order or self-coordinating system governing the allocation pattern of a market economy can also be observed in welfare economics.[3] Applying the organizational concept to a market system in order to derive Pareto optima and comparing the results with allocational features of real economies, it became possible to identify a plethora of cases of market failure. And since the information problem was also abstracted when considering government action, it became equally possible to devise interventions that could remove the identified deficiencies of the market process.

Transaction Costs and Catallaxy

More recently, neoclassical welfare economics has been assessed with respect to its implied market theory from a point of view that may appear unrelated to Hayek's problem of knowledge. Here, the focus has been on the costs incurred when carrying out market transactions and their consequences for matching supply and demand. Ultimately, Coase and Demsetz were aiming at an assessment of those cases of market failure that had been established by applying Pigouvian welfare economics, which neglects transaction costs.[4] The assessment led to diverging theoretical results and to an attack on neo-

---

sophisticated the model itself may be. The whole exercise is reduced to a logical problem that can only be solved because it is set up as if all relevant information were accessible to a single mind. The market process, as a process of self-coordination based on limited subjective knowledge, is excluded by assumption.

3. Hayek (1976, 109) uses the term *catallaxy* "to describe the order brought about by the mutual adjustment of many individual economies in a market." The adjustment itself is brought about by the acquisition and competitive use of partial individual knowledge through the price mechanism. To quote Hayek again: ". . . the price mechanism operates as a medium of communicating knowledge which brings it about that the facts which become known to some, through the effects of their actions on prices, are made to influence the decision of others" (125).

4. See Coase 1960; Demsetz 1964, 1968, and 1969. For a circumspect presentation of the theory of property rights, cf. Krüsselberg 1983.

classical welfare economics. The attack was no doubt as vigorous as Hayek's criticism, but it was more readily accepted.

It may have been easier to accept the criticism by the Chicago school because it did not question general equilibrium theory as such. Rather, it was presented as an extension of neoclassical microeconomics where the costs of market transactions were integrated into partial equilibrium models. The neoclassical approach remained basically untouched. On the other hand, criticism by the Austrian school stressed the necessity for a "theory of complex phenomena" (Hayek 1967) to avoid determinism and to allow a genuine theory of catallaxy as a source of order in an evolutionary context.[5]

It will be our central purpose to show that the Chicago criticism leaves a lot of the analytical potential of the transaction costs approach unexploited because of its equilibrium bias. If the consequences of transaction costs for allocation are examined without prior limitations associated with the problem of knowledge, it becomes evident that the equilibrium model involves inadequate abstractions. Their removal promises to provide elements for a basis from which an evolutionary market theory could be developed.

Transaction Costs, Equilibrium, and Evolution

As a first step in our analysis, it is useful to introduce the concept of transaction costs. So far, it seems that no general convention concerning the content and analytical use of such a concept has been established. As we will show in due course, this is at least partly a consequence of efforts to mold the concept in a way that fits the general equilibrium approach. In the following discussion, we concentrate on transaction costs that reflect a use of resources to coordinate allocation through the market process. Coordination costs within organizations (such as firms) will not be analyzed. However, this does not mean that the possibility of substituting organization costs for those of market transactions (Coase 1960; Williamson 1975) is considered to be irrelevant from the point of view of acquisition and exchange of information.

Sunk Costs of Market Transactions

From an institutional point of view, market transactions involve agreements on an exchange of property rights or components of such rights. This implies that the rights and their exchange are secured. Corresponding legal protection is provided by what Lachmann (1963, 66) has defined as "external institutions." They represent an important part of the economic constitution of a

---

5. See Furubotn and Pejovich 1972, 1138, 1157.

society with a market-oriented economic system. External institutions consist mainly of legal provisions

—defining beyond doubt who can exclusively dispose of property rights,
—making contracts for the exchange of property rights enforceable, and
—setting procedural rules that allow disputes between private agents, which may arise when property rights are executed or disposed of, to be settled.

Characterizing these institutions as external to the market system emphasizes the fact that they represent a legal framework within which economic agents can operate. The provisions themselves cannot be changed by the economic agents, even if they were to agree on such a change. A change in external institutions can only be accomplished by the political process of legislation, in which economic agents can participate as private citizens and members of the electorate.

Internal institutions of the market system differ from external ones precisely in the sense that they can be developed by market participants during the process of exchanging property rights. Important internal institutions are, for example, general conditions of sale, standard contracts, product standards, and general business practices. By setting standards and modes of practice, internal institutions reduce that part of a contract that requires specific negotiations.

From an allocational point of view, the development of external as well as internal institutions incurs sunk costs. In the case of external institutions, the legal framework has the economic properties of a public infrastructure.[6] But internal institutions also have properties of public capital goods to the extent to which they can be used repeatedly throughout time. As elements of private self-regulation they frequently emerge from a widespread business practice or custom. And customs themselves represent the outcome of an evolutionary process in which rules emerge because they frequently turn out to be mutually acceptable to economic agents.[7]

---

6. An answer to the question of "How far is Vienna from Chicago?" has been attempted by Paqué (1985), who analyzes the methodology of the two schools of dogmatic liberalism. For a broader analysis, see Buchanan (1975, chap. 7); a brief characterization can be found in Streit (1987, 3ff.).

7. This leaves open the fascinating question of how rules emerge and of how the most adequate rules are selected. The question stands for a whole research program that is still far from being consolidated and cannot be discussed here. However, it should be mentioned that, so far, two general approaches are employed, an evolutionary approach in the tradition of the Scottish moral philosophers and a contractarian approach with affinity to neoclassical thinking. The first approach is closely related to Hayek's work, whereas Buchanan figures prominently in the second approach.

Sunk Transaction Costs and General Equilibrium

Sunk costs of transactions do not cause particular problems for equilibrium theory as long as they can be considered as given. However, this means that a possible demand for changing the corresponding institutions, which may develop in the course of their use, is excluded from the analysis. In the case of external institutions, such a feedback between the market process and the controlling institutions could be ignored on the grounds that changes involve the political decision process that is not part of allocation theory.

The exclusion of changes in internal institutions is more difficult to defend. Here, it is necessary to assume that the economy in question is characterized by a twofold optimum:

—an institutional optimum, in which sunk transaction costs are at a minimum and where further reductions in their level can be safely excluded,
—a Pareto optimum, which precludes the development of new objects as well as new modes of transaction.

These assumptions imply that economic agents are incapable of developing institutional and material innovations.

If these assumptions are accepted, sunk costs of transactions do not render the stability conditions of a general equilibrium invalid. It can be argued that the costs incurred when operating within a specific institutional framework will diminish over time and thus remove potential allocational distortions. Hence, the specific content of the corresponding rules and regulations can be excluded from the stability analysis of a general equilibrium. Furthermore, it is plausible to assume that given institutions may even tend to reinforce the stability of an equilibrium. This would apply if individual uncertainty about the economic consequences of an institutional framework were reduced in the process of adjustment to the framework. At the end of the adjustment process, economic behavior could be expected to be perfectly stabilized within the given institutional framework; hence it would no longer be a source of uncertainty.

If, however, the assumptions that permit an equilibrium analysis are rejected, an evolutionary theory of economic institutions can be developed. Consequently, the following questions are among those likely to be found on the corresponding research agenda.

—What exactly are the evolving regulatory properties of external and internal institutions and what is their allocational impact?
—Which economic forces can help to explain changes in internal and

external institutions and, hence, help to establish a feedback of market transactions to their institutional framework?[8]

The institutional branch of evolutionary economics will not be pursued any further here. For our purposes, it is important to keep in mind that

—investment in external and internal institutions represents sunk costs of transactions from an allocation point of view;
—the institutional framework for market transactions has an informational content in the sense of stabilizing the behavior of economic agents with the likely consequence of reducing individual uncertainty;
—the institutional framework is basically open to innovative objects and modes of transaction and to respecifications that may become desirable as a feedback from the evolving economic and social system;[9] and
—sunk costs of transaction do not represent an obstacle to general equilibrium if they are assumed to be at an ultimate minimum and if the framework is closed to innovation.

Current Costs of Market Transactions

In the following discussion, we concentrate on those coordination costs that represent current costs of market transactions. These costs differ from sunk costs because they are incurred when individual exchanges of property rights or changes of components of such rights are initiated, enforced, and controlled. The connection with individual transactions is clearly established by Coase.

In order to carry out a market transaction it is necessary to discover who it is that one wishes to deal with, to inform people that one wishes to deal and on what terms, to conduct negotiations leading up to a bargain, to draw up the contract, to undertake the inspection needed, to make sure that the terms of the contract are being observed, and so on. (1960, 2)

---

8. Using an approach based on communication theory that was suggested by Luhmann (1987), Hutter tries to analyze the interdependence between the economy and the legal system. He starts from the following proposition: "If the economy produces the law, it produces its own preconditions" (1989, 2).

9. Obviously, this proposition only applies to the economic constitution of a society characterized by Max Weber (1985, 399) as a "contract society" and by Franz Böhm (1966) as a "society of the private law." Feudal societies or societies showing significant feudal elements do not seem to have a large evolutionary potential, precisely because they tend to rely on a rather inflexible (material) law as opposed to the flexible (formal) law that is characteristic of the economic constitution of a contract society (cf. Röpke, 1983).

As these examples indicate, current costs of market transactions arise because, initially, economic agents do not know exactly

—who will be the partner in a transaction,
—under what conditions an exchange can be made mutually acceptable, and
—whether the promised properties and, hence, the values of the objects of a transaction will really hold true (see Schüller 1983b, 158ff.).

Bringing together supply and demand requires searching and signaling, establishing the terms of exchange makes negotiating as well as contracting necessary, and securing the realization of a contract involves controlling. Viewed more closely, all efforts at solving these problems attempt to reduce the individual uncertainty of the economic agents involved. Ultimately, acquisition and exchange of knowledge is required. Hence, it can be argued that current costs of market transactions represent, in fact, costs of information or—perhaps better—communication costs.[10]

Current Transaction Costs and General Equilibrium

Within a neoclassical perspective, from which the concept of current transaction costs was originally developed, these costs were also considered to be information costs. This holds particularly true for the costs of searching and signaling as demonstrated, for example, by Stigler (1971). The next analytical step was to treat information as a commodity (e.g., Arrow 1971, 147). After that, it became seemingly possible to optimize information efforts. In the case of a search for price quotations, for example, it became analytically plausible for a seller to have to equate the marginal costs of search with the expected increase in receipts (Stigler 1971, 66).

The implication for equilibrium analysis was that transaction costs could be treated like costs of substitution. As soon as they were considered comparable to transportation costs, they did not cause additional problems.[11] From

---

10. See Hutter 1989, 15ff. Dahlmann (1979), to whom Hutter also refers, was probably the first to propose this view.

11. Having identified transaction costs as costs of information, Dahlmann (1979) makes a clear distinction between these costs and costs of transportation. However, when trying to relate information costs to the existence or nonexistence of a Pareto optimum, he abandons the distinction. Since an equilibrium analysis in the Pareto-Walras tradition neither allows for a market process nor for uncertainty, Dahlmann loses sight of the initial distinction as soon as he discusses optimality conditions (1979, 152). Interestingly enough, a similar shift in reasoning can be found in a well-received survey of the theory of transaction costs by Bössmann (1982). At first, Bössmann notes that there appears to be a consensus with regard to transaction costs being different from costs of production (1982, 665). However, after having noted the possible rele-

this point of view, transaction costs prevent the equalization of rates of substitution. But it is possible to realize riskless profits or net savings as long as the deviations are not at a minimum.

However, the neoclassical answer to the problem of information had to face "a fundamental paradox in the determination of demand for information: its value for the purchaser is not known until he has the information, but then he has, in effect, acquired it without cost" (Arrow 1971, 148). As a consequence, an optimization of information efforts by equating marginal costs and return becomes impossible. In the case of information, unlike that of a commodity, the assessment of its utility cannot be separated from its use.[12]

Given current transaction costs, individual agents are faced with a two-tiered decision problem. First they have to decide on the size of their information efforts without being able to optimize. Only after acquiring and exchanging information can they make a choice about what they know. The implication for general equilibrium theory is that the problem of information can only be handled in a way compatible with the basic analytical approach by resorting to an abstraction that is obviously inadequate in view of the previously mentioned paradox.

Current Transaction Costs and Rational Choice

Interestingly enough, it was an Austrian, Mises, who first insisted that all economic decisions should be interpreted as questions of a pure logic of choice. However, it is difficult to see how this logic could be applied to decisions about information efforts. Limited information diminishes the possibility of gains from trade. But decisions to acquire additional knowledge do not represent a rational choice in the microeconomic sense. Ignorant agents can decide to devote resources to the acquisition of knowledge, but they are unable to choose between specified quantities of information, since they do not know what they are getting for their information effort. They cannot make a rational choice, but they can choose to search. If they do this, they cannot be certain that they will find something that leads to a net gain from the conse-

---

vance of information economics in this context, she turns to models that are used to explain the effects of imperfect information on the existence and properties of a market equilibrium (666). Posing the question in such a way, we would argue, necessarily implies that a distinction can no longer be made between transaction costs and transportation costs. And this is exactly the result at which Bössmann arrives, namely that transaction costs are quite similar to transportation costs or other impediments to a smooth exchange of goods (669).

12. Arrow himself uses the paradox to derive "a strong case for centralized decision making" (1971, 149) from the viewpoint of optimal allocation. And since he assumes "an existing stock of information" (148) that must be accessible to a central agency, the problems resulting from knowledge that is dispersed among individual economic agents and that changes in an unpredictable way are excluded by definition.

quent commodity choice when the information costs incurred are taken into account.

As far as the consequent commodity choice is concerned, it is equally possible, from a non-neoclassical point of view to apply the pure logic of choice. However, it is impossible to question its rationality or to develop degrees of rationality by using a perfectly informed observer as a point of reference. The Olympian model of rationality (Simon 1983, 23) is no longer sustainable. What remains is a concept of subjective rationality.

Regarding the problem of search, one could try to retain the stability of a stationary system by proposing that the information set to which the search efforts of an economic agent are directed should be considered as constant and "external" to the agent. In this way, the set (as such) seems to consist of objective data to which the individual agent can adjust. However, the agent is bound to recognize that he or she has to decide whether his or her state of knowledge requires search efforts or not (without being able to employ the logic of choice). Hence, he or she gains a degree of informational autonomy which he or she cannot have when this decision situation is compared with the conventional microeconomic model. As a consequence, the "external" set of data loses its objective relevance to the individual decision. What matters is not the set of market data per se, but which elements of the set the individual agent has found. The subjective autonomy described cannot be penetrated by allocation theory. The economic agent must, on his or her own, evaluate his or her state of knowledge and define levels of aspiration considered as satisfying. If he or she can link up with previously experienced states of knowledge, it is possible that levels of aspiration gain a dynamism that again is inaccessible to equilibrium theory (see Witt 1992, chap. 3).

The subjectivity of search and discovery goes even further than previously thought. Straightforward opportunities to gain from trade are not what the economic agent can track down. Such opportunities are in no way self-evident. Or, as Boulding (1977, 84) has stated: "Alternatives do not usually have the courtesy to parade themselves in rank and order on the drill ground of our imagination." They have to be discovered through a subjective and possibly creative act of cognition. The act itself can be conceived of as an effort to relate a newly found piece of information to the image or knowledge structure that an economic agent has with respect to his or her economic environment. Hence, our point of view also differs from the conventional search models with regard to the required acts of cognition. Opportunities to gain from trade cannot be found. They have to be developed by acts of cognition that can, themselves, be innovative and can contribute to economic evolution.

Furthermore, it is also important to note that, contrary to the commodity view of information, search in the sense in which it is used here cannot be riskless. If an economic agent has discovered new opportunities to trade, their exploitation may or may not lead to a net return on search costs. However, this result cannot influence the decision to engage in information efforts ex ante. And ex post it is impossible to change the information costs incurred. The information, as such, will then be used irrespective of how costly it was to obtain.

A way to reduce the search problem to analytically manageable proportions that is frequently observed is to close the set of possible pieces of information. Consequently, this allows parametric uncertainty to be introduced by defining a probability density function with respect to the closed set. Whether the probabilities are called objective or subjective does not change anything with regard to the implied abstraction that is relevant here. It is suggested that the individual knows almost everything he or she could try to find out except for the fact that a certain piece of knowledge—that is, a market datum—is only relevant to him or her with a known probability. In this way, the intractable autonomy of the individual would be removed by assumption. The assumption is inadequate since, in a situation of search, the individual only knows that there may be something he or she does not know; whether there is actually something and what it is can only be revealed after a search effort has been made.[13]

Finally, the intractability of current transaction costs with the pure logic of choice also becomes evident when cost components different from those incurred by the search for transaction opportunities are considered. Negotiation costs are a particularly striking case in point. Even if the search for potential partners to a transaction is closed, no partial rational choice between the transaction opportunities is possible by perfectly anticipating the negotiation costs. And it is obvious that quite a number of internal institutions have evolved precisely to reduce this highly uncertain cost component, for example, standardized contracts and general conditions of sale. Once these institutions are accepted as such, a transformation of formerly current costs of transactions into sunk costs has taken place.

---

13. For a critical assessment of models in which search is optimized, see Witt 1992, chap. 3. Witt argues, as we do, that optimization is only feasible if the set of possible events is a closed set. Only then can individuals form probabilities related to the elements of the set. However, if a probability density function exists, there is no longer any analytical room for search because what can be found is already known. For similar reasons, it is also possible to criticize neoclassical models of innovative behavior in the tradition of Dasgupta and Stiglitz, Kamien and Schwartz, as well as Reinganum (for a survey of these models, see Kamien and Schwartz 1982, chaps. 4 and 5). The analogy with a race means that the models are deterministic at the outset. With the competitors and the price—a singular innovation—given, the problem is reduced to a manageable game with R&D being the only action parameter. And we can agree with Witt (1992, chap. 2) who argues that, after having set up the model in such a way, practically everything that makes innovation highly uncertain and incalculable is excluded from the analysis.

Costs of Transaction versus Costs of Substitution

Our last remark allows further clarifications to be made concerning the relationship between sunk and current transaction costs, on the one hand, and substitution costs, on the other. Sunk costs of transactions can be considered development costs for external and internal institutions. The informational content of these institutions consists of the constraints imposed on the behavior of economic agents who are either obliged to conform to them (external institutions) or who commit themselves to do so (internal institutions). In this way, institutions reduce uncertainty. This means, in turn, that potential current transaction costs are saved compared to a situation in which the institution in question does not exist. The costs incurred in developing the institution are sunk.

However, in order to operate within the institutional framework, it must be familiar to the economic agents and—where necessary—be adapted or supplemented to serve individual transactions. The costs of making economic agents familiar with institutions become sunk costs of transactions as soon as the corresponding knowledge is used repeatedly. What remains as a source of current transaction costs is the task of adapting or supplementing the institutional framework to make it fit to individual transactions. For example, being familiar with the law of contracts does not free economic agents completely from negotiating and formulating the terms of an individual contract and, thus, from incurring current transaction costs.

What remains to be analyzed are the allocation effects of current transaction costs compared with substitution costs such as transportation costs. In the neoclassical approach, there is no differentiation because, as we discussed, information is treated as a commodity. As a consequence, current transaction costs add to those deviations between rates of substitution that survive effective arbitrage. Furthermore and like other costs of substitution, transaction costs are considered to be impediments to perfect competition because they reduce the transparency of markets. However, the economic agents pay for information in the same way as they do, for example, for transportation. Hence, they exploit all the substitution possibilities that offer more than a compensation for substitution costs, including current costs of transaction.

In the case of the commodity approach, the agents know exactly as much as they need to know. Transaction costs, like (other) substitution costs, would produce gaps of substitution that remain open, although they are known. From a non-neoclassical point of view, however, it is the knowledge problem that makes the difference between the allocational consequences of current costs of transaction and costs of substitution. Current costs of transaction leave an unknowable number of substitution gaps open. Those gaps that happen to be discovered will be closed, to the extent to which it is profitable to do so in the light of the costs of substitution, whereas the incurred transaction costs will be treated as forgone.

As far as the effects of current transaction costs on competition are concerned, it is not a deviation from perfect competition, and hence from perfect knowledge, that matters from a non-neoclassical (Hayekian) point of view, because the solution of the knowledge problem is considered to be inseparable from market action. As we show in the following section, it is highly problematical to make any direct comparison between two totally different concepts of competition: competition as a stationary, fixed-point problem defined by a perfectly informed outside observer on the one hand and an evolutionary, subjectivist approach to what is conceived of as a process of discovery on the other hand. What can be said at this stage, with respect to the allocational gains in terms of exploitable opportunities of substitution that may be identified by competition as a discovery procedure, is the following. Current transaction costs are the price to be paid in order to have a chance, not the guarantee, of discovering opportunities to gain from reallocation. These gains are elements of a potential of unknowable size.[14] And the potential has to be conceived of as an open set because innovation must be permitted.

According to the Hayekian discovery procedure, the competitive market process makes dispersed fragments of economically relevant knowledge accessible. The problem of "use of knowledge in society" is analyzed from the point of view of the individual agent, who has to trade by applying his or her limited knowledge based on search and experience. It is this subjectivist approach that not only allows evolutionary elements to be introduced, but also constitutes the basic difference between Hayek, on the one hand, and Schumpeter as the most frequently cited proponent of the evolutionary perspective in economic theorizing, on the other. In his *Theory of Economic Development,* Schumpeter (1968) retained the Walrasian model to explain those variables he treated as endogenous to his model, that is, prices and quantities. However, this also meant that he had accepted the informational requirements of the Walrasian model. As an important consequence, economic development could only be conceptualized as the result of shocks inflicted upon the model by the (new) data. These shocks were personalized (by Schumpeter) as the dynamic entrepreneur who was able to innovate and perform competitive imitation.

By accepting the Walrasian model as the core of his concept, Schumpeter

---

14. This view also represents an important difference from the view proposed by Kirzner and that of scholars pursuing his approach (e.g., O'Driscoll). Since they still maintain general equilibrium as a reference system, an external observer can assume that a fixed potential of profits exists that is accessible through entrepreneurial activities. Most probably, this result is closely related to the dominant affinity to the arbitrageur that can be found in Kirzner's image of the entrepreneur.

defined the source of innovation as exogenous. As an important consequence, the discussion focused on the technological content of an innovation and disregarded the concomitant problem of knowledge.[15] The Schumpeterian entrepreneur was only required to inject innovation into the system. His or her job consisted of "the setting up of new production functions" (Schumpeter 1939, 87). Because the approach was basically a neoclassical one, Schumpeter could not initiate a critical review of mainstream economics, although he drew attention to an evolutionary phenomenon.[16] His entrepreneur was welcomed as a useful extension, whereas his sociological and historical insights could be referred to without leaving the basic line of reasoning. The suppression of the knowledge problem was spotted by Hayek (1945, 530), who deplored Schumpeter's use of the notion of "datum" as a barrier to the understanding of the evolutionary market process.

Transactions, Knowledge, and Catallaxy

The evolutionary approach stresses the inseparability of the solution of the knowledge problem from market action. Hence, it is important to analyze the consequences of transactions for the dissemination of economic knowledge.

Stationary versus Evolutionary
Interpretations of Arbitrage

As a starting point, it may be useful to clarify possible differences between the two approaches by considering the process of arbitrage, in which knowledge also ranks highly in the neoclassical approach. From a neoclassical, detached, and informed view of the allocation process, opportunities for arbitrage can only exist in a situation of disequilibrium. For them to persist, it is necessary to assume imperfect information. From an evolutionary point of view, imperfect information offers chances to discover allocational gains and to be rewarded by entrepreneurial profits. If such profitable opportunities are discov-

---

15. For a discussion of the widely ignored knowledge problem in innovation policy, which cannot be outlined here, see Streit 1984b.

16. The technological bias that still dominates neo-Schumpeterian analyses is revealed by the questions on the corresponding research agenda compiled, for example, by Kamien and Schwartz (1982, 107). Basically, the questions center around the problem of how to allocate R&D in the case of a specified innovation, whose introduction is subject to a race between market participants. Besides the analogy itself, which we have already questioned, it is important to note the abstraction introduced by discussing innovation as a simple production problem with R&D as the input variable. In fact, this once more allows the use of the conventional theory of the firm, which is practically a black box adjustable to the requirements of general equilibrium and which has also been criticized by Kamien and Schwartz themselves.

ered, a process of arbitrage may be induced that in turn will lead to their disappearance.[17]

This kind of reasoning does not differ markedly from the one used with the partial model of arbitrage. The model leads to a competitive equilibrium if information is conceived of as a commodity. In order to be able to bend the evolutionary approach toward the equilibrium approach, it is necessary to close the set of discoverable gains from trade. If this set is exposed to a process of discovery causing transaction costs, it can be expected that the economy will approach competitive equilibrium by a process of trial and error. In order to initiate a consecutive process of discovery, it is only necessary to introduce a new set of opportunities, that is, to expose the system to an exogenous shock caused by new technologies, new tastes, and so on.

With respect to transaction costs, it can be argued that they must be incurred in a situation of disequilibrium in order to move toward equilibrium. These costs would, in principle, become irrelevant if equilibrium could be reached without new shocks (see Wegehenkel 1981, 19). In this way, it seems possible to introduce an evolutionary approach, although it is still the familiar neoclassical adjustment process. As a procedure, it is quite typical for the neo-Austrian interpretation of the market process, but, as a consequence, evolutionary arguments are converted into an extension of the neoclassical model.

Hence, it is necessary to check whether this extension is possible without resorting to an assumption that has to be considered inadequate in light of the phenomenon in question. If it is possible for an economic system to improve in terms of transparency, as suggested by the neoclassical handling of the evolutionary problem, the state of knowledge of all individuals about the market data must approach the state of perfect knowledge. Hence, it is reasonable to treat the state of knowledge like a capital good of the "continuous input–point output" type. Informational activities of entrepreneurs then can help to build up a stock of knowledge, and, during the process of imitative arbitrage, this stock would turn into a public good (cf. Arrow 1971, 148).

---

17. Such a neoclassical interpretation of the transaction costs approach has been provided by Wegehenkel (1981, 22ff.). Assuming that transaction costs have to be incurred in order to move from a state of disequilibrium to one of equilibrium, it can be stated that, in equilibrium, transaction costs must be zero with all preferences being revealed (27). This is quite in line with the Kirznerian tradition already discussed. However, why transaction costs should be equal to entrepreneurial profits in disequilibrium, as suggested by Wegehenkel, remains to be explained. Furthermore, it is difficult to see how Hayek (1937)—as suggested by Wegehenkel (27)—should have come to this kind of approach, which differs markedly from his view of the market process. Finally, it can be doubted that the approach is evolutionary in a proper sense. To point to ever-changing economic data (Wegehenkel 1981, 27) is not enough to move from ad-hocery to systematic explanation.

However, the informational concept of current transaction costs does not allow such an analogy to be used. If an agent acquires information by incurring transaction costs, the value of the information depends on when it was acquired. The discovery of an opportunity for profitable exchange reflects information about the present. This information may quickly become outdated from an evolutionary point of view but not from the neoclassical, stationary one. Hence, it is not possible to add pieces of knowledge about the present to those about the past. Or, in terms of the analogy, in order to be able to identify a piece of information as an addition to the stock of knowledge, it is necessary to know the rate of depreciation. The question concerning the actuality of a given stock of knowledge cannot simply be ignored.[18]

The analogy should clarify how restrictive the assumptions must be if economic agents are to become perfectly informed about market data even if these data are initially considered as a closed set. The most convenient but also the most implausible assumption would be that it is sufficient to incur transaction costs only once in order to be informed about all profitable transaction opportunities. The second possibility is to assume a sequence of informational efforts and to ask whether it is still plausible to assume that the set can be considered as closed or whether the set actually does change as a consequence of sequential discovery. To confirm this, it can be argued that not only are newly discovered opportunities eliminated at a profit when they are exploited, but new opportunities are also created, which are waiting to be discovered. In this case and from the point of view of an outside observer, the value of the stock of accumulated knowledge would be depreciated by attempts to increase it.

The Informational Content of Pecuniary External Effects

What has, in fact, been questioned in the preceding section is the way in which market interdependence enters the equilibrium approach. The differences between this approach and the evolutionary approach can be demonstrated by again referring to arbitrage. For example, if competing firms are considered, a process of arbitrage may be triggered if one of them discovers a new and profitable transaction opportunity that causes costs to fall. The additional profits from exploiting the opportunity will give an incentive to the successful entrepreneur to expand his or her capacity by attracting more resources. The unintended consequence on the output side will be that his or her expansion will tend to lower prices in the corresponding market and exert

---

18. Stigler (1962, 97) has pointed out the potential obsolescence of information. But when introducing his analogy between a capital good and knowledge as a stock (103), he ignores the necessity for depreciation, probably because such a depreciation is not conductive to equilibrium.

pressure on his or her rivals by weakening their position in the competition for resources. From a neoclassical point of view, the rivals are induced to imitate the pioneer. Having defined the borders of the market in question, it is clear who exerts competitive pressure on whom. And the market signals also reveal how the pressure can be answered, namely either by imitating the pioneer or by no longer bidding for resources, that is, by reducing capacity.

Although a partial analysis of a market characterized by similar transactions can also be useful from the point of view of an evolutionary theory, there remain three basic differences when compared with the neoclassical approach.

—In order to make evolution possible, it is not useful to endow the economy with a predetermined, stationary set of similar transactions called markets; instead, it is important to allow new types of transactions and markets to develop endogenously.
—The evolutionary approach does not focus on the physical reallocation of resources, but rather on the concomitant process of information.
—Market signals are considered to be abstract in the sense that they appear as changes in the values of exchange of property rights; however, they do not provide information about the causes of those changes.

This points to a theoretical concept that usually does not attract much attention in neoclassical analysis: the Scitovscian concept of pecuniary external effects. The concept does not require the advance definition of who is competing with whom. It does not exclude the possibility that a discovery may lead to new markets. And it allows changes in market values of property rights or in components of such rights to be considered as information conveyed, in a coded form, in the Hayekian sense (see Hayek 1976, 117) and not as a Marshallian message concerning substitution necessities.[19]

According to Hayek, price movements include abstract information. They synthesize a multitude of conditions of demand and supply that no single agent can be expected to know or, in fact, is required to know. The agent who realizes a loss in the market value of one of his or her property rights usually does not know anything about what caused this negative pecuniary effect. Equally, he or she is not told how to adjust to the new situation. In a system

---

19. An attempt to express the Marshallian view in a formal way has in fact been made by Radner (1979) in the context of a rational expectations equilibrium. In order to arrive at a "revealing full communication equilibrium" it is necessary to map different economic signals into distinct price vectors. This allows the (private) information that has entered a price vector to be inferred by observing the (public) market price. For a criticism of this procedure and of the related analytical results in the case of futures markets, see Streit 1984a, 392ff.

that is based on the division of knowledge, this kind of information cannot automatically be communicated. It must be discovered.

The fact that information is conveyed in a coded form through pecuniary external effects is not compatible with the concept of parametric steering through relative prices that is required to make a general equilibrium possible. If current transaction costs have to be incurred, changes in relative prices are not the initial market signal. Only after the discovery of individual prices is it possible to exclusively relate them to one another. Prices that have not been discovered must necessarily be left out of any consideration. This is even more true for prices that do not yet exist, namely those of innovations. And individuals engaging in innovative efforts are not only likely to interpret the same market signals in a different way; they are also likely to search for prices different than the ones that agents who commit themselves to adjustment might search for.

What can further be discovered is not a fixed set of prices but, rather, notions of intended terms of trade. Prices and other conditions of trade are themselves objects of negotiation in a competitive environment. And the intensity of competition depends, to a considerable extent, on the willingness of the economic agents to engage in attempts to propagate and discover information about old and new substitution possibilities. However, such a sequential process of competitive formation of transitory prices is simply beyond the scope of an equilibrium approach.[20]

Arbitrage, Imitation, and Innovation

Negative pecuniary external effects provide an incentive for achieving a better combination of property rights, but this is not possible without incurring costs of transaction. As outlined above, the corresponding informational efforts can only produce results that are unknown in advance. Hence, it must be concluded that negative pecuniary effects induce a response by an agent that is predictable with certainty neither by him or her nor by an outside observer. If this were not so, the market system would not have an endogenous propensity to innovate.[21]

---

20. See Röpke 1980, 145ff.; Streißler 1980, 54ff. An attempt to set up a model including at least some features of this process, for example the occurrence of innovations, has been made by Witt (1985).

21. Hayek repeatedly stresses the nonparametric character of market signals in the sense that they are abstract and do not offer lines of appropriate economic action. But sometimes he appears to ignore this important deviation from the equilibrium approach. The following passage may serve as an example (Hayek, 1976, 116–17): "The remunerations which the market determines are, as it were, not functionally related with what people have done, but only with what they ought to do. They are incentives which as a rule guide people to success, but will produce a

Hence, it does not follow, even from a partial analysis of arbitrage, that successful competitors will necessarily engage in imitation. It is also possible that they may discover an opportunity to innovate through their efforts to respond to the negative pecuniary effect that they realized. Only in the stationary version of the problem (and with prices revealing a predetermined and specific knowledge), can it be concluded that imitators will be attracted by the prospect of profits.

As a general consequence, stationary market theory leads to a predetermined sequence of events, that is, successful use of a discovery (innovation), imitation, equilibrium, new discovery. Schumpeter constructed his theory of innovation basically along those lines. However, this cyclical pattern is not convincing from the point of view of transaction costs.[22] In connection with pecuniary external effects as a coded form of information, the fact that current costs of transaction allow for an important evolutionary possibility has been ignored: for a new process of arbitrage to be triggered, it is not necessary for the preceding one to be terminated. Innovation and not merely imitation can be a market response to innovation.

From the point of view of knowledge, this possible market response means that new knowledge obtained by incurring transaction costs cannot turn obsolete only "behind the innovator's back." The obsolescence can even be induced by his or her initial information effort. In an economy approaching a Walrasian equilibrium, the economic agents would permanently add to their knowledge by engaging in informational efforts. In the case of an evolutionary market process, they may even learn something new without being able to tell whether they have made a net gain of knowledge.

Concluding Remarks

We hope we have shown how essential it is for evolutionary market theory to take into account

---

viable order only because they often disappoint the expectations they have caused when relevant circumstances have unexpectedly changed."

22. For a presentation and critique of the Schumpeterian innovation cycle, see Witt 1992, chap. 2. To a limited extent, Schumpeter's abstraction from the knowledge problem has been reduced more recently by Nelson and Winter (1982). They concentrate on the acquisition of new technical knowledge that allows the improvement of production processes. In terms of the neoclassical definition, technical progress is made dependent upon investment in R&D. However, as has been argued, for example by Witt (1992), the approach remains nonevolutionary, although its stochastic properties might suggest otherwise. Furthermore, it is exclusively supply oriented and, hence, merely an extension of the theory of the firm. This means that the informational content and the evolutionary qualities of the competitive market process still remain to be explored.

—the division of knowledge as a concomitant of the division of labor, and
—the relationship between transaction costs and the dispersion of knowledge in a market economy.

However, as soon as these key concepts are used in economic analysis, recognition of the explanatory limits of neoclassical equilibrium theory becomes unavoidable. And these limits can only be overcome by resorting to assumptions that must be considered inadequate in view of the required reduction of the knowledge problem. Ultimately, the necessary abstractions merely lead to new names for well-known problems, some of which have already been solved.

Furthermore, the information-oriented interpretation of the process of coordination through market transactions—the catallaxy—also precludes reasoning in terms of disequilibrium analysis. What appears to be a potential source of market failure from the point of view of disequilibrium turns out to be a driving force when judged from an evolutionary perspective. The endemic imperfection of individual knowledge about transaction possibilities, on the one hand, and the coded information provided by market signals, on the other, make the system open to evolutionary processes. And only in such a system does the Hayekian interpretation of competition as a discovery procedure have analytical value. The same applies to the Schumpeterian dynamic entrepreneur if he is not conceived as a deus ex machina, injecting new technologies at random into an inherently stationary Walrasian system.

Admittedly, it turns out to be very difficult to leave behind the homely ground of a well-established theory. Furthermore, evolutionary market theory is not likely to acquire the formal stringency of equilibrium analysis. However, it may be consoling to remember what Schumpeter had to say about new ways of thinking.

> The history of science is one great confirmation of the fact that we find it exceedingly difficult to adopt a new scientific point of view or method. Thought turns again and again into the accustomed track even if it has become unsuitable and the more suitable innovation in itself presents no particular difficulties. The very nature of fixed habits of thinking, their energy-saving function, is founded upon the fact that they have become subconscious, that they yield their results automatically and are proof against criticism and even against contradiction by individual facts. But precisely because of this they become drag-chains when they have outlived their usefulness. So it is also in the economic world. (1968, 16)

REFERENCES

Arrow, K. J. 1971. "Economic Welfare and the Allocation of Resources for Invention." In *Economics of Information and Knowledge*, ed. D. M. Lamberton, 141–59. Harmondsworth: Penguin.
Barzel, Y. 1985. "Transaction Costs: Are They just Costs?" *Zeitschrift für die gesamte Staatswissenschaft* 141:4–16.
Blaseio, H. 1986. *Das Kognos-Prinzip: Zur Dynamik sich selbstorganisierender wirtschaftlicher und sozialer Systeme*. Berlin: Duncker und Humblot.
Böhm, F. 1966. "Privatrechtsgesellschaft und Marktwirtschaft." *ORDO* 17:75–151.
Bössmann, E. 1982. "Volkswirtschaftliche Probleme der Transaktionskosten." *Zeitschrift für die gesamte Staatswissenschaft* 138:664–79.
Boulding, K. E. 1981. *Evolutionary Economics*. Beverly Hills, Calif.: Sage.
Boulding, K. E. 1977. *The Image: Knowledge in Life and Society*. Ann Arbor: University of Michigan Press.
Buchanan, J. M. 1975. *The Limits of Liberty: Between Anarchy and Leviathan*. Chicago: University of Chicago Press.
Buchanan, J. M. 1980. "Rent Seeking and Profit Seeking." In *Toward a Theory of the Rent-Seeking Society*, ed. J. M. Buchanan, R. D. Tollison, G. Tullock, 1–15. College Station: Texas A&M University Press.
Coase, R. H. 1960. "The Problem of Social Cost." *Journal of Law and Economics* 3:1–44.
Dahlmann, C. J. 1979. "The Problem of Externality." *Journal of Law and Economics* 22:141–62.
Demsetz, H. 1964. "The Exchange and Enforcement of Property Rights." *Journal of Law and Economics* 7:11–26.
Demsetz, H. 1968. "The Cost of Transacting." *Quarterly Journal of Economics* 82:33–53.
Demsetz, H. 1969. "Information and Efficiency: Another Viewpoint." *Journal of Law and Economics* 12:1–22.
Fehl, U. 1983. "Die Theorie dissipativer Strukturen als Ansatzpunkt für die Analyse von Innovationsproblemen in alternativen Wirtschaftsordnungen." In *Innovationsprobleme in Ost und West*, ed. A. Schüller, H. Leipold, and H. Hamel, 65–89. Stuttgart: Gustav Fischer.
Fehl, U. 1986. "Spontaneous Order and the Subjectivity of Expectations: A Contribution to the Lachmann-O'Driscoll Problem." In *Subjectivism, Intelligibility, and Economic Understanding: Essays in Honor of Ludwig M. Lachmann on his Eightieth Birthday*, ed. I. M. Kirzner, 72–86. London: Macmillan.
Furubotn, E. G., and Pejovich, S. 1972. "Property Rights and Economic Theory: A Survey of Recent Literature." *Journal of Economic Literature* 10:1137–62.
Georgescu-Roegen, N. 1976. *The Entropy Law and the Economic Process*. Cambridge, Mass.: Harvard University Press.
Hayek, F. A. 1937. "Economics and Knowledge." *Economica* 4, n.s. no. 13: 33–54.
Hayek, F. A. 1945. "The Use of Knowledge in Society." *American Economic Review* 35:519–30.
Hayek, F. A. 1967. "The Theory of Complex Phenomena." In *Studies in Philosophy,*

Politics, and Economics, ed. F. A. Hayek, 22–42. London: Routledge and Kegan Paul.
Hayek, F. A. 1976. *Law, Legislation and Liberty.* Vol. 2, *The Mirage of Social Justice.* Chicago: University of Chicago Press.
Hayek, F. A. 1978. "Competition as a Discovery Procedure." In *New Studies in Philosophy, Politics, Economics, and the History of Economic Ideas,* ed. F. A. Hayek, 179–90. Routledge and Kegan Paul.
Hesse, G. 1983. "Zur Erklärung der Änderung von Handlungsrechten mit Hilfe ökonomischer Theorie." In *Property Rights and ökonomische Theorie,* ed. A. Schüller, 79–109. Munich: Vahlen.
Heuß, E. 1965. *Allgemeine Markttheorie.* Tübingen: Mohr, Polygraphischer Verlag.
Hoppmann, E. 1980. "Gleichgewicht und Evolution: Voraussetzungen und Erkenntniswert der volkswirtschaftlichen Totalanalyse. In *Festveranstaltung der Wirtschaftswissenschaftlichen Fakultät der Julius-Maximilian-Universität Würzburg zum 75. Geburtstag von Erich Carell,* 19–39. Baden-Baden: Nomos.
Hutter, M. 1989. *Die Produktion von Recht.* Tübingen: Mohr.
Kamien, N. I., and Schwartz, N. L. 1982. *Market Structure and Innovation.* Cambridge, Mass.: Harvard University Press.
Kirzner, I. M. 1973. *Competition and Entrepreneurship.* Chicago: University of Chicago Press.
Kirzner, I. M., ed. 1986. *Subjectivism, Intellegibility, and Economic Understanding: Essays in Honor of Ludwig M. Lachmann on his Eightieth Birthday.* London: Macmillan.
Krüsselberg, H. G. 1969. *Marktwirtschaft und ökonomische Theorie: Ein Beitrag zur Theorie der Wirtschaftspolitik.* Freiburg im Breisgau: Rombach.
Krüsselberg, H. G. 1983. "Property Rights und Wohlfahrtsökonomik." In *Property Rights und ökonomische Theorie,* ed. A. Schüller, 45–77. Munich: Vahlen.
Lachmann, L. M. 1963. "Wirtschaftsordnung und wirtschaftliche Institutionen." *ORDO* 14:63–77.
Luhmann, N. 1987. *Soziale Systeme: Grundriß einer allgemeinen Theorie.* Frankfurt: Suhrkamp.
Nelson, R. R., and Winter, S. G. 1982. *An Evolutionary Theory of Economic Change.* Cambridge, Mass.: Harvard University Press.
Paqué, K. H. 1985. "How Far is Vienna From Chicago? An Essay on the Methodology of Two Schools of Dogmatic Liberalism." *Kyklos* 38:412–34.
Radner, R. 1979. "Rational Expectations Equilibrium: Generic Existence and the Information Revealed by Prices." *Econometrica* 47 (3): 655–78.
Röpke, J. 1977. *Die Strategie der Innovation.* Tübingen: Mohr.
Röpke, J. 1980. "Zur Stabilität und Evolution marktwirtschaftlicher Systeme aus klassischer Sicht." In *Zur Theorie marktwirtschaftlicher Ordnungen,* ed. E. Streißler and Ch. Watrin, 124–54. Tübingen: Mohr.
Röpke, J. 1983. "Handlungsrechte und wirtschaftliche Entwicklung." In *Property Rights und Ökonomische Theorie,* ed. A. Schüller, 111–44. Munich: Vahlen.
Schmidtchen, D. 1983. *Property Rights, Freiheit, und Wettbewerbspolitik.* Walter Eucken Institut, Vorträge und Aufsätze no. 89. Tübingen: Mohr.
Schüller, A., ed. 1983a. *Property Rights und ökonomische Theorie.* Munich: Vahlen.

Schüller, A. 1983b. "Property Rights, Theorie der Firma, und wettbewerbliches Marktsystem. In *Property Rights und ökonomische Theorie,* ed. A. Schüller, 145–83. Munich: Vahlen.

Schumpeter, J. A. 1939. *Business Cycles: A Theoretical, Historical, and Statistical Analysis of the Capitalist Process.* Vol. 1. New York: McGraw-Hill.

Schumpeter, J. A. 1968. *The Theory of Economic Development.* Harvard Economic Studies, vol. 46. Oxford: Basil Blackwell.

Simon, H. A. 1983. *Reason in Human Affairs.* Oxford: Basil Blackwell.

Stigler, G. J. 1962. "Information in the Labor Market." *Journal of Political Economy* 70 (Supplement): 94–105.

Stigler, G. J. 1971. "The Economics of Information." In *Economics of Information and Knowledge,* ed. J. M. Lamberton, 61–82. Harmondsworth: Penguin.

Streißler, E. 1980. "Kritik des neoklassischen Gleichgewichtsansatzes als Rechtfertigung marktwirtschaftlicher Ordnungen." In *Zur Theorie marktwirtschaftlicher Ordnungen,* ed. E. Streißler and Ch. Watrin, 38–69. Tübingen: Mohr.

Streit, M. E. 1984a. "Information Processing in Futures Markets: An Essay on Adequate Abstraction." *Jahrbücher für Nationalökonomie und Statistik* 199:385–400.

Streit, M. E. 1984b. "Innovationspolitik zwischen Unwissenheit und Anmaßung von Wissen." *Hamburger Jahrbuch für Wirtschafts- und Gesellschaftspolitik* 29:35–54.

Streit, M. E. 1987. "Economic Order and Public Policy: Market, Constitution, and the Welfare State." In *Efficiency, Institutions, and Economic Policy,* ed. R. Pethig and U. Schlieper, 1–21. Berlin: Springer.

Weber, M. 1985. *Wirtschaft und Gesellschaft: Grundriß der verstehenden Soziologie.* 5th ed. Tübingen: Mohr.

Wegehenkel, L. 1981. *Gleichgewicht, Transaktionskosten, und Evolution: Eine Analyse der Koordinierungseffizienz unterschiedlicher Wirtschaftssysteme.* Tübingen: Mohr.

Williamson, D. 1975. *Markets and Hierarchies: Analysis and Antitrust Implications.* New York: Free Press.

Witt, U. 1985. "Coordination of Individual Economic Activities as an Evolving Process of Self-Organization." *Economie Appliquée* 37:569–95.

Witt, U. 1992. *Individualistic Foundations of Evolutionary Economics.* Cambridge: Cambridge University Press. Forthcoming.

CHAPTER 9

The Implementation of Industrial Policy in an Evolutionary Perspective

Alexander Gerybadze

The Evolution of Industrial Policy: Empirical Evidence, Problems, and Possible Solutions

The postwar era has been characterized by increasing government involvement in the process of economic and technical change in most industrialized countries. A growing share of government expenditures, the advent of interventionist policies, and the alleged success of some countries with strong government involvement have fueled the debate on industrial policy. A country's wealth and international competitiveness tends to depend more and more on its *created* comparative advantage, on human capital, technology, and industrial organization, that can deliberately be influenced—at least to a certain extent—by public policy.[1]

This emphasis on created comparative advantages has given rise to theories of strategic trade policy.[2] Inasmuch as international trade increases the linkage between nation-states, effective industrial policies in any one country will strongly affect competitiveness, welfare, and employment in other countries. In order to preempt first-mover advantages of others, each country will increase its expenditures on industrial policy, bringing about a sharp rise in global spending.[3]

Resulting changes in industrial policy can be described both in quantitative and qualitative terms. The leading industrialized countries have increased R&D as a percentage of GNP from a level of 2.0 percent in 1970 to a range of 2.7 to 2.9 percent in 1987, and will be approaching 3.0 percent by 1990. Together with a considerable growth of GNP, this has resulted in increases of

---

1. See U.S. Department of Commerce 1985; Thurow 1987.
2. See Helpman and Krugman 1985; Krugman 1986.
3. This effect was reported in a number of recent studies and is used as an argument for increased spending in almost every "white book on industrial policy" published by governments in the major countries.

R&D expenditures by a factor of four to six between 1971 and 1985.[4] Furthermore, we have also experienced major qualitative changes in the focus, design, and functioning of industrial policy. Over the years, it has become more active and forward oriented, as opposed to passive and structure conserving, more R&D and science based, and more international in scope. Industrial policy has become increasingly concerned with the generation of major scientific and technical advances and with the facilitation of innovation in industry.

Another very important feature of industrial policy is the increasing emphasis on cooperation at regional, national, as well as international levels. Increasing investments required for new generations of technologies, together with shortened product life cycles and growing risks of obsolescence often lead to situations in which additional innovations can only be attained through a joining of forces by different market participants. Large and risky R&D investments increasingly call for collaborative developments at national and regional levels, as well as for international strategic alliances by even the largest firms. Government agencies are more frequently than ever approached to support and facilitate these processes.[5]

This growing significance of interventionist industrial policies, which are increasingly directed toward joint activities and cooperative ventures, cannot on its own be used as a justification for policy. Government intervention creates its own inherent costs and distortions. It is essential to ask, for any proposed public support of cooperative private activity, whether collaboration and government involvement is a necessary condition for a specific improvement, for example, a new technology, organization, or behavior, and whether public support policies can really be organized and implemented effectively.

Even though it may be difficult to answer these questions unambiguously for a specific political decision, we can learn from past experience; numerous well-reported cases can provide us with enough empirical evidence to analyze and explain the strengths and weaknesses of industrial policies. Some alleged success stories seem to indicate that the following conditions are important.

- Targets or missions for industrial policy must be sufficiently clear and specific.
- The attempted change must lead to a Pareto-superior situation.
- The public agency must "listen carefully" to the key decision makers and find an appropriate joint strategy.

---

4. While the United States and West Germany have both increased their R&D spending by a factor of four, Japan has attained a factor of six. See BMFT 1988, 25.

5. Government involvement in precompetitive joint industrial activities is a major policy issue in the United States (e.g., Sematech), in Europe (EUREKA, ESPRIT), and in Japan, even though it is very difficult to implement successfully. It requires a formulation of joint goals and a coordination of activities at local, regional, national, as well as supranational levels.

- The strategies of individual agents together with the proposed joint strategy must be compatible.
- The appropriate financial, organizational, and human resources must be mobilized within the required time-horizon.

If these conditions are met, public programs may succeed in supporting a certain group of firms and in attaining the desired outcome. Policies pursued within the Japanese information technology industry, for the early postwar development of the U.S. aerospace industry, or for the French avionics and space sector can all be considered successful in this respect.

On the other hand, there are numerous examples of failures of industrial policy reported for several countries. Past attempts to support the British aircraft industry in the 1960s and 1970s; the semiconductor and computer industry in Britain, France, and West Germany; or the early support of the Japanese computer industry did not lead to the expected results. One or more of the following reasons is always among the key explanatory factors for failures of industrial policy.

- Targets or missions are ambiguous and controversial.
- Situations prevail in which some agents will gain, while others expect to lose from an attempted change.
- Public agencies try to "impose a program" or a new policy on firms.
- Strategies of individual actors and strategies of government agencies are incompatible with each other.
- Certain key resources, for example, finance, people, or time, cannot be mobilized at the critical level or in the right combination.

These requirements, which can explain ex post why some programs were successful while others have failed, are rather difficult to simultaneously verify and fulfill in most real-life situations. Since decisions related to industrial policy are complex and uncertain, and since cooperation between competing firms and public agencies is often very difficult to realize, we usually have neither a reliable method nor the information needed for judging ex ante whether a proposed policy will show good or bad results. What we need in such a situation is not a method that tells us, once and for all, in which technologies to invest and which type of specific support policy to pursue. Such an approach of constructivist rationalism cannot be feasible for situations with a high degree of uncertainty, bounded rationality, and unpredictable behavior. Instead, we need a joint problem-solving process or mechanism that helps us to decide rather early, and at several consecutive intervals, whether certain success conditions are most likely to be fulfilled, whether the key participating actors will behave in a compatible way, and whether we can preclude an unacceptable risk of failure for an attempted collaborative program.

Such a joint problem-solving mechanism is a major ingredient for a new type of industrial policy that is embedded in a systemic evolutionary approach.[6] According to this approach, the agent of collective action is "endogenized,"[7] and proposes an appropriate type of joint solution interactively with the key decision makers. It is the purpose of this chapter to outline how such a joint problem-solving mechanism can be designed and implemented. I will outline my arguments in favor of this proposed new approach to industrial policy in the following sequence.

1. I will begin by describing a typical problem situation: some firms within an industry consider a certain type of new behavior, y, that would be superior to x, an established mode of activity (e.g., a widely accepted technology). Within a simple analytical model, an adjustment or coordination problem is explained through the fact that resistant firms do not apply the new behavior, y, "because most other firms don't do it."
2. I will then show that there are ways for solving this problem by using four different types of industrial policy. Supply-side incentives, demand-side support policies, regulation and legislation, as well as policies supporting cooperation and networking can all be helpful in facilitating the desired adaptation process. It will be argued, however, that each type of policy has its specific advantages and disadvantages. Applied separately, each type of policy can help to overcome problems, but will also create new ones.
3. I will then argue that there is a strong need for a political entrepreneur, who has to discover novel solutions for solving a specific problem and who has to make sure that he or she gets enough support for implementation. The political entrepreneur will strongly influence and control the joint problem-solving process by subdividing the task, by finding a new combination of policies, and by selecting an appropriate form of organization.

A Model of Change through Interdependent Activities

The following model, which is based on an article by Witt (1991), describes a group of firms $(F_1, \ldots, F_n)$ that are characterized by a certain routine be-

---
6. Malik (1984) describes the systemic evolutionary model as a better alternative to the constructivist technomorph model for all situations in which an organization has to cope with complexity and with environmental change.

7. See Witt 1991 for an interesting description of the "endogenous public choice theorist."

havior x, but that may individually consider switching to an alternative mode of behavior, y. Behavior y can be described in terms of using a new technique (innovation), of modernizing the industrial structure (restructuring), of applying a certain product or safety standard (standardization), or as a move toward improved environmental control. Insofar as comparisons between techniques are considered, my approach is very similar to the modeling of choices between competing technologies that are characterized by network externalities and increasing returns to adoption (Arthur 1985, 1988 and 1989; Katz and Shapiro 1986; Cowan 1987 and 1989; David 1987; David and Bunn 1987).[8]

A considerable number of innovations are characterized by the interrelatedness between autonomous firm decisions: the advantage of company i switching to behavior y will depend on whether firm j applies the new behavior. We thus assume in our model, that firm i's return, r_i, obtained from interaction with firm j, depends on which kind of behavior is chosen by j. The simultaneous adoption of behavior y by both firms will lead to a Pareto-superior situation, while a mixed solution (firm i applies y, while firm j applies x) will result in a Pareto-inferior situation, both in comparison with the status quo where all firms apply x:[9]

$$r_i(y_i,y_j) \geq r_i(x_i,x_j) \geq r_i(y_i,x_j) \quad \text{and} \quad r_i(x_i,y_j) \tag{1}$$

for all $i = 1, \ldots, n$, the strict inequality being satisfied for at least one i.

Each firm will then consider the choice between x and y in accordance with the expected payoff, depending on the behavior of the other firms in the industry. As a result, the relative share of firms adopting behavior y, given by $p(y) = 1 - p(x)$ will be of crucial importance. If firm i intends to switch to behavior y, its expected return will be:

$$E[r_i(y)|p(y)] = p(y)r_i(y_i,y_j) + [1 - p(y)]r_i(y_i,x_j). \tag{2}$$

This will be compared to the expected return from behavior x:

$$E[r_i(x)|p(y)] = [1 - p(y)]r_i(x_i,x_j) + p(y)r_i(x_i,y_j). \tag{3}$$

---

8. These models analyze the choice situation for two competing *new* technological designs, while I concentrate on a comparison between a dominant, established technique, and a new technique that has to fight an uphill battle against increasing returns to adoption attained through the widespread use of the established technique.

9. Such a model specification is appropriate for situations in which an innovating firm has early-mover disadvantages. As an example, the switch toward a new standard causes high costs and comparatively low returns if the standard is not accepted by other firms. This situation is similar for environmentally conscious firms that have to pay directly for the adoption of cleaner equipment or processes, but that also have to bear the damages caused by other, polluting firms.

Any firm behaving rationally will switch to behavior y only if

$$E[r_i(y)|p(y)] > E[r_i(x)|p(y)], \qquad (4)$$

which will depend on the relative share of other firms already adopting y. The threshold level can be calculated by solving inequality 4 for p:

$$p^* = \frac{r_i(x_i,x_j) - r_i(y_i,x_j)}{r_i(x_i,x_j) + r_i(y_i,y_j) - 2r_i(y_i,x_j)}. \qquad (5)$$

Behavior y can be expected to be chosen with probability 0 by each firm as long as $p \leq p^*$, and with probability 1 for $p > p^*$. All firms for which the strict inequality $r_i(x_i,x_j) > r_i(y_i,x_j)$ in equation 1 applies will remain hesitant and will wait until enough others have decided to apply behavior y. As long as the percentage of nonhesitant firms in the population n is considerably smaller than p*, no change will be initiated.

> *Result 1 (Resistance to Change).* Even though behavior y is Pareto superior if chosen collectively by all firms, the expectation that a majority of firms will not opt for the new behavior will cause most firms to remain hesitant. As a result, threshold level p* will not be attained, and Pareto-inferior behavior x will be dominant.

Now suppose there is some entrepreneurial potential explained by differences of firms within the industry. Some firms will evaluate expected returns from behavior y more highly than others,[10] and/or they may display a certain preference for innovation and social responsiveness. The following conditions can explain why some firms will move ahead more rapidly in applying behavior y than others.

- Some firms can gain much more from innovation than they would lose from resistant behavior of others:

$$r_i(y_i,y_j) - r_i(x_i,x_j) \gg r_i(x_i,x_j) - r_i(y_i,x_j).$$

- Firms set up effective subgroups and communication networks in which the likelihood of interaction with "early innovators" is increased, while contacts with "defecting" noninnovators are minimized.[11]

---

10. Some firms can switch from x to y at lower cost than others, partly depending on capital commitments related to older technologies; differences in firm size can explain return differentials generated from innovation. In addition, firms are different with respect to their expectations and their risk preference.

11. This strategy of focusing interactions on subgroups of "similar-minded," cooperating

- Some firms are optimistic with respect to the behavior of others:

  $E_i(p) > p^*$ for $i = 1, \ldots, n'$, $n' < n$.

- Some firms may not be simple profit maximizers, or they may pursue additional goals favoring behavior y.[12]

If at least one of these conditions holds, some companies will initiate a change in behavior and will generate an adaptation process through which threshold level p^* may eventually be attained.

> *Result 2 (Innovation and Diffusion).* In spite of the prevailing resistance to change, entrepreneurial activity explained by diversity within a population of firms will trigger a switch to behavior y. If there are enough innovating firms in the industry, they will generate an adaptation process through which threshold level p^* will be attained. This again will cause all other, resistant firms to apply behavior y.

Results 1 and 2 describe two extreme outcomes, the first of which could indicate a need for coordinated behavior that might either be achieved through some form of government intervention or through collaboration between firms. Meanwhile, the second result will often be the outcome of a competitive market process for which government involvement is either not necessary, or where its activities can be limited to an early initiating role.

Most real-life situations, in contrast, will be characterized by movements between these two results, sometimes with an open final outcome. Entrepreneurial activity may or may not be strong enough and coordinated in the appropriate way to generate the momentum needed for attaining threshold level p^*. Any change process can thus end up in two directions, either the final success of a superior mode of behavior y (result 2), or in a faltering of innovative activity that will result in the prevalence of behavior x (result 1). It is this second type of "indecisiveness" that is often used as an argument by promoters of industrial policy. Countries with a more dedicated type of industrial policy can, it is said, be more successful in innovations that require a high degree of complementarity and interrelatedness between independent market participants.[13]

---

agents has been described by Axelrod (1985). Relatedly, empirical diffusion research has shown many examples in which innovations have spread within a subpopulation of individuals akin to each other, before they became disseminated within a wider population.

12. Some companies apply rules such as "always buy the most modern equipment" or "be ahead of others in technology or with respect to environmental responsiveness."

13. In his analysis of Japanese industrial policy, Freeman (1988) emphasizes the important role of the "national system of innovation." It is primarily for complex technologies with a very

Any proposition for the solution of such a coordination problem, however, must seriously consider the problem of how the collectively superior behavior y can reliably be identified ex ante, particularly in situations with high uncertainty and in which competitors experiment with different types of behavior (e.g., alternative technological designs). This problem is addressed within the "competing-technologies models" by Arthur (1988), Cowan (1987 and 1989), and David and Bunn (1987). Cowan (1989) shows that a central coordinator may be helpful in identifying a certain route of behavior that will eventually turn out to be collectively superior. However, if the evolution of competing technologies is intrinsically unpredictable, if arbitrary early successes have strong implications for adoption decisions and for increasing returns to adoption, and if information is unfavorably distributed among decision makers, the central coordinator will run a high risk of betting on the wrong horse, that is, of selecting a technology that may finally turn out to be inferior. Furthermore, a decision once made by a central coordinator may subsequently lead to troublesome lock-in situations, if economic or political obligations and interdependencies undermine the flexibility needed to switch later on to a modified or new route of ultimately superior behavior.[14]

It thus appears that industrial policy can be effective only under very specific conditions that relate both to the underlying choice situation and to the ways it is implemented. The true existence of a critical mass or coordination problem is a necessary requirement for this. Furthermore, a central coordinator must be able to collect a bundle of information that is superior in terms of potential risk reduction to the information available to individual agents. Finally, he or she must be able to implement a policy that is supported by individual agents and will lead to self-enforcement. Any attempt to argue in favor of a certain type of industrial policy will thus have to prove that there really is a critical mass problem of the type described here, that critical requirements related to information and implementation can be fulfilled, and that there is no better alternative organizational solution.[15]

Alternative Policies for the Support of Industrial Innovation

In order to solve the critical mass problem and to attain the degree of coordination needed for innovation, public institutions may be important for both

---

high degree of interrelatedness (such as computer-integrated manufacturing, high-definition television, or advanced telecommunication [ISDN]), for which some form of an industrial policy similar to the Japanese approach appears to be advantageous.

14. For an illustrative description of serious "lock-in" encountered by public decision makers and industrialists during the Concorde project, see Hayward 1983. A similarly interesting account is the description of the German fast breeder reactor program (see Keck 1981).

15. Teece (1989) shows that the growing need for strategic coordination can be responded

empirical and theoretical reasons. In most empirical cases, a number of existing public institutions will either define the boundary conditions for the working of private markets, or public agencies themselves will act as key participants in the competitive process. Theoretically, public involvement can be justified for reasons of market failure, although additional shortcomings within the political and administrative decision-making process have to be taken into consideration. In particular, it must be asked whether public agents are in control of the relevant information needed to assess the relative advantage of a proposed new solution (e.g., behavior y). Furthermore, it is important to know whether political agents can make sure that a certain program to promote y will get the right political momentum.[16] Finally, the expected benefits of a program have to more than outweigh its additional costs, particularly in terms of transaction and agency costs.

Such an overall evaluation of prospects and limitations of industrial policy, however, needs to be complemented by a careful analysis of very specific policies and support schemes. Public institutions can pursue four different routes of activity. They can

1. provide supply-side incentives through which the cost of certain critical inputs or activities are reduced;
2. pursue demand-side related policies such as public procurement;
3. define and influence the regulatory and legal framework; or
4. facilitate and support networking activities and cooperation.

I will show that any of these four areas of public involvement will only help to solve part of the coordination problem I have outlined. I will argue that the most effective type of policy will be a specific combination of all four types of activity, which are implemented through a self-referential process.

Supply-Side-Oriented Policies

Let us suppose that the switch from behavior x to behavior y requires some specific inputs that firm i has to acquire at cost $c_i(y)$. These specific inputs can include the use of existing research facilities, the setting up of in-house R&D, or the hiring of highly skilled personnel. Public institutions can have an influence on lowering the cost of these inputs by providing the appropriate research infrastructure, by subsidizing R&D performed in industry, and by providing the appropriate facilities and services for education and training.

---

to alternatively through integration, strategic alliances, industrial policy, or through a combination of these governance modes.

16. There is a corresponding critical-mass problem at the political level, relating to the tedious consensus-building process. Only if this political consensus building is easier to achieve than interfirm coordination, can industrial policy be justified.

Through any of these supply-side policies, which can discriminate enough between inputs specifically used for x and y, the expected return $r_i^s(y)$ for a subsidized innovator will be increased:

$$E[r_i^s(y)|p(y)] > E[r_i(y)|p(y)], \qquad (6)$$

while the expected return from behavior x remains unaffected:

$$E[r_i^s(x)|p(y)] = E[r_i(x)|p(y)]. \qquad (7)$$

Innovative firms will find it more rewarding to apply new behavior y and will initiate a change process that will eventually help to attain critical mass p^*. However, such a supply-side-oriented policy will only work effectively as long as the public agency can control the key information needed to assess the relative advantage of techniques, their risk profile, as well as their cost structure.

In order to be effective, the state agency needs to know which type of behavior (y vs. x) is really the best, which specific inputs are required for y, and how it can discriminate best by supporting y without unwillingly also supporting x. In most industrial markets, however, the relevant know-how about alternative routes of behavior, their risk and return profile, and about specific inputs required for each activity is kept hidden as strategic information that is only available to particular firms. Public agencies are most often at an informational disadvantage and will be dependent on information transmitted from these firms.[17] Both innovative companies favoring behavior y and conservative firms favoring x will provide tactically selected information by either "glorifying" the relative advantage of y, or by overemphasizing costs and risks involved with a change from behavior x to y.

This information dilemma of the government agency is more likely to be solved in situations in which the target (e.g., behavior y) is unambiguously clear, and where the implications of a decision in favor of y can reliably be assessed.[18] Given such favorable circumstances, government agencies can

---

17. Firms engaged in rivalrous competition have an incentive to distort information. This may have a seriously negative impact on the quality of information available to the public coordinator. Only for certain configurations of rivalry and resource ownership distribution between firms will public agents be able to secure the appropriate quality of information. The description of public policy experiences within different industries in the United States (see Nelson 1982) shows significant differences with respect to the quality of information transmitted to public decision makers.

18. This can explain why supply-side policies tend to be more successful in countries that want to imitate a more advanced rival (as, for instance, the Japanese efforts to emulate U.S. firms during the 1970s). See, particularly, Nelson 1984 for that argument.

pursue appropriate courses of action. Even if the degree of uncertainty with respect to behavior y is high, a central coordinator can have a strong role as long as an information asymmetry applies in favor of the state, that is, the public agency knows more than any single firm. This last requirement can be fulfilled in situations in which public institutions themselves have a strong influence on the choice of behavior and on the selection of specific inputs, primarily in regulated markets. Furthermore, if public agents are involved in cooperation and networking activities, they can often exploit synthetic information that the individual firms do not possess. However, these favorable circumstances will only be valid under very specific conditions, which clearly reduces the scope of applications for which supply-side support politics can effectively mobilized.

Demand-Side Policies

Public agencies can also create incentives for the application of behavior y through purchasing and procurement policies. They can support product innovation directly by buying new products with certain specifications. Or they can exert an influence on production technology by purchasing only from companies using a new process. Similarly, public agencies can offer a premium price to any manufacturer using a new product or process, thereby increasing the return to early innovators and the likelihood of a switch to behavior y. If government purchases represent a considerable share of the total market, this type of policy will entice enough firms to apply new behavior y, thereby reaching critical level p^*, which will then lead to further adaptation processes within the group of resistant firms. Apart from representing a major part of the market, government should also be the final customer and should control a major part of the relevant know-how about the products, their uses, and about specific inputs required.[19] These prerequisites for an effective purchasing policy constrain the application potential of such demand-side inducements to innovation. In addition, the requirement that government represents a large market share and controls the relevant know-how always bears the risk of monopsonic behavior with a stifling impact on innovation and a preference for very costly overspecification.[20]

---

19. This is a major problem in the telecommunication or transportation sector, where government agencies act "as if" they were the final customer. The introduction of ISDN by the German PTT shows how major innovation decisions are carried forward without knowing enough about either the final users of the new service or about their specific requirements.

20. Furthermore, the typical bureaucratic decision-making processes, together with "cameralistic" controlling procedures, rarely allow for procurement policies explicitly favoring innovation.

The Regulatory and Legal Framework

Government institutions influence innovation processes and cooperative activities in industry through a number of policies constituting the regulatory and legal framework, such as market and antitrust regulation, tax policies, public regulation in the field of health, environment and safety, social policies and labor relations, as well as through foreign trade and export policies.[21] Market and antitrust regulation together with tax policies define an important set of boundary conditions, specifically for innovations that require a certain degree of coordination between competing firms. The initial introduction of new behavior y often requires joint efforts of several firms (e.g., joint R&D or the agreement on a joint standard) as well as active campaigning by an agent of collective action. Public coordinators can play a strong role in mediating decisions for the formation of dominant designs and in influencing the standard-setting process. Of course, the regulatory and legal framework must be in accord with, and not antagonistic to, this type of coordination. Collaborative activities of firms during the standard-setting process must be compatible with antitrust regulation and, if possible, financially supported by tax policies. In some countries, in contrast, the regulatory and legal framework causes some serious impediments to joint industrial activities.[22]

Health, environment, and safety regulation can both stimulate and stifle innovation, depending on the political and administrative framework applied. A target- or objective-oriented policy in general appears to be more suitable than the prescription of a specific technical solution. Instead of forcing all firms to apply a certain behavior, y, government agencies should set targets that allow all firms to select their most appropriate technical solutions depending on their specific resources and in accord with ongoing technical change. Public regulation must also be in compliance with the planning horizon of firms. Clear signals and predictable targets mean greater security for planning new projects. A higher degree of innovation will be achieved than if regulatory requirements change erratically.

Networking and Cooperation Policy

Government institutions at both the regional and national level can help facilitate coordination processes by sponsoring workshops and active networks, by setting up demonstration plants, and by supporting appropriate institutions for

---

21. For a more detailed and systematic survey of the impact of the regulatory and legal framework on innovation, see ISI 1989.

22. Particularly in the United States, antitrust regulation is a serious constraint for many forms of interfirm collaboration.

the dissemination of know-how.[23] By providing support and credibility at the public level, public institutions can help overcome the dilemma of the agent of collective action. Public involvement in this fermentation process does not need to be very costly and centralistic. Instead, government can rely on existing communication networks and institutions, for which often only minor adaptations may be needed. This kind of soft and bottom-up policy certainly has many advantages, but it also has a number of constraints. It relies on weak ties and on existing, historically grown social relationships and institutions. As such, it is hard to plan and organize and requires a long time-horizon, which most people in politics and within the administration often cannot sustain.

The advantages and disadvantages of all four alternative types of industrial policy are summarized in table 1.

A New Design for Industrial Policy

All four types of policies described in the preceding section can help to overcome an organizational dilemma caused by resistant firms that are only willing to adapt to new behavior y if enough other firms do so first. At the same time, no policy is available at zero cost, and each of the four types has its specific disadvantages and shortcomings (see table 1). The question is then posed: Can we design a certain new system or framework of policies that helps to reduce or balance these shortcomings and may result in a more favorable cost-benefit relationship? In particular, we will ask:

1. Can we solve the organizational problem by subdividing the tasks and by focusing on an area that is more likely to lead to the desired solution?
2. Can we exploit interdependencies and synergies between different types of policies such that a combination of them will lead to improvements?
3. Can we design an appropriate new form of organization that can be regarded as informationally efficient and more suitable for change?

I will argue that all three "design characteristics" will help to overcome the coordination problem outlined in the preceding section. They should be regarded as behavioral principles for the implementation of industrial policy within an evolutionary perspective.

---

23. The Agricultural Extension Service in the United States has often been cited as a classical, and quite successful, public support program.

TABLE 1. Advantages and Disadvantages of Alternative Policies

Type of Policy	Advantages	Disadvantages and Shortcomings
Supply-side incentives	Can provide strong incentives to firms Can be applied very selectively (fine-tuning)	Requires very specific know-how on the side of the public agency
Demand-side policies	Can provide strong incentives to firms Helps to clearly define customer needs and missions	Requires very specific know-how on the side of the public agency Only applicable to areas where government is a major customer
Regulatory and legal framework	Can clarify the rules and boundary conditions for private activity Can provide clear signals for innovation	Provokes shirking behavior Cannot be very specific and selective. The more specific: —the higher the information needs for the central agency, —the higher the cost of control and implementation, and —the more stifling on decentralized innovation activities Not very flexible: —must be encoded in law —market participants require stable and reliable guidance
Networking and cooperation policy	Mobilizes existing communication networks Powerful mechanism to support decentralized innovation activities	Very difficult and time consuming to create where it does not already exist Absence of strong incentives, e.g., complementary financial funds, can lead to disintegration

Subdivision of Tasks

All too often, organizational problems are caused by seemingly insurmountable complexity. A reduction of complexity through specific organizations or through problem-solving mechanisms, if feasible, is often the most appropriate way to proceed. Private firms face this problem continuously; they solve it by forming business units and by assigning them specific tasks and responsibilities. The situation is similar for the design of industrial policy, for which complexity can be reduced by forming a subgroup of agents, by addressing only a specific subset of potential new behavior, and by defining incremental steps or stages. The first method consists of an identification of small groups, for example, conversation circles or communication networks, the members of which are more akin to a certain new behavior, y.[24] Members of such subgroups prefer to interact among themselves and will thus realize $r_i(y_i,y_j)$ with a much higher probability than the rest of the population. Behavior y will diffuse more rapidly within the subgroup, and, once all members have been converted, they can go on evangelizing other subgroups.[25] The success of industrial policy is crucially dependent on such a selection of early believers. However, if uncertainties are high, and if decisions once made have binding effects on future choices, government agencies can easily get locked into technological trajectories favored by a few biased decision makers in industry.

A related problem is caused by the openness and complexity of the choice set. For many empirical decisions there is no simple and clear-cut choice situation involving only two types of behavior, x and y. Instead, different actors come up with several alternative solutions $(y_1, \ldots, y_m)$, which may be real or only imaginary alternatives.[26] Many firms will simply be hesitant, because they are troubled by the sheer complexity of the choice situation. In such a situation, an agent of collective choice can achieve remarkable results by concentrating the attention of the participating firms on a simple, binary subset of choices.

If the switch from behavior x to behavior y involves a very large step, which most firms are not willing to undertake, change can be initiated by incrementalizing the process.[27] The task performed can be subdivided so that firms can apply behavior y at a lower activity level until they convince each other and move on to full conversion. As an example, the adoption of new industrial processes is facilitated if a firm can try out a process for one plant first, before it is applied for all other plants at later stages. Accordingly, it has often proven helpful for industrial policy purposes to devise simple mechanisms for incrementalizing the early adoption process, for example, through demonstration plants, trial equipment at user premises, leasing arrangements, and so forth.[28] One special way of incrementalizing can be applied to multi-

---

24. This is described as a subgame of agents in Witt 1991.

25. The early internal dynamics of the Christian and other religious movements can be explained by a similar pattern.

26. This is especially the case for early phases of an industry or a technology, during which a dominant design has not been established.

27. To teach children how to use stairs, one would start by letting them climb short, slightly inclined staircases.

28. For a description of the important role of task partitioning during the innovation process, see von Hippel 1990.

stage processes. Firms can be more easily convinced to start with a first phase if they are left with an option to continue or not, depending on the outcome of this initial step. Industrial innovations can easily be subdivided in that way (concept phase, research, development, prototype development, first manufacturing, etc.). For large, complex, and risky technologies, relatively cheap models can be tested well before expensive key components and scaled-up systems are developed and utilized.[29] An important role of the agent of collective action is to devise an appropriate method of sequential decision making, which most involved firms will find acceptable.

> *Result 3 (New Partitioning of Tasks).* One of the key roles legitimizing the early involvement of a political entrepreneur[30] will involve the collection of information on the potential subgroup of agents and their expectations, on a focused subset of choices, and on new ways of subdividing and incrementalizing change processes. The political entrepreneur will use this information to design a new kind of problem-solving process that will improve the feasibility of a joint solution.

The collection of information is a very important first step for exploring the feasibility of a certain new solution and policy. It is also a major step in the consensus-building process and will lead to more stable and lasting support for the later implementation stages. The early collection of information will also, in most cases, be much cheaper than the attempted implementation of a new policy that turns out at a very late date to be feasible only with great difficulty or not even feasible at all.

Combination of Policies

Economists have a preference for partial analytical modeling and tend to analyze the effect of a single policy compared to a situation with no political influence at all. They tend to neglect the interaction effect of several policies

---

29. Industrial policy would benefit considerably if political decision makers followed this incremental, though systematic, approach. Unfortunate counterexamples (e.g., nuclear reactor programs, some cable television projects, or defense procurement decisions) demonstrate that heavy losses of billions of dollars can be incurred if irreversible investment decisions are made before a dominant design has been established or before political consensus is attained.

30. Similar to the role of the private entrepreneur as the "innovating agent who organizes inputs according to his ideas of the new possibilities for producing and selling commodities" (Witt 1992, chap. 2), the role of the political entrepreneur consists in organizing inputs according to his or her ideas of the new possibilities for designing, adapting, and implementing policies and public choice situations. See also Picot, Laub, and Schneider 1989 for an analoguous description of the role of a political coordinator.

that are often pursued in parallel at a certain activity level. This interaction effect may sometimes have an unforeseen negative impact, but it can also lead to a reciprocal strengthening of policies, each of which would have its own deficiencies if applied separately.

It is one of the tasks of a political coordinator to explore the political choice set and to assess the potential outcome of a new combination of instruments. In many empirical situations, different types of policies are applied in parallel, but they are not coordinated in the most appropriate way.[31] The collective choice agent can help identify the opportunities for a more coherent and integrated type of industrial policy. In his or her role as political entrepreneur, he or she will discover and propose new bundles of policies, for example, the strengthening of supply-side inventives through appropriate demand-side-oriented policies or the support of networking and cooperation initiatives through complementary financial incentives.[32]

Result 4 (New Combination of Policies). The second important task of the political entrepreneur involves the collection of information on the choice set for political instruments, on positive, or harmful, effects of these policies anticipated by different actors, and on new forms of combining different policies which were so far uncoordinated. He or she will propose new bundles of policies, and he or she also has to anticipate whether certain critical events or some subgroups of actors can undermine the coordinated political program.

Forms of Organization

The preceding arguments in favor of the agent of collective action will evoke the question of whether we overextend the role of public agencies in the direction of some kind of new Leviathan. As Witt (1991, sec. 2) formulates the argument originally put forth by Buchanan (1977), ". . . it is unclear how proposals on social rearrangements, developed by the theoretician on the basis of normative individualism, will be launched into the actual political process and thus exposed to the required test." Do I propose that "a normative public choice theorist suggests changes that self-interested politicians or the judiciary have to implement?" According to my view, this would be a false approach.

---

31. A typical example is the industrial policy for the German aerospace industry, where four different ministries each pursue their own goals and policies. The joint impact would be much stronger if policies could be coordinated more effectively across agencies. See Little 1987.

32. It is often reported that regional initiatives receive a strong thrust through the announcement of central government to support the initiative. This signaling effect has a strong impact on unifying independent agents; the symbolic effect is often much more important than the volume of financial funds.

Instead, I suggest an approach in which the spontaneous organization of private firms or individuals is the driving element. Government activity must be a resultant and/or a facilitating element for the self-referential change process initiated by the firms and individuals involved. Consequently, the public choice theorist must be endogenized and has to work both as a moderator of information supplied to him or her and as a catalyst for activities pursued at a decentralized level.

The endogenized political choice agent will collect information about individual interests, claims, and choices preferred, about opportunities for joint solutions, and about the feasibility of specific government activities. He or she will then support the self-organizing system through a new form of policy that is most suitable for the targets to be achieved and is most likely to be supported and implemented. This procedure of endogenizing the political choice agent is very information intense, and its feasibility will thus depend on whether a system can be devised that saves on information costs. Otherwise, the "bottleneck in information processing that the central coordinating agency creates,"[33] which is the major argument against constructive rationalism, would similarly apply for the endogenized public choice theorist. This bottleneck in information processing can only be overcome by finding an information-efficient mode for the endogenous change process. This requires a certain organizational structure, within which a coordinator is selected who serves as the network node. Such a network node can economize on information costs because the number of binary interactions between private firms and public agents will be reduced considerably. The actual degree of information efficiency of this intermediary will depend on whether a coordinator can be selected who has better and cheaper access to the relevant information, and whether the risk of filtering information by a self-interested coordinator can be minimized.

Certain organizational requirements must be fulfilled so that the coordinator can effectively play his or her role and attain a desired outcome at acceptable cost. These requirements can be expressed in the following way.

1. A coordinator must be selected who knows both industry and government well enough, who can mobilize existing communication links to both sides, and who is located at the right place and organization in order to get continuous support.[34]

---

33. This argument was repeatedly put forward by Hayek (1978). See Witt 1991, sec. 2 for a detailed examination of the potential role as well as the restraints on an "endogenized public choice agent," who operates within a "normative individualism" framework of reference.

34. Experience shows that it is often very helpful if the coordinator is working for a mixed public/private organization that will be accepted by industry because of similarities in objectives, decision rules, and communication patterns, but which also has close access to government

2. The coordinator has to act as a mediator of exchanges and must be in control of scarce resources, both of which are necessary to establish binding relationships with both government and industry.
3. The coordinator must have an appropriate bridgehead on both sides, that is, industry and government. He or she must be supported and controlled by both a political champion and an industry champion.

The industry champion will strengthen the communication links between the coordinator and industrial firms, and he or she will support the implementation process. At the same time, he or she has to control the activity of the (self-interested) coordinator. Similar tasks have to be fulfilled by the political champion, acting within the political process and/or within the public administration.

> *Result 5 (New Organization).* A new form of organization is required that can economize on information and transaction costs. Within this organization, the political coordinator acts as network node and has to maintain close communication links to both government and industry. The coordinator must control scarce resources and has to maintain binding relationships through real transfers. His or her success depends strongly on the support (and control) by strongly committed persons at high level, acting as bridgeheads, both within government and industry.

Conclusions

I have outlined both the scope and the limitations of a specific form of industrial policy aiming at the facilitation and coordination of change processes that are characterized by a high degree of interrelatedness between economic agents. Many empirical change processes, particularly those involving complex and systemic new technologies, are strongly affected by coordination and critical-mass problems similar to the ones outlined in the second section. To overcome such coordination problems, decision makers in industry and government increasingly call for interventionist types of policies. I have tried to show that industrial policy may provide appropriate solutions, even though the corridor within which it can operate effectively is rather narrow. Since the economic, political, and organizational requirements outlined in the third and fourth sections are often quite difficult to fulfill, indus-

---

institutions. Such mixed public/private institutions have often proven to act as a very effective network node for industry restructuring programs, for regional policy, and for collaborative R&D programs.

trial policy does not necessarily lead to the intended results. Successes of industrial policy, rare though they are, seem to depend on a unique combination of favorable circumstances.

This does not necessarily imply that key requirements for effective industrial policy cannot be safeguarded and controlled. If implemented within an appropriate perspective, that is, with unambiguous targets in mind, through the bundling of information, and on the basis of a coherent, bottom-up process, industrial policy can work effectively within specific areas. It must be built around a joint problem-solving process that requires

1. that specific tasks and objectives are selected and focused on,
2. that a new and carefully selected bundle of policies is orchestrated, and
3. that an appropriate form of organization, together with the right people and their specific roles, is chosen.

Within the framework of such a new type of industrial policy implemented within an evolutionary perspective, the endogenized coordinator acts as a political entrepreneur who discovers new ways of solving a problem jointly with all agents involved. He or she does not operate within a framework of constructivist rationalism, presuming full knowledge about the best possible solution; nor does he or she attempt to impose an authoritarian policy upon a group of firms. Instead, he or she tries to grasp the movements and undercurrents for a specific empirical change-situation. His or her principal aim is to discover an improved, practicable solution, for which he or she can convince the key decision makers. A typical sequence of such a discovery procedure (or joint problem-solving process) may involve the following five steps, which are shown in more detail in table 2.

1. Collect early information in order to be able to reduce complexity and to define a manageable subproblem or task.
2. Gather information about choice opportunities, claims, and activities of the major decision markers involved.
3. Develop strategies and find out if there is a core of joint strategies and a need for cooperative activities.
4. Design an appropriate set of policies and incentive mechanisms and review it with the parties involved.
5. Implement, manage, and evaluate the process over a consistently long enough time span.

This proposed framework can provide an appropriate model and a strong tool for solving similarly complex change processes for a number of different

TABLE 2. Major Steps for New Industrial Policy Formulation and Implementation

Step	Objectives to Be Achieved
Assess the present status of the industry or region	—Focus on specific tasks and objectives —Identify major players and decision makers —Analyze major driving forces
Assess future changes for the industry or region	Identify and analyze —Market trends —Technology trends and possibilities for substitution —Competitive forces and strategies —Changes in industry structure
Analyze strategies of firms and their compatibility	—Marketing and product strategies —Technology strategies —Strategies for cooperation and joint activities
Develop strategy for industrial policy and collaboration	—Require acceptance of industrial policy —Select appropriate policies and instruments —Select best method of coordinating the industrial policy framework
Implement and adapt appropriate policies	—What should be done in public institutions by whom? —Cooperation between public institutions —Cooperation between industry and government —Consecutive evaluation —Adaptive learning and improvement

application areas such as industrial R&D and innovation, industry restructuring and modernization, development planning for both developing countries and for new industries, and for regional policy as well as for environmental and resource policy.

REFERENCES

Allesch, J., ed. 1988. *Regional Development in Europe*. Berlin: de Greuyter.
Arthur, W. B. 1985. "Competing Technologies and Lock-in by Historical Events: The Dynamics of Allocation under Increasing Returns." Stanford University Center for Economic Policy Research, Revised Paper no. 43.
Arthur, W. B. 1988. "Competing Technologies: An Overview." In Dosi et al. 1988, 590–607.
Arthur, W. B. 1989. "Competing Technologies, Increasing Returns, and Lock-in by Historical Events." *Economic Journal* 99:116–31.
Axelrod, R. 1985. *The Evolution of Cooperation*. New York: Basic Books.
BMFT. 1988. *Bundesbericht Forschung 1988*. Bonn: German Federal Ministry for Research and Technology.

Buchanan, J. M. 1977. *Freedom in Constitutional Contract: Perspectives of a Political Economist.* College Station: Texas A&M University Press.
Cowan, R. 1987. "Backing the Wrong Horse: Sequential Technology Choice under Increasing Returns." Ph.D. diss. Stanford University.
Cowan, R. 1989. "Backing the Wrong Horse: Sequential Choice among Technologies of Unknown Merit." Stanford University. Mimeo.
Dasgupta, D., and Stoneman, P. L., eds. 1987. *Economic Policy and Technological Performance.* Cambridge: Cambridge University Press.
David, P. 1987. "Some New Standards for the Economics of Standardization in the Information Age." In Dasgupta and Stoneman 1987, 206–39.
David, P., and Bunn, J. 1987. "The Battle of Systems and the Evolutionary Dynamics of Network Technology Rivalries." Stanford University. Mimeo.
Dosi, G.; Freeman, C.; Nelson, R.; Silverberg, G.; and Soete, I.; eds. 1988. *Technical Change and Economic Theory.* London: Pinter.
Eliasson, G. 1987. "Industrial Targeting: Defensive or Offensive Strategies in a Neo-Schumpeterian Perspective." In Giersch 1987, 333–60.
Ergas, H. 1987. "Does Technology Matter?" In Guile and Brooks 1987, 191–245.
Freeman, C. 1982. *The Economics of Industrial Innovation.* 2d ed. Cambridge, Mass.: MIT Press.
Freeman, C. 1988. *Technology Policy and Economic Performance: Lessons from Japan.* London: Pinter.
Gerybadze, A. 1988a. *Raumfahrt und Verteidigung als Industriepolitik? Auswirkungen auf die amerikanische Wirtschaft und den international Handel.* Frankfurt: Campus.
Gerybadze, A. 1988b. "Strategic Management of Endogenous Regional Development Strategies." In Allesch 1988, 55–71.
Giersch, H., ed. 1987. *Free Trade in the World Economy: Toward an Opening of Markets.* Tübingen: J. C. B. Mohr.
Guile, B. R., and Brooks, H., eds. 1987. *Technology and Global Industry: Companies and Nations in the World Economy.* Washington, D.C.: National Academy Press.
Hayek, F. A. 1978. "The Errors of Constructivism." In *New Studies in Philosophy, Politics, Economics, and the History of Economic Ideas,* ed. F. A. Hayek, 3–23. Chicago: University of Chicago Press.
Hayward, K. 1983. *Government and British Civil Aerospace: A Case Study in Postwar Technology Policy.* Manchester: Manchester University Press.
Helpman, E., and Krugman, P. R. 1985. *Market Structure and Foreign Trade: Increasing Returns, Imperfect Competition, and the International Economy.* Brighton, Sussex: Wheatsheaf Books.
ISI. 1989. *Der Einflußwirtschafts- und gesellschaftspolitischer Rahmenbedingungen auf das Innovationsverhalten von Unternehmen.* Report to the Federal Minister of Economics. Karlsruhe: Fraunhofer-Institut für Systemtechnik und Innovationsforschung (ISI).
Katz, M. L., and Shapiro, C. 1986. "Technology Adoption in the Presence of Network Externalities." *Journal of Political Economy* 94:822–41.
Keck, O. 1981. *Policymaking in a Nuclear Program: The Case of the West German Fast Breeder Reactor.* Lexington, Mass.: Lexington Books.

Krugman, P. R., ed. 1986. *Strategic Trade Policy and the New International Economics.* Cambridge, Mass.: MIT Press.
Little, A. D. 1987. *Maßgebliche Einflußfaktoren für die Entwicklung der technologischen Leistungsfähigkeit der deutschen Avionikindustrie im Vergleich zu Frankreich und Großbritannien.* Report to the Federal Minister of Research and Technology. Bonn: Federal Ministry of Research and Technology.
Lorenzen, H. P. 1985. *Effektive Forschungs- und Technologiepolitik: Abschätzung und Reformvorschläge.* Frankfurt: Campus.
Malik, F. 1984. *Strategie des Managements komplexer Systeme.* Bern: Haupt.
Mowery, D. C., and Rosenberg, N. 1982. "The Commercial Aircraft Industry." In Nelson 1982, 101–61.
Nelson, R. R., ed. 1982. *Government Support of Technical Progress: A Cross-Industry Analysis.* New York: Pergamon Press.
Nelson, R. R. 1984. *High Technology Policies: A Five-Nation Comparison.* Washington, D.C.: American Enterprise Institute for Public Policy Research.
Nelson, R. R. 1986. "The Influence of Links with Science, University Research, and Technical Societies on Industrial R&D and Technical Advance." Columbia University. Mimeo.
Nelson, R. R. 1987. "Institutions Supporting Technical Change in the United States." Columbia University. Mimeo.
Nelson, R. R., and Winter, S. G. 1982. *An Evolutionary Theory of Economic Change.* Cambridge, Mass.: Belknap Press.
Picot, A.; Laub, U.; and Schneider, D. 1989. *Innovative Unternehmensgründung.* Heidelberg: Springer.
Teece, D. J., ed. 1987. *The Competitive Challenge: Strategies for Industrial Innovation and Renewal.* Cambridge, Mass.: Ballinger.
Teece, D. J. 1989. "Technological Development and the Organization of Industry." Paper presented to the International Seminar on Science, Technology, and Economic Growth, Paris.
Thurow, L. C. 1987. *Zero-Sum Solution: A Radical Blueprint for Economic Growth.* 2d ed. Harmondsworth: Penguin.
U.S. Department of Commerce. 1985. *Global Competition: The New Reality.* Report of the President's Commission on Industrial Competitiveness. Washington, D.C.: U.S. Government Printing Office.
von Hippel, E. 1990. "Task Partitioning: An Innovation Process Variable." *Research Policy* 19:407–18.
Witt, U. 1991. "The Endogenous Public Choice Theorist." *Public Choice.* Forthcoming.
Witt, U. 1992. *Individualistic Foundations of Evolutionary Economics.* Cambridge: Cambridge University Press. Forthcoming.

Contributors

Alexander Gerybadze is presently senior researcher at the University of Heidelberg in Germany, where he received his Ph.D. in economics in 1981. He has worked as a research fellow at Stanford University and as a senior management consultant with Arthur D. Little International. For many years he has advised the federal government in Germany on industrial policy issues, especially in aerospace industry and information technologies.

Werner Güth is professor of economics, especially economic theory, at the University of Frankfurt in Germany. His major research interests are in game theory, experimental economics, and applications of game theory to social decision problems.

Günter Hesse is professor of economics at the University of Würzburg in Germany. He previously held a Heisenberg scholarship from the German Research Foundation for several years that enabled him to conduct extensive studies of the theory and history of socioeconomic evolution in the very long run.

Hans-Paul Schwefel is professor of applied computer sciences at the University of Dortmund in Germany. He lectures in the field of systems analysis with emphasis on nonlinear dynamics. His main area of research lies in the understanding of evolutionary phenomena and in imitating evolutionary principles for computer-aided problem solving.

Manfred E. Streit is professor of economics at the University of Freiburg. He has held positions previously at the University of Mannheim, the European University Institute in Florence, and the University of Reading, United Kingdom. His major research fields are principles of economic policy, constitutional economics, and competition policy.

Viktor Vanberg is professor of economics at George Mason University and editorial director at the Center for Study of Public Choice. He is coeditor of *Constitutional Political Economy*.

Peter Weise is professor of economics at the University of Kassel in Germany. His research fields include microeconomics, applications of synergetics to socioeconomic problems, and business cycle theory.

Joseph A. Weissmahr is an international consultant in Zurich, Switzerland. Trained as a chemist, he has held numerous positions in chemical industry and research management in the United States, South America, and Europe. His research focuses on economic growth, development, and long-range planning. He is an active member of the European Study Group for Evolutionary Economics.

Gerhard Wegner is assistant professor at the University of Witten-Herdecke, the first private university in Germany. He gained his doctorate in economics at the University of Mannheim.

Ulrich Witt is professor of economics at the University of Freiburg in Germany. He has done research on evolutionary concepts in economics for a decade and has published extensively on this research. He is at present chairman of the European Study Group for Evolutionary Economics.

Menahem E. Yaari is director of the Institute of Advanced Studies at the Hebrew University, Jerusalem. He has held positions previously at Stanford University; Yale University; the University of California, Berkeley; Cambridge University; and the London School of Economics. His research fields include mathematical economics, game theory, and experimental economics.

Name Index

Abel, W., 83, 89, 99
Abramovitz, M., 79
Adams, J., 3, 18
Albert, H., 114, 120
Alchian, A. A., 6, 16
Aldrich, H., 6, 16
Allen, P., 3, 17, 62
Allesch, J., 171
Arrow, K. J., 134, 135, 141, 147
Arthur, W. B., 9, 16, 17, 35, 47, 155, 171
Ashby, W. R., 49, 50, 62
Axelrod, R., 157, 171

Bäck, T., 53, 62
Baldwin, W. L., 10, 17
Bandes, W., 43, 48
Barzel, Y., 147
Beckmann, J., 85, 92, 99
Bergson, H., 78
Berman, H. J., 114, 120
Binswanger, K. E., 4, 17
Birdzell, L. E., 105, 111, 113, 119, 121
Blaseio, H., 126, 147
Böhm, F., 133, 147
Boserup, E., 86, 88, 89, 99
Bössmann, E., 134, 147
Boulding, K. E., 3, 6, 17, 71, 73, 79, 126, 136, 147
Box, G. E. P., 53, 56, 62
Boyd, R., 6, 17, 32, 34
Braudel, F., 83, 99
Bray, F., 88, 99
Brennan, G., 118, 120
Brooks, S. H., 51, 62, 172

Brown, H. P., 82, 83, 99
Buchanan, J. M., 6, 14, 17, 125, 131, 147, 172
Bunn, J., 155, 172

Cage, R. A., 83, 99
Caldwell, J. C., 86, 89, 99
Cameron, R., 82, 99
Campbell, D. T., 118, 120
Cassel, G., 87, 99
Chao, K., 89, 99
Clark, C., 99
Clark, N., 3, 17
Coase, R. H., 125, 129, 130, 147
Cooper, J. P., 88, 99
Cowan, R., 155, 172
Crafts, N. F. R., 92, 99
Curtin, P. D., 100
Cyert, R. M., 6, 17

Dahlmann, C. J., 134, 147
Dantzig, G. B., 56, 62
Dasgupta, D., 172
David, P., 9, 16, 17, 155, 172
Day, R. H., 3, 9, 17
De Bresson, C., 3, 18
De Gregori, T. R., 84, 100
De Groot, M. H., 4, 18
Demsetz, H., 15, 18, 129, 147
Dennell, R., 88, 100
Doob, J. L., 38, 47
Dosi, G., 11, 18, 172

Eccles, J. C., 10, 19
Eger, T., 43, 47
Eigen, M., 7, 18

177

Name Index

Eliasson, G., 172
Ergas, H., 172
Eysenck, H. J., 47

Favreau, R. F., 51, 62
Fehl, U., 126, 147
Ferguson, A., 112, 120
Fisher, F. M., 4, 18
Fletcher, R., 53, 62
Foster, J., 3, 18
Frank, R. H., 33, 34
Franks, R., 51, 62
Freeman, C., 6, 11, 18, 157, 172
Furubotn, E. G., 18, 130, 147

Gabisch, G., 8, 18
Gaertner, W., 35, 47
Gallmann, R. E., 93, 100
Georgescu-Roegen, N., 90, 100, 126, 147
Giersch, H., 172
Gordon, W., 3, 18
Gouldner, A. W., 33, 34
Graff, H. J., 83, 89, 100
Granovetter, M., 12, 18, 42, 47–48
Greenberg, D., 100
Grefenstette, J. J., 53, 62
Gerybadze, A., 172
Guile, B. R., 172
Güth, W., 34

Haag, G., 9, 13, 18, 20, 40, 48
Haken, H., 9, 18, 46, 48
Hannan, M. T., 6, 18
Hanusch, H., 3, 18
Hayami, Y., 81, 88, 100
Hayek, F. A., 13, 15, 18, 106, 107, 109, 111, 114, 115, 116, 118, 120, 125–31, 139–41, 143, 144, 147–48, 168, 172
Hayward, K., 158, 172
Heiner, R. A., 6, 18
Helpman, E., 151, 172
Hesse, G., 81, 83, 84, 86, 90, 100, 148
Heuß, E., 101, 126, 148

Hirschman, A., 45, 48, 116, 120
Hirshleifer, J., 3, 6, 18, 19
Hoffmeister, F., 53, 62
Holland, J. H., 13, 19, 53, 62
Holliday, R. H., 88, 101
Hooke, R., 53, 62
Hoppmann, E., 126, 148
Hothersall, D., 36, 48
Humphrey, W. S., 82, 101
Hutter, M., 126, 134, 148

Ingrao, B., 5, 19
Israel, G., 5, 19

Jeeves, T. A., 53, 62
Jones, E. L., 89, 101, 113, 120
Jones, S., 36, 48
Junna, C., 3, 17

Kamien, M. I., 10, 19, 137, 148
Kanefsky, J. W., 82, 101
Katz, M. L., 155, 172
Kauffman, S. A., 19
Keck, O., 158, 172
Kirzner, I. M., 15, 19, 126, 139, 141, 148
Kleinknecht, A., 11, 19
Komolos, J., 101
Kraft, M., 35, 46, 48
Kravis, I. B., 88, 101
Krelle, W., 37, 48
Krugman, P. R., 151, 172
Krüsselberg, H. G., 126, 129, 148
Kuczynski, M., 79
Kunter, M., 83, 101
Kuznets, S., 71, 81, 101
Kwasnicka, H., 62, 63
Kwasnicki, W., 62, 63

Lachmann, L. M., 6, 19, 120, 126, 130, 148
Landes, T., 35, 46, 48
Lantane, B., 36, 48
Laub, U., 173
Law, J., 101
Leach, G. L., 87, 101

Leibenstein, H., 120
Leith, H., 95, 103
Lesourne, J., 9, 19, 37, 48
Lewin, K., 36, 48
Lewis, D., 16, 19
Lewis, W. A., 81, 101
Lindert, P. H., 83, 101
Little, A., 167, 173
Locke, J., 68, 79
Lorenz, H.-W., 8, 18, 45, 48
Lorenzen, H. P., 173
Loschky, D., 83, 101
Lucas, R. E., 4, 19
Luhmann, N., 133, 148

Malik, F., 154, 173
Manley, G., 82, 101
March, J. G., 6, 17, 19
Marti, K., 54, 63
Marx, K., 71, 76, 79
Matyas, J., 54, 63
May, R. M., 45, 48
Maynard Smith, J., 7, 19, 24, 30, 34
Mead, R., 53, 55, 63
Mendels, F. F., 92, 101
Menger, C., 6, 19, 74, 79
Mensch, G., 9, 18–19
Mirowski, P., 5, 19
Mokyr, J., 83, 101
Mowery, D. C., 173
Mueller, S., 6, 16
Müller, J., 85, 101
Munson, J. K., 51, 63
Musson, A. E., 82, 102

Nebel, A., 91, 102
Nelder, J. A., 53, 55, 63
Nelson, R. R., 3, 11, 19, 71, 79, 107, 120, 145, 148, 160, 173
Neumann, J., 49, 63
North, D. C., 4, 19, 112, 121

Ockenfels, P., 33, 34
Odum, E. P., 88, 102
Olsson, U., 83, 102

Paque, K. H., 131, 148
Pejovich, S., 130, 147
Penrose, E., 19
Perkins, D. H., 88, 102
Petty, W., 68
Picot, A., 173
Pöppel, E., 84, 102
Popper, K. R., 10, 19, 109, 121
Powell, M. J. D., 53, 62, 63
Prigogine, I., 9, 19

Quesnay, F., 68

Radner, R., 143, 148
Rastrigin, L. A., 51, 63
Rechenberg, I., 51, 63
Reid, D. A., 102
Ricardo, D., 70, 79
Richerson, P. J., 6, 17
Richter, R., 15, 18
Röpke, J., 126, 133, 148
Rosenberg, N., 105, 111, 113, 119, 121, 173
Rosenbrock, H. H., 53, 63
Rubin, A. I., 51, 63
Ruthenberg, H., 88, 102
Ruttan, V. W., 4, 17, 81, 88, 100, 105, 121

Saalfeld, D., 92, 102
Sahlins, M., 87, 102
Salehi-Isfahani, D., 88, 102
Schaffer, J. D., 53, 63
Scherer, F. M., 11, 20
Schlicht, E., 46, 48
Schmid, M., 6, 20
Schmidt-Trenz, H. J., 117, 121
Schmidtchen, D., 117, 121, 148
Schneider, D., 173
Schofield, R. S., 82, 103
Schull, J., 62, 63
Schumpeter, J. A., 4, 10, 20, 74, 79, 119, 121, 139, 140, 145–46, 149
Schurr, S. H., 93, 102
Schwartz, N. L., 10, 19
Schwarz, L. D., 83, 103

Schwefel, H.-P., 53, 55, 56, 60, 63
Scitovsky, T., 45, 48
Scott, J. T., 10, 17
Selten, R., 7, 20, 23, 24, 34
Shackle, G. L. S., 6, 20
Shapiro, C., 155, 172
Silverberg, G., 9, 20, 35, 48, 172
Simon, H. A., 6, 20, 78, 79, 136, 149
Slicher von Bath, B. H., 83, 102
Smith, A., 69, 70, 79, 89, 102
Soete, I., 172
Sonnenblum, S., 93, 102
Soong, R., 12, 18, 42, 47, 48
Stanislaw, J. A., 82, 101
Stewart, G. W., 53, 63
Stigler, G. J., 134, 142, 149
Stolper, W. F., 10, 20
Stoneman, P. L., 172
Streißler, E., 144, 149
Streit, M. E., 131, 140, 143, 149
Sugden, R., 12, 20

Teece, D. J., 158, 173
Thomas, K., 102
Thornton, R., 102
Thünen, J. H., 88, 102
Thurow, L. C., 151, 173
Tollison, R., D., 112, 121
Tranter, N. L., 83, 102
Trivers, R. L., 24, 33, 34

Vanberg, V., 110, 115, 121
Van Damme, E., 7, 20, 23, 24, 30, 34
von Hippel, E., 165, 173

Wagner, A., 103
Walter, H., 95, 103
Watt, J., 70
Weber, M., 133, 149
Weber-Kellermann, I., 91, 103
Wegehenkel, L., 141, 149
Weidlich, W., 9, 13, 18, 20, 40, 48
Weise, P., 35, 43, 46, 47, 48
Weissing, F., 23
Wiener, N., 63
Williamson, D., 130, 149
Williamson, J. G., 83, 101
Williamson, O. G., 15, 20
Winston, G. C., 37, 48
Winter, S. G., 3, 20, 145, 148, 173
Wiseman, J., 6, 20, 118, 121
Witt, U., 7, 8, 12, 20, 23, 34, 35, 48, 108, 111, 121, 126, 136, 137, 144, 145, 149, 154, 165, 167, 168, 173
Wolfson, M., 5, 20
Wood, D. O., 93, 102
Wrigley, E. A., 82, 103
Wuketits, F. M., 6, 20

Young, G. A., 34

Zeeman, E., 43, 48

Subject Index

Access to resources, 84
Adaptation, 50, 154, 157, 161; innovation of, 84, 87–88, 93, 99
Adoption, 155, 165; increasing returns to, 155, 158
Agricultural Extension Service, 163
Agriculture: employment, 90; labor force, 81, 94; production, 86–87, 90; productivity, 88
Analogy between biology and economics, 7
Anthropocentricity, 71, 74
Anticonformity, 40–41, 43–45
Antitrust regulation, 162
Arbitrage, 140, 142, 144
Artificial intelligence, 49
Austria: economics, 6, 8, 15; position, 7; school, 125, 130

Behavioral theory of the firm, 5–8
Behavior: chaotic, 46; demographic, 85; problem-solving, 108; reciprocal, 23, 27, 33
Bottom-up process, 170

Capital, 72; formation of, 93, 97; intensity of, 88, 91
Catallaxy, 129
Catastrophe theory, 43
Chicago school, 130
Civilization, 89
Classical political economy, 89
Collective action, 163
Collective choice, 115
Collective experiment, 115–18

Communication: costs, 134; network, 156, 163
Comparative advantages, 151
Competition, 61, 106, 112–14, 118, 127, 139; as discovery process, 109; of technologies, 155, 158
Computer revolution, 49
Conformity, 40–41, 43–46
Constitutional choice theory, 14
Constructivist rationalism, 153, 170
Contract, 134
Conversation circles, 165
Cooperation, 152, 159, 161; policy of, 162
Coordination, 127, 162; problem of, 154, 158, 163
Coordinator, 170; central, 158, 161, 168
Costs: communication, 134; negotiation, 137; organization, 130; reciprocation, 26; substitution, 138; sunk, 130, 131, 133, 137; transaction, 15, 129, 132, 134–35, 138, 141, 145; transportation, 134
Creativity, 7–8, 14, 72, 73, 84
Critical mass, 9, 16, 158
Customs, 131
Cybernetics, 49

Darwinian theory, 6, 7, 108
Data, 136
Decentralization, 113, 118–19
Demand-side related policies, 159, 161
Demonstration plants, 162, 165
Desire to reciprocate, 32

Subject Index

Development economics, 14
Development planning, 171
Diversity, 61
Diffusion, 157
Discovery, 141–42
Dynamic evolutionary process, 31

Economics: growth in, 71, 81–103, 105, 111, 113–14; subjectivist, 6–7, 15
Economies of scale, 93
Education and training, 159
Effective purchasing policy, 161
Effectiveness, 83–84
Energy, 14, 73, 76–77, 86, 94; consumption of, 83, 94, 97; efficiency of, 87; flow of, 72–73; per labor hour, 93; solar, 73, 77; use of, per worker, 94
Engel's law, 81
Entrepreneur, 140; activity of, 157; potential for, 156
Environment, 162; control by, 155
Equilibration, 50
Equilibrium, 4–6, 8–9, 11, 129, 134, 141; partial, 130; theory of, 125–28, 132, 136, 146
ESPRIT, 152
EUREKA, 152
Evolution, 26, 49; approaches of, 3, 5–7, 11, 13–14, 140; biological, 33; cultural, 13, 15, 32, 106–112, 114, 115; dynamics of, 33; game theory of, 12; market theory of, 130; strategies, 12, 23–24, 31, 33, 50
EVOP (evolutionary operation), 55
Experiments, 105–6, 109, 111–12, 114–18; institutional, 114
Export policies, 162
Externality problem, 110

Factory organization, 93
Federalism, 118
Field of socioeconomic forces, 37
Fire engine, 69–70
Food chain, 89

Force of preference, 40
Free good, 77
Frequency dependency effect, 12, 16

Game, symmetric, 29
Genetics: algorithms in, 13, 53; evolution of, 32, 33; mutations in, 26
Gift of nature, 68, 70
Government, 112; involvement of, 152, 157
Gradient, 53
Groping-in-the-dark, 61
Growth. *See* economic growth
Growth theory, 13–14; theory, neoclassical, 87

Health, 162
Homeostatic automation, 50
Homo economicus, 76
Human brain, 49

Imagination, 6–7, 10
Imitation, 144
Incrementalizing, 165
Industrialization, 14, 81–82, 89, 92–94
Industry: champion, 169; policies, 151–173; restructuring, 171
Information, 135, 142–43; asymmetry of, 161; autonomy of, 136; as a commodity, 134; complete, 24; dilemma of, 160; imperfect, 127, 140; incomplete, 33; perfect, 33
Innovation, 4, 10–11, 14, 83, 105, 111, 113, 119, 137, 140, 144, 155, 157, 162, 172; of firms, 160
Innovators, early, 156
Institutional optimum, 132
Institutions, 106–7, 109, 112, 114, 116; external, internal, 131, 132, 138; innovation of, 107, 114
Internal model, 53
Invention, 10
ISDN, 161

Knowledge, 14–15, 33, 73, 74, 106, 125, 127, 138, 139, 142, 145–46;

dissemination of, 163; division of, 128; perfect, 141

Labor, 72; theory of value in, 67, 71, 76
Land, 72; use systems, 88
Learning: algorithms, 49; behavior, 27; online, 56; ontogenetic, 49; phylogenetic, 49; rules, 13
Legal framework, 131
Legal systems, 133–34
Leviathan, 167
Lock-in, 158
Logistic equation, 45

Market coordination, 15; failure of, 129, 159; interdependence of, 142; process of, 157; transactions of, 133
Mediator of exchanges, 169
Meliorization, 50
Methods, 53
MIMD, 55
Moderator, 168
Monte Carlo strategy, 50
Motion equation, 42
Mutants, 30–31
Mutation, 27; correlated, 56; rate of, 55

Natural selection, 3, 6
Neoclassicism: analysis, 143; approach, 138; economics, 4–7, 10, 15; theory, 36, 128
Network: activities, 159, 161; externalities, 155; node, 168
New bundles of policies, 167
New technique, 155
Nonlinear dynamics, 8–9, 12, 16, 35
Novelty, 8–10

Opportunity trap, 58
Optimization, 4–6, 8, 11, 15, 50
Organizational/institutional innovations, 105–6
Overadaptation, 57

Pareto optimum, 132
Pareto-superior situation, 152, 155

Partitioning of tasks, 166
Pecuniary external effects, 142, 144
Photosynthesis, 77
Physiocrats, 67
Pleiotropy, 56
Political and administrative framework, 162
Political champion, 169
Political coordinator, 167
Political entrepreneur, 154, 167, 170
Political momentum, 159
Polygeny, 56
Population: principle, 54; theory, 86
Positive-sum game, 69, 77
Preferences, 35–36; theory, 12; variation over time, 45
Prejudices, 62
Prices, 144
Prisoner's dilemma, 12, 32–33, 110, 119
Private property, 68
Problem-solving, 153, 170; behavior, 108; mechanism, 154, 164
Procurement policies, 161
Production factors, 13, 14, 67
Productivity, 76
Profit, 71, 76–77
Property rights, 130–31, 143; in land, 89
Public: good, 110, 119; infrastructure, 131; involvement, 159

R&D, 151–52, 171
Rational choice, 135
Rational expectation equilibrium, 143
Rationality, 136
Recession, 57
Reciprocal mechanism, 34
Recombination, 58
Reduction of complexity, 164
Regional policy, 171
Regulatory and legal framework, 159
Replication, 7, 13
Reproductive success, 23, 25, 30–31
Requisite variety, 59

Subject Index

Research infrastructure, 159
Resistance to change, 156
Retaliatory precommitment, 32
Routine, 106–7, 109
Rules, 106–7, 114–16

Satisficing, 6, 8
Search: blind, 51; costs, 137; creeping random, 51
Seasonality, measure of, 94
Selection, 7; pressure, 58; soft, 58
Self-organiztion, 9, 35–36, 46; system of, 168
Self-referential process, 159, 168
Self-reinforcing processes, 35–36
Sematech, 152
Sequential decision, 166
Sexual inheritance, 56
Social interaction, 36
Social pressure, 40
Sociobiology, 7
Solidarity, 61
Spontaneous order, 129
Spontaneous organization, 168
Stages, implementation of, 166
Stagnation, 57
Standard of living, 82
Standard-setting process, 162
Standardization, 155
State, 112–13
Strategic alliances, 152

Strategy: evolutionary, 12, 23–24, 31, 33, 50; mixed, 30; undominated, 27
Structural transformation, 81
Subjectivist approach, 139
Substitution gap, 138
Success: rate of, 51; of industrial policy, 170
Supply-side incentives, 159
Surplus value, 71
Survival of the fittest, 51
Systems analysis, 62

Target, 152, 162
Tax policies, 162
Technology: progress of, 71, 81, 83; trajectories of, 165
Time, 73, 78–79
Trade policy, 151
Trial-and-error, 49, 108, 109, 114–15, 118

Uncertainty, 132, 134, 137
Utility function, 38–39, 43

Variation, 7, 13

Wealth, 75
Welfare: economics, 129; theory, 126
Work, 76

Zero-sum game, 68–69, 77